"*Not Done Yet* is a gift to the church. The antithesis of formulas, gimmicks, program-heavy strategies, and other unnatural approaches, this book presents an evangelism that is based on friendship, real church, and changing culture. One senses in these pages a gifted evangelist who is sharing her secrets of bearing witness to the beauty and power of the gospel."

Al Tizon, affiliate associate professor of missional and global leadership at North Park University, executive minister of Serve Globally, Evangelical Covenant Church

"Beth Seversen has successfully developed a book on evangelism that appeals to the scholar and the church leader. In a North American culture filled with gloomy statistics, she shows there are bright spots where young people are participating in Christian communities and committing to lives as disciples of Jesus Christ. More than this, she shows how local congregations can increase their evangelistic illumination to join these bright spots."

Mark R. Teasdale, E. Stanley Jones Associate Professor of Evangelism at Garrett Evangelical Theological Seminary

"If your ministry is interested in reaching young adults, *Not Done Yet* is a strong primer."

James Choung, vice president for strategy and innovation with InterVarsity Christian Fellowship/USA, author of *True Story* and *Longing for Revival*

"Grounded in careful research on emerging adults and the churches that are reaching them, Beth Seversen's *Not Done Yet* provides a hope-filled portrait of vibrant faith in the next generation. More importantly, she offers clear and practical guidelines for how churches can welcome, include, and equip the twentysomethings around them. A must-read for church leaders!"

David Setran, Price-LeBar Professor of Christian Formation and Ministry at Wheaton College

"The spiritual journeys of emerging adults are dynamic and varied, yet too often churches have reduced their experiences to one (typically negative) narrative. As a result, most churches start with the wrong perceptions and offer emerging adults something far from good news. Seversen's project is a breath of fresh air that gives ministry leaders a better view for understanding those navigating their third decade of life. Read this book if you want to be informed and if you dare to rethink the ways you are supporting emerging adults in your community."

Steven Argue, associate professor of youth, family, and culture at Fuller Theological Seminary

"Beth Seversen provides both robust research and practical suggestions to guide churches to fulfill the mission of God in this generation."

Jay Moon, professor of evangelism and church planting at Asbury Theological Seminary

"With a pastoral heart for young adults who are disconnected from faith communities, Dr. Seversen helps churches understand the unique spiritual journeys of young adults and how they are seeking a place to belong and contribute."

Joyce Koo Dalrymple, pastor of discipleship and connections at Wellspring Alliance Church, Wheaton, IL, and a former attorney

"Every church needs to follow this mandate: reach the next generation or die trying. Beth Seversen has made a great contribution to answer the question, *How?* With an unusual front-line experience combined with big-picture research, Dr. Seversen offers insightful clues for ordinary church leaders."

Mark Ashton, lead minister of Christ Community Church in Omaha, Nebraska

"Beth delivers a much-needed and inspirational model for engaging emerging adults! The model of engagement in *Not Done Yet* is comprehensive, insightful, and most importantly, research based. Beth is right on in pointing out that the key to attracting and keeping emerging adults in the church is getting them to serve, to belong missionally even when they don't fully identify with the entire mission of the church."

R. York Moore, national director of catalytic partnerships for InterVarsity Christian Fellowship

"*Not Done Yet* has clearly captured the calling on the church in North America to reach emerging adults in the name of Jesus Christ. Dr. Beth Seversen provides an encouraging voice of challenge and presents a pathway for the church to regain trust with millennials and Gen Z."

Tim Ciccone, director of youth and young adult ministry for the Evangelical Covenant Church

"Dr. Seversen's groundbreaking work demonstrates that reaching today's young adults is not a lost cause but is in fact likely if we intentionally engage in risky yet proven practices that connect them to the life of the church. This book will be a seminal text in my evangelism courses for years to come."

Craig Hendrickson, associate professor and program head, missional leadership, Moody Bible Institute

"*Not Done Yet* is an important book for anyone who wants to understand how to reach the next generation! Author Beth Seversen combines her passion for evangelism with solid research and practical tools to give us a guide for how to engage younger adults. The church will either grow older and smaller or younger and larger. This book is essential for the future of the church!"

Dave Ferguson, lead visionary at NewThing, author of *Hero Maker: Five Essential Ways for Leaders to Multiply Leaders*

Not Done Yet

Reaching and Keeping Unchurched Emerging Adults

Beth Seversen

An imprint of InterVarsity Press
Downers Grove, Illinois

InterVarsity Press
P.O. Box 1400, Downers Grove, IL 60515-1426
ivpress.com
email@ivpress.com

InterVarsity Press® is the book-publishing division of InterVarsity Christian Fellowship/USA®, a
movement of students and faculty active on campus at hundreds of universities, colleges, and schools of
nursing in the United States of America, and a member movement of the International Fellowship of
Evangelical Students. For information about local and regional activities, visit intervarsity.org.

All Scripture quotations, unless otherwise indicated, are taken from The Holy Bible, New International
Version®, NIV®. Copyright © 1973, 1978, 1984, 2011 by Biblica, Inc.™ Used by permission of Zondervan.
All rights reserved worldwide. www.zondervan.com. The "NIV" and "New International Version" are
trademarks registered in the United States Patent and Trademark Office by Biblica, Inc.™

While any stories in this book are true, some names and identifying information may have been changed to
protect the privacy of individuals.

Cover design and image composite: Cindy Kiple
Interior design: Jeanna Wiggins
Images: color paper montage: © imran kadir photography / Moment Collection / Getty Images
         male silhouette: © Mads Perc / Digital Vision / Getty Images
         church illustration: © Vipul Umretiya / DigitalVision Vectors / Getty Images

ISBN 978-0-8308-4157-8 (print)
ISBN 978-0-8308-4197-4 (digital)

Printed in the United States of America ♾

InterVarsity Press is committed to ecological stewardship and to the conservation of natural resources
in all our operations. This book was printed using sustainably sourced paper.

Library of Congress Cataloging-in-Publication Data
A catalog record for this book is available from the Library of Congress.

P 25 24 23 22 21 20 19 18 17 16 15 14 13 12 11 10 9 8 7 6 5 4 3 2 1

Y 37 36 35 34 33 32 31 30 29 28 27 26 25 24 23 22 21 20

To Mark, Meredith, Kate,
Audrey, Trevor, and Chris,

who sacrificed so much
for my dreams to be realized!
Kingdom dreams still come true.

"I will pour out my Spirit on every kind of people:
Your sons will prophesy, also your daughters.
Your old men will dream, your young men
will see visions. I'll even pour out my
Spirit on the servants, men
and women both."

JOEL 2:28 *THE MESSAGE*

Contents

Introduction – 1

1 Journeying – 9
*The Long, Winding Road
to Identity Formation*

2 Initiating – 27
*Walking Together
Toward Commitment*

3 Inviting – 39
*No Need to Believe
to Come to Church*

4 Welcoming – 49
*Open the Door and
See All the People*

5 Changing – 63
*Creating an
Invitational Culture*

6 Including – 76
*The Superglue for
Emerging Adults*

7 Involving – 92
Contributing Before Committing

8 Investing – 106
The Church Is Here for You

9 Leading – 121
What's a Leader to Do?

10 Attracting – 150
*Connecting Evangelism,
Discipleship, and Mission*

11 Revisioning – 170
*Evangelism Inside
the Church Box*

12 Balancing – 187
*Orthodox Distinction
and Culture Engagement*

13 True North – 203
*I Just Wanted to Know
You Were for Real*

Acknowledgments – 221

Notes – 223

Introduction

B en transferred from Loyola University to a local college near the Midwest metropolis where he grew up. Through his younger sister's influence, Ben, an unchurched young adult, began to hang around an active evangelical church near his home. Paul, the church youth pastor, invited him to help with the youth group and then to join the high school mission trip to Guatemala. There, Ben made a first commitment to follow Jesus.

In time, Ben and his college-age brother and sister began to cook for their friends on Friday nights. Sometimes they pulled out a guitar and sang songs, including Christian music. The gathering grew to twenty and then thirty college students and young people pursuing careers. They went skiing over winter break, and Ben came alongside and gently cared for each young adult. The lead pastor reached out to Ben and connected with him regularly for mentoring and prayer, and the church offered Ben the "chapel" on Friday nights.

This community became Access, a young-adult ministry of the church with thirty to sixty young adults showing up on Sunday nights and eventually Sunday mornings for worship led by Ben and friends. Many were new to church and not yet following Jesus.

Ariana, a young adult on the church support staff, tended the fledgling group, which drew young people, including "nones," those who don't identify with any type of religion, and "dones," those who have given up on church attendance. The Access community invited people to speak each Sunday on topics significant to emerging adults' faith and purpose. For this community of young adults, "church" was anything but irrelevant. It was an essential part of their social routine.

The Other Side of the Coin

However, groups like this are far from common. Much research from the past decade or so shows that North American congregations are losing many more young adults than they're gaining—at least among the youngest emerging adults: eighteen- to twenty-three-year-olds. When we look at individuals' religious trajectories during their young-adult years, we see that many more of them experience a decline in religious faith and practice (63 percent) than growth (8 percent).

The term *dones* is fitting for those who have "been there, done that" and dropped out of church for twelve months or longer. How are bright-spot churches reaching one of the least-reached, least-churched (especially the younger eighteen- to twenty-three-year-olds), and the least-supported cohort in terms of social services and church support? This question drove me to research that small minority of young adults growing in religious service attendance, prayer, and salience, which led me to study the pathways that bright-spot churches create to serve the preconversion journeys of emerging adults. To better understand how to engage unchurched young adults effectively, it's critical that we know what's happening in churches that effectively evangelize emerging adults.

We also need to listen to the stories of emerging adults who are experiencing spiritual transformation. And we need to hear the stories of bright-spot churches, which have proven effective at reaching and retaining former nones (the religiously unaffiliated) and dones (church dropouts). What is going right in the churches that are effectively evangelizing them?

How can North American churches have an impact on emerging generations? What would success even look like these days? What would it take to get young adults to come to church—and to stay there? Is anyone doing it? My research on the spiritual journeys of emerging adults—a group I roughly define as nineteen to twenty-nine years old—suggests that the answer is yes.

The Good News

The small percent of young adults growing in their faith stand out in a culture of indifference and disillusionment. And this has led me to uncover a new script being written in certain churches scattered across North America. When researching my own denomination, the Evangelical Covenant Church, I discovered a breathtaking phenomenon: there are churches that young adults really like. In these churches it's normal to see emerging adults making new faith commitments to Christ, attending church regularly, growing in prayer and service, and prioritizing their relationship with Jesus. These churches aren't common, but they exist. I call them *bright-spot* churches, because they stand out in a landscape where most young adults find religious faith anything but compelling.

Churches I researched for this project are writing a new narrative: emerging adults like Jesus and they also like church. That may surprise you, because lots of young adults do not like church. Many of them look at the church and feel disillusionment, hurt, or indifference.

Here's some good news: we can learn a lot from these churches. Through interviews with young new Christians and their pastors across North America, I found that churches reaching and keeping unchurched emerging adults have attitudes and practices in common. Churches seeing faith develop among unchurched young adults share similar social and cultural patterns—patterns other churches can adopt and learn. Some churches are effectively making connections. Some are even connecting with emerging adults who have never set foot in a church building or have given up on the church.

This book aims to identify why these churches stand out when it comes to understanding emerging adults, how they make Christian faith, community, and service attractive to them, and how they guide them along the path to spiritual transformation.

Encountering the Gospel at Church

Over the course of my research, I found that non-Christian emerging adults are connecting to the church as an early step in their faith journey, usually by attending the main Sunday service at the invitation of a Christian friend. They are then assimilated into the church community in formal and informal ways. Lead pastors play a significant role in their faith journeys by having an evangelistic and invitational ethos and by communicating the Christian faith in culturally relevant ways. As cultural brokers, pastors help emerging adults navigate new experiences, taking what is unfamiliar and making it familiar. Emerging adults' journeys to faith progress along pathways of compelling Christian community, service that makes a difference, and mentoring and leadership development that provides care and accountability. They encounter the gospel in churches' main services, small group settings, and one-on-one meetings with pastors or leaders in coffee shops, pubs, and other third space venues.

As cultural brokers, pastors help emerging adults navigate new experiences, taking what is unfamiliar and making it familiar.

Most significantly, churches contribute to emerging adults' pre-conversion process through the following nine initiatives. Each will be explored further throughout the book:

▶ initiating, inviting, including, involving, and investing in emerging adults—immediately

▶ encouraging emerging adults to engage in Christian community and behave like Christians before they believe and commit

▶ incorporating and retaining emerging adults before or during the evangelization process

▶ engaging in evangelism inside the church

▶ promoting retention activities, such as service projects within and outside the church

▶ blending evangelism and retention strategies

▶ joining young adults in mutual risk-taking

▶ serving as moral communities in which like-minded friends support, legitimate, and help maintain faith

▶ orienting emerging adults in a collective Christian identity that provides meaning, belonging, expectancy, and reaching aspirations, and that helps them navigate the tension of remaining both culturally distinct and culturally engaged

In the following pages I will break down all these findings, give illustrative examples, and provide clarity. For now, I simply list the findings to give you a sense of the path our learning curve will follow.

Studying Bright-Spot Churches

The information in this book is based on original qualitative research on churches reaching and incorporating young adults, both the formerly unchurched or churchless—identified by George Barna and David Kinnaman in their book *Churchless* as those who in the past six months attended church only on special occasions like holidays and funerals—and the nones, those who self-identify on surveys as having no particular religious affiliation. I offer it to you as one denomination's story to help us—the church—address our urgent need to research effective ways of evangelizing emerging adults in an increasingly post-Christian context so we can provide guidance to churches that long to become more fruitful among young adults in North America.

This book focuses on bright-spot churches that stand out because of the number of new faith commitments they have retained among emerging adults aged eighteen to thirty-three. To qualify for this study, churches had to see not only a minimum of eight new faith commitments among their emerging-adult population in the past twelve months but also had eight new converts become active in the church in some way. So churches in this study were unusually successful at connecting to, evangelizing, and incorporating emerging adults into the church.

How these churches connect with and nurture unchurched young adults into the faith is the crux of my research. As the data is from a small qualitative study, the research is suggestive, not prescriptive. Yet it adds to our understanding of how effective churches reach and retain emerging adults in our contemporary cultural context.

Telescoping the Findings: The Five Practices

Effective churches connecting to, reaching, and incorporating emerging adults engage in five distinct practices that set them apart. These practices, discovered in my research, are helpful in reaching and retaining emerging adults and work well both for individuals immersed in post-Christian culture and for those coming from church-saturated backgrounds. This is partly because almost all emerging adults explore the meaning of their own identity. The application of the "five I's" in a church culture of enthusiasm for participation—for believers and not-yet-believers alike—also helps explain the success of churches that prioritize invitation. They set high expectations for active participation in Christian community and service among both committed disciples and non-Christian newcomers.

Let's call the five practices *invitational* because the church culture of bright-spot churches is welcoming, hospitable, and accepting of unchurched people. Unchurched folks are on churched people's radars. Let's call these practices *missional* because these bright-spot churches focus discipleship not only inwardly on becoming rooted in Christ but also outwardly on engaging God's mission of loving our unchurched neighbors and restoring broken people and communities. For simplicity, I will refer to them as the five practices or the five invitational practices (see fig. 0.1).

These five practices will be further explained, but for now, here's an overview:

1. *Initiating.* Initiate relationships and live missionally with unchurched people where you work, live, and recreate.

2. *Inviting.* Enthusiastically extend invitations to church activities and events where people are warmly welcomed.

3. *Including.* Radically include unchurched people into compelling Christian community and small groups.

4. *Involving.* Encourage young adults to contribute, serve, lead, and grow in ways they believe make a difference. Do this even before their faith commitments are intact and fully developed.

5. *Investing.* Church leaders and congregation members invest in unchurched visitors through mentoring, care, and leadership development.

Here's some insider information, the nonpublic backdrop behind the success of bright-spot churches and what gives them the advantage in reaching young adults: they don't let any time pass before they engage newcomers to their church in the five invitational practices.

These five practices are not necessarily sequential, and part of their effectiveness is due to these churches intentionally and immediately connecting to emerging adults through each of the practices to draw them into the life of the church and without much time passing between each practice.

Figure 0.1. Five practices of churches reaching emerging adults

Consequently churches engaged in the five practices grow in attractiveness to young adults. The more emerging adults are recipients of the practices, the more attractive their churches become, and the more they invite their unchurched friends and family to connect to their new churches. As a result, churches implementing the five practices are growing through new faith commitments that stick.

Cultural Intelligence and Identity Exploration

Evangelistically successful church cultures are relevant, easily accessible, and porous. In this type of church, non-Christians are swiftly engaged, invited, included, involved, and invested in by the church. Newcomers are not left at the margins to figure out unfamiliar church culture on their own. Instead they're connected with cultural informants who help them jump in, and they receive mentoring from leaders who communicate a credible Christian faith with clarity and cultural fluency.

New paradigms of evangelism and incorporation reflect the fact that emerging adults are often evangelized inside the church, becoming incorporated into the church community before or during the evangelization process. Churches reach younger generations in part by taking risks, giving them opportunities to explore, experiment, and try on Christian identity before fully committing to faith in Christ. In doing so, these churches facilitate a preconversion process by providing for the identity construction that characterizes young adults' lives.

Throughout this book you'll read the stories of young adults who come from unchurched backgrounds and are connecting to churches through invitations to serve and mentor. Their stories will reveal how pastors and churches take risks to invest in those who are not fully formed in their faith, inviting them into opportunities to contribute and serve and to find and own their identity as Christ-followers.

This book is for anyone who longs to reach the growing number of unchurched young adults and incorporate them into the life of the church. It's written with the goal of helping pastors, laypeople, and ministry leaders understand the unique spiritual and religious identity journeys of today's emerging adults. My prayer is that it will be used actively as a resource for both leadership insight and personal renewal.

At the end of each chapter, you'll find helpful tools for reviewing the big ideas from that chapter, for starting group discussions, and for following up with practical action steps. By the end of this book, my hope is that you will have deeper knowledge and compassion for the young adults in our midst who, though they may seem hopelessly disconnected from traditional faith communities, are more open than you may think to relationships, conversations, and experiences that can move them closer to an authentic commitment of faith in Jesus Christ.

1

Journeying

THE LONG, WINDING ROAD
TO IDENTITY FORMATION

T o become adults, we take a long, winding road from adolescence to adulthood. The road metaphor aptly describes the journey toward forming an identity. And we can't read much on young-adult identity without running into Jeffrey Arnett's description of early adulthood. A professor of psychology at Clark University, Arnett coined the term *emerging adulthood* to refer to a unique and distinct developmental life phase between adolescence and mature adulthood, roughly from age eighteen to twenty-nine. During emerging adulthood, young adults increase in their independence from family and other support systems, experience seismic change, and explore the world, themselves, and endless possibilities. Arnett uses the metaphor of a long and winding road to depict this prolonged transitional period, which runs from exiting teen years to entering adulthood. Emerging adulthood is sometimes divided between younger (eighteen to twenty-three) and older (age twenty-four to twenty-nine) emerging adults.

Although not everyone agrees that emerging adulthood is a distinct developmental phase or that emerging adulthood happens at a certain age, most agree that there is a time period in which people transition from adolescence to adulthood. Obviously, it's during this season of life that people make life-impacting decisions regarding education,

vocation, life partnership, geographic location, housing, and community. First, let's nail down some terminology before we explore a few of the
characteristics of this life phase just before adulthood.

Sorting Out Our Terms

While *emerging adulthood* refers to the developmental stage that extends
between adolescence and adulthood (usually ages eighteen to twenty-
nine), the millennial generation refers to people born between 1981 and
1996, according to Pew Research. Postmillennials, also called Generation Z, were first born in the year 1995, according to Seemiller and Grace,
or 1997, according to Pew Research. Scholar James Emory White marks
the birth years of Generation Z as between 1995 and 2005. Designating
generational years for cohorts isn't an exact science; it is simply a way to
describe people who were impacted by similar social, economic, political,
and technological events or changes in history like the Great Depression,
World War II, the Kennedy assassinations, the Cold War, and 9/11. Since
there is no one authoritative body that determines generational birth
dates for our purposes, let's imagine the start year for Generation Z was
1995, and that they experienced 9/11 in kindergarten and arrived on the
college scene as freshmen in 2013.

Combined, the two youngest generational cohorts make up about half
of the US population, with Generation Z (25.9 percent) at one percentage point ahead of millennials (24.5 percent). For a time, the 78 million
millennials made up the largest generation in American history and
were the most racially diverse segment of American society. Generation Z has surpassed millennials in both size and ethnic diversity.

I will use the terms *emerging adults, young adults,* and *young people* synony-
mously. Frequently I will refer to Generation Z and millennials or to both
of them as "emerging generations." But my primary focus will be on *emerging adults* as a descriptor for people in their twenties and early thirties.

I won't describe the differences in the two generations. Much already
has been written on millennials—much of it negative. But you won't find
any millennial bashing here, only a deep appreciation for a generation

seeking to find their place in the world. Generation Z may be less familiar and is the focus of much current study. For a quick primer on Generation Z, I recommend *Generation Z: A Century in the Making* by Corey Seemiller and Meghan Grace, and I defer to James Emory White's summary of the defining markers of this newest generation: recession marked, Wi-Fi enabled, multiracial, sexually fluid, and post-Christian. He writes,

> So who are Generation Z? They are growing up in a post-9/11 world. They are experiencing radical changes in technology and understandings of family, sexuality, gender. They live in multigenerational households, and the fastest-growing demographic within their age group is multiracial.

Rather I will focus on looking at these two groups collectively within the category of "emerging adulthood" as it relates to the heart of this study: churches reaching and keeping young adults. Neither of the newest emerging generations attend church much. Only two-fifths (41 percent) of Generation Z attend weekly religious services, while only 27 percent of millennials attend weekly services once or more. This book is about Christian churches that care about those dismal statistics and are pointing these emerging generations toward Christ.

In the face of the general decline in religious attendance among emerging adults in North America, logical questions emerge: How are churches reaching the small minority of dones and nones among emerging adults who are increasing in religious Christian faith and church attendance? How are churches reaching the least-reached, least-churched generations, especially the younger eighteen- to twenty-three-year-old group? Let's start by taking a quick stock of what we know about young adults through a developmental lens.

The Characteristics of Emerging Adulthood

Much of the literature proposing the concept of emerging adulthood refers to it as a transitory stage with five common features also first identified by Arnett:

1. identity exploration answering the question "who am I" and trying out various life options especially in love and work

2. instability in love, work, and places of residence

3. self-focus and figuring out how to manage life independently

4. feeling in-between, in transition, neither adolescent nor adult

5. possibilities and optimism, when hopes flourish and people have an unparalleled opportunity to transform their lives

The trail through emerging adulthood is confusing and complicated. For research I traveled to Burning Man, a self-expression arts festival held annually over Labor Day in Black Rock City, Nevada, and attended by some sixty thousand adherents. The following is an excerpt from an interview with a female millennial attending Burning Man.

I entered college as a statistics major, and I graduated with an accounting degree. I went to work for a Big Four. I hated it! I was miserable. So I got a new job. My boyfriend and I had dated four years, and we broke up for three and a half years. We just started dating again. I left accounting and went to recruiting, and now I recruit for a startup in San Francisco. . . .

Spirituality is a belief in something bigger, I think. That's how I would define god too. I wouldn't say god is Jesus. I would say god is just like a higher being. . . . I feel like I can always pray. I pray, like, every night. . . . I always believed in god, which I wouldn't really classify as like a Christian God or anything. And I try to meditate a lot and understand my inner self, like Zen meditation. . . .

I like to party, fine. Doing drugs seven days a week? No. . . .

What am I looking forward to or longing for? I value my friends really highly, so good relationships. I'd like to settle down. Right now I live in San Francisco, and there is a decent amount of partying. I look forward to settling down a little bit more, having a house, a couple of kids, just enjoying myself, a good career. Sounds kind of boring, but is sounds really nice.

This twenty-seven-year-old woman explores her identity in terms of what company she will work for, who her life partner will be, and where she will live. Besides her identity exploration, we observe instability, self-focus, transition or in-betweenness, and an optimistic outlook toward a more stable future. Her story clearly fits the five distinctive marks of emerging adulthood and is illustrative of many young adults' journeys.

Besides the religious and spiritual lives of emerging adults, Christian Smith, professor of sociology at the University of Notre Dame, and his research team also looked at the underbelly of young adulthood through interviews with eighteen to twenty-three year olds. They wanted to discover how broader cultural influences shape young people's behaviors and relationships. In *Lost in Transition* they describe the dark side of emerging adulthood, also using five descriptors. Smith found some emerging adults are disposed toward many of the same morally misguided behaviors, addictions, and social problems their parents struggle with, including moral confusion, recreational sex, unlimited technology, routine intoxication, serious addiction to alcohol and drugs, and massive consumerism. The difference is young adults engage these destructive behaviors with a greater intensity than their parents due to wider exposure to and availability of contraceptives, information, drugs, alcohol, and purchasing ease while at the same time living in a much more morally relaxed society.

For instance, today's technology gives young people far greater access to pornography and sexual stimuli than was available to their parents. And for many emerging adults, cultural shifts depreciate their sense of certainty and give them a universalist outlook. For many emerging adults, life in a postmodern context is more self-constructed, subjective, and morally relative than that of their moms and dads. For example, a bright eighteen-year-old student in my introductory course on the Bible this semester raised his hand and asked, "Isn't sin a social construct?"

Delaying Adulthood As We Know It

Back in the day, yet not that long ago, adulthood was defined by the social markers of leaving home, completing an education, gaining financial independence, marrying, and starting a family—and for those of privilege, home ownership. But let's be real: those conventional markers are now delayed for Americans for all sorts of reasons that have to do with the economy: job instability, access, and the need or pressure for higher education or specialized training, extended financial dependency on parents and family, and recreational sex due to easily acquired birth control. Young adults are for these reasons extending their transition to adulthood and suspending for an undetermined amount of time a career, marriage and family, and homeownership or even rental.

Social forces, particularly the global economy, undermine stable and lifelong careers. Cultural trends like increasing use of artificial intelligence, companies not replacing retirees, and needing more education or training to compete for employment in the job market contribute to a delay in fully entering adulthood. Many young adults are supported financially by their parents through their twenties to mid-thirties. Smith reports parents spend an average of $38,340 on each of their young adult children between their kids' ages of eighteen and thirty-four. For all these reasons emerging adults statistically are not marrying or starting families as much or as early, compared to past generations.

Fifty-nine percent of millennials are not married. Eighty-three percent do not have children. These two factors contribute to delays in identity commitments and, I suspect, in delays in commitments to a religious identity. In the past, young adults stopped participating in church for a few years then returned once they had a stable career, married, and started their families. Think about it. Between 1950 and the latest census, the median age of women marrying for the first time rose from 20.3 to 27, and the median age of marriage for men rose from 22.8 to 29. The debate continues about whether or not young adults will return to church once they marry and start a family.

Today's young adults take a nine- to eleven-year break from church after high school. Many who study the religious lives of young adults see the delay in marriage and family formation as the key reason they are not practicing their faith. Rodney Stark, an influential figure in sociology of religion, says not to worry about this too much. Young adults are simply sleeping in and learning to manage their lives on their own, like they always have. When they eventually settle down, marry, and have kids, they'll be back to church. Yet the verdict is out on whether or not churched dropouts will return to church after five, ten, or fifteen years away.

Delaying Commitments to Identity _always growing_

Developmental psychologists believe human identity develops throughout our life span and is never complete. But young adults are on the apex of a significant identity stage, making some of their most important decisions affecting the rest of their lives.

When we talk about identity, we refer to questions like, Who am I? What am I going to do with my life? What groups will I commit to? In the United States, personal identity includes one's goals, values, beliefs, group memberships, and roles. The guru of identity work and life-stage development, Erik Erikson (1902–1994), is still respected for his theory of eight stages of identity development from a life span perspective, especially his work among adolescents and his concept that culture influences development. Identity is a sociological concept focused on the search for self and how self relates to the wider social context.

Identity is considered fluid, mutable, and adaptable over time as societies change and develop. It is also believed to vary according to social contexts—that is, people may juggle multiple identities and switch them according to whether they are with their family, with friends, or at work. We may manage multiple identities corresponding to the various roles in life we have—I am a professor, a minister, a wife, a mother, and a friend. The groups people associate with contribute to their sense of identity. Children of immigrants, for example, often modify their ethnic identity, having different identities depending on the social context they're in at a given time and place.

Erikson believed that the work of identity is the most important work of adolescence and saw identity as the sense of who one is as a person and as a contributor to society. He believed that although people develop their sense of identity throughout life, there is a significant identity stage that takes place during adolescence (ages twelve to eighteen). Jeffrey Arnett later proposed that the period of emerging adulthood is when identity development is a major task and has similarities to the same maturation tasks Erikson outlined among high school-aged youth. Still, over time, the two major questions in developing identity have remained much the same: Who am I? and What is my place in the world?

Today, these questions are most acute during young adulthood and worked out within what Erikson called a "psychosocial moratorium" or a reprieve from responsibilities like work and family, when young adults get to play and experiment with future roles and land on their moral and ideological commitments. During this season of life, young adults explore and form their personal and social identities—their self-concept: who they are, what they think about themselves, who they will become, what group or groups they will belong to, what they want to do with their lives, what vocation they will pursue, their beliefs and what perspectives they will adopt, what romantic partner they will journey with through life, and basically how they view the world. Marcia built on Erickson's work and proposed an identity model with four stages or quadrants: diffusion, foreclosure, moratorium and achievement to describe and measure identity exploration and commitment. For our purposes in considering how churches are connecting to and supporting young adults, I am focusing on just moratorium. Setran and Kiesling describe moratorium as "individuals in moratorium actively explore ideas and lifestyles without having committed to them."

Because there are fewer expectations for young adults to be responsible and keep commitments among people of privilege in the United States during emerging adulthood, young people are able to experiment with their roles. Often this period of "social moratorium" or "moratorium" takes place in institutions like the university campus—at least for the privileged—or internships, apprentices, trade schools, working at summer camp, and so forth. These types of structures can assist or block the process of identity cohesion. Informal identity processes and not just structures also are likely to lead to positive and cohesive identity formation. These include supportive parents, supportive adults, and supportive communities, which are all necessary during young-adult years for healthy and cohesive identity formation. Approaches that are less supportive, such as when young adults are isolated, discourage identity exploration and commitment and can lead to what psychologists call "identity procrastination."

The Balancing Act

Young adults need a healthy balance of both personal agency and community to pull off a healthy, cohesive identity. They need to act with deliberate agency, making independent choices in order to develop and grow intellectually, occupationally, and psychosocially. Making their own decisions and becoming responsible for themselves helps them prepare for adult roles. When they don't have those opportunities to express and act with personal agency, young adults tend to procrastinate and to become passive and chaotic in their identity exploration, which may interrupt or delay the formation of their identity. This disruption causes them to be driven by circumstances and impulse, making them unprepared for adult roles.

While it's important for young adults to act with agency, they also need a supportive community that encourages them to explore an identity that is not isolated from supportive parents, adults, and community. In the United States there's an increasing absence of supportive community and adults during this stage. Increasingly, choices of a college, career, location, housing, and spouse are made independently, apart from supportive community. Identity work is seen more and more as one's personal and subjective choice. Cultural observers argue that social identity has eroded in the United States and is replaced by personal choice and guided by self-selected affinity groups. When identity work excludes a supportive family, adults, and mentors, identity formation can lead to anxiety and apathy. Without a supportive community, identity exploration may be aimless, and young adults find themselves stuck.

Think about it. When those life choices that young adults used to make in the context of a supportive family and community are now made with very little guidance from older adults, they are left responsible for their own critical decisions, and the consequences of their independent choices have long-term effects. For example, they may take on enormous college debt to get a degree that has no practical use in a career and as a result end up working as a barista and living at home overwhelmed, isolated from meaningful community, and depressed.

During this significant period of identity exploration, it is also not uncommon for emerging adults to lack much support from society and from churches at this crucial time in their lives, and they often drop out of organized religion as a result. Robert Wuthnow, professor of sociology at Princeton University, points out that most churches offer few programs or assistance to young people once they graduate from high school. It's not until they get married and or have children that churches jump back into providing means of support and encouragement through premarital counseling and childcare and parenting classes and other forms of social support. Young adults are pretty much left on their own to figure life out.

Supportive communities at this acute identity stage are important because they help organize identity pathways across ethnic groups. Identity commitments are nurtured when emerging adults are involved and integrated into normal structured communities like university life, trade schools, apprenticeships, and church. Community and religious involvement are important contexts that foster positive identity formation. What is great about community involvement is that it often provides multiple opportunities for exercising agency. Community participation especially seems to link to identity formation when the activities and groups young adults belong to are infused with positive values and ideologies.

Involvement in religious communities and activities provides a positive context for identity formation. Through religious involvement, emerging adults are supported in finding meaning and purpose, making sense of difficulties, receiving opportunities to experiment with beliefs and to assess their value, and taking opportunity to engage with a moral community that supports their values and gives them a moral framework. Basically, social research confirms that religious communities help young adults integrate a cohesive identity. Being religious is actually associated with positive identity outcomes, like learning the social skills and behaviors needed for work and friendship. Religious contexts encourage emerging adults to get their focus off themselves and on to others and the world, to find meaning and purpose in a faith community, and to understand their place in "the universe and eternal scheme" of things.

The Role of Mentors in Finding Identity

Mentors play a positive role in a young adult's identity development. In the church and Christian communities, mentors help young adults internalize beliefs and behavior. They offer accountability and support for young adults to find the courage and strength to say no to temptations, unhealthy choices, and destructive behaviors. In their book on discipling emerging adults, Richard Dunn and Jana Sundene write, "In every country and culture, the key factor that determines whether young adults are thriving or simply surviving is always the same: the availability and accessibility of teachers, coaches, pastors, friends and mentors who are committed to investing in their spiritual vitality."

Sharon Daloz Parks, a pioneer in young-adult development theory, argues that a mentoring community is the ideal resource for guiding identity development among emerging adults. Mentoring communities help young adults reach their potential and are places where emerging adults can imagine their futures and see how they can contribute to making the world better. Without mentors and mentoring communities in the twentysomething years beyond college, emerging adults may flounder in their identity development.

Faith communities provide a social structure that buffers religious identity, keeping people from caving in to the pressures of competing identities that are countercultural to kingdom values and norms. In Christian groups, campus ministries, and residential Christian colleges, young adults are less likely to give up their religious identity. Parks argues that mentoring communities are very significant in emerging adults' formation of meaning, purpose, and faith. Within supportive Christian communities like churches and campus ministries, emerging adults find the resources and support to make and to continue religious identity commitments.

Delaying Religious Commitments

Religious identity construction may not be acute until a person's late twenties or early thirties, when commitments to career, marriage, and family are finally made. Such delayed commitments to marriage and family may make returning to church difficult for emerging adults. Of course, the verdict is still out on whether young adults who grew up in church then dropped out after high school will return to church. Their memories of church from ages twelve to sixteen or eighteen are certainly not as sharp and vibrant as their unchurched memories from ages eighteen to twenty-seven or twenty-nine. Among earlier generations, religious commitments were postponed for a few years after the completion of high school; today they are delayed by two to three times that amount.

All these delays—landing a job with financial security, purchasing a home, marrying, having kids, identity formation, and commitments—lengthen the time that emerging adults are disconnected and detached from church. The longer emerging adults are absent from church, the more foreign church culture and life may appear to them. What's to say that when they finally do marry and have children, they will come back—especially when their new habits, friendships, and social groups are formed outside church? What's to say that they will go back to attending church?

Christian Smith, who has worked with the largest and longest study of emerging adults, concluded that, due to social change and upheavals, emerging adulthood is extended far longer than for previous generations of young adults. It is possible that with these societal changes extending young adulthood, conversion may also be prolonged. So evangelism may need to look different than it has. The chapters to come will reveal some of these generational differences as we explore the spiritual journeys of young adults and how churches are reaching and keeping them.

During their identity construction, many emerging adults will disassociate from their parents' religious associations and views, likely because they need to differentiate from their parents. For young adults, religious disaffiliation seems to cause less family tension than other disassociations. Since most young adults care about their parents, their parents' opinions, and their relationship with their parents, not attending religious services may be one of the least stressful forms of detachment. One result of religious disassociation from parental choices is that young adults in the United States, in seeking to form their own religious commitments today, cobble together their religious identities partially in isolation from their parents and independent from older adults.

Being absent from church for a long time may make it more difficult for a young adult to return—a phenomenon not seen in former generations. Recommitting may not be easy. Jonathan Hill, who studies the impact of higher education on religious commitment, writes,

> If young adults spend a long time outside the church developing meaningful networks of relationships and establishing career trajectories, then they may be less likely to return even if they do marry and have children. Understanding the full implications of this extended period of disengagement appears to be the next step in understanding religion in early adulthood for the current generation.

It is also important to ask, what are the implications of delayed religious identity formation for reevangelism, incorporation, and discipleship among those absent for a decade or so? For young adults who have conformed to the ways of the world in their attitudes, destructive behaviors, and syncretistic theology, it will include an orientation or reorientation in christocentric and orthodox theology.

When I traveled to the Burning Man festival, I interviewed eighteen- to thirty-five-year-olds about their religious journeys and identities. Most of the young adults I interviewed grew up in Christian, Jewish, or Mormon homes, but they were very eclectic in their spiritual beliefs and practices.

The Sacred Spaces Villages Camp at Burning Man offered an imposing variety of spiritualities to choose from. To give you a sense of what I
mean, here are some of the spiritual movements and practices I saw represented on the menu boards: Alchemy, Deeksha Prayer Circle, Buddhist
Wisdom, Kirtan, Yoga, Healing Arts, Sound Healing, Native Wisdom,
Shamanism, Krishna Consciousness, Transcendence, Ambient Trance,
and Sacred Geometry. The syncretistic pluralism on display was often
bewildering: many attendees were happy to give away rocks with special
powers or take drugs in an effort to gain an esoteric experience of heightened awareness—while still holding to certain Christian beliefs from
their upbringing.

Bricoleur, a term that has its roots in the work of French social anthropologist Claude Levi Strauss, was popularized in the United States by
Robert Wuthnow, who used the word *bricolage* to refer to young adult's
religion and their reuse of available materials and whatever is at hand to
solve problems and create new tools—something like spiritual tinkering.
Many of the young people I met at Burning Man were spiritual bricoleurs
or do-it-yourselfers. They had a cut-and-paste approach to religion or
spirituality, picking and choosing from a plethora of choices and
resources to put together a spiritual life that worked for them.

Experimenting with Christian Identity

Churches effective in reaching and incorporating unchurched young
adults seem to be helping with identity exploration by supporting
cohesive identity development. Bright-spot churches provide the social
moratorium that Erikson believed to be crucial to identity development.
That moratorium may look different in each church, but a pattern
emerges where young adults have opportunity to experiment with roles
and identity commitments in various Christian social settings, such as
young adult internships, and incorporating emerging adults into communities like small groups and mentoring communities. When churches
give emerging adults the opportunity to explore and experiment with
Christian identity through belonging to a church and becoming involved

in a Christian community, those young people are likely to make new faith commitments, including committing to Christ.

Churches that do well at serving emerging adults give them opportunities to "try on" and "try out" Christian identity. By participating in Christian community and Christian practices like prayer, worship, Bible reading, small groups, and service, emerging adults explore and experience Christianity. The church community, its small groups, and its ministries function

When churches give emerging adults the opportunity to explore and experiment with Christian identity through belonging to a church and becoming involved in a Christian community, those young people are likely to make new faith commitments, including committing to Christ.

like those institutions and structures described by Erik Erikson's social moratorium, in which young adults take a recess from their normal life and play in a new sandbox, experimenting with Christian identity. They try Christianity on to see if it fits, to see if it's comfortable. They have a space and a place to consider whether it is the faith community and the Christian worldview they want to commit to at a time when they are exploring identity commitments.

I believe bright-spot churches are giving emerging adults room to explore what it means to identify as a believer in Christ. By attending worship, small groups, or ministries and by participating, they experiment with adhering to the norms and values and practices of the Christian community. All the while they also observe the community and the way community members live out their faith and lives in the way of Jesus, caring for one another and for the broader community. What I appreciate about these standout churches is that they have high expectations for non-Christians, but they don't pressure them. They offer invitations to a culture where everyone is welcome and invited and expected to serve and enjoy community—but are not coerced or obligated to do so. This type of participation and contribution lets emerging adults experiment before deciding whether a Christian identity commitment will work for them.

One of the most critical findings in my study is that churches that effectively help emerging adults move forward in their conversion journeys provide them opportunities to try out Christian identity before committing to it. Practically, that means they give non-Christian young adults access to Christian community and involvement that aligns with and affirms emerging adulthood as a life stage in which identity exploration is an intense part of young adults' work and in which they settle on identities that are most satisfying to them. For these standout churches, community participation, religious involvement, and mentoring catalyze young adults' new and renewed faith commitments. So supportive community and religious involvement truly do propel identity formation.

CHAPTER REWIND

The process of becoming an adult has gotten significantly longer in the last several decades due to the global economy and changing cultural expectations and factors. In turn, identity exploration and formation have too. Young adults are consolidating their ethical, moral, and belief commitments during emerging adulthood to form their values, norms, and identity. The conversion process is often extended, in part due to identity exploration taking longer.

This is the season when emerging adults make commitments to intimate relationships and work associations. When they do so with the assistance of supportive adults, mentors, and mentoring communities, they experience productivity and competence, which are essential to healthy identity work. Community and religious involvement help emerging adults find meaning in their lives, make sense of difficulties, and experiment with and critique contradicting beliefs and belief systems, ultimately rejecting some and integrating others into their identity.

Plenty of evidence demonstrates that in the recent past, people were first invited to engage in a supportive Christian community where they experienced belonging and then came to faith in Christ in that community. However, the emerging adults in my investigation followed a slightly different spiritual journey toward faith in Christ. They participated not only in supportive community but also in the social moratorium that bright-spot churches provide, where they are able to experiment with Christian faith and practice through community and involvement. Certain steps in these emerging adults' conversion process allowed them to experiment with Christian identity within a moral, life-giving Christian community that validated pursuing a new identity commitment. And this enhanced their spiritual journey. Giving young adults space, time, community, and roles greases their wheels and ultimately leads to commitments to the Christian faith.

When church leaders, pastors, mentors, and mentoring communities guide emerging adults during this identity stage, they provide space for emerging adults to try on Christian identity to see if it's right for them, and they land on what developmental psychologists call a cohesive identity.

Specifically, when church leaders, pastors, mentors, and mentoring communities guide emerging adults during this identity stage, they provide space for emerging adults to try on Christian identity to see if it's right for them, and they land on what developmental psychologists call a cohesive identity. Basically, as the church community assists young adults in figuring out how the world works, where they fit in, and how they can contribute to making it a better place, they assist young adults in their identity work, and this work encourages their spiritual journeys, concluding in new and renewed faith commitments.

STARTING THE CONVERSATION

▶ How are you inspired or challenged by how young adults explore and form identities?

▶ Who are the young adults attending your church, and who are the supportive church adults in their lives?

▶ How does your church guide emerging adults toward vocation? How does it help unleash gifts and passions by offering them opportunities and communities in which they can find purpose and their place in the world God created?

ACTION STEPS

Know who's out there. Identify the young adults between the ages of eighteen and thirty-five attending your church—and their friends.

Know where they are. Identify any communities within your church that young adults are a part of.

Draw them in. Connect young adult church attendees to supportive church adults and mentoring Christian communities.

2

Initiating

WALKING TOGETHER TOWARD COMMITMENT

Nathan had grown up in an unchurched family in the Pacific Northwest, considered himself agnostic, and had only one close Christian friend throughout high school and college. He told me he knew his friend went to church, but Nathan didn't talk about religion growing up and didn't really know what it was.

When his old high school friend invited him to join a young-adult camping trip with some of her church friends, Nathan was naturally skeptical. But several guys on the trip reached out and asked him to join a church-sponsored sports activity. Despite his apprehension that he may be indoctrinated, Nathan started playing Frisbee with a bunch of people that went to that church. When he heard his new teammates talking about their pastor and their church community in positive and non-stereotypical ways, Nathan became curious. But he was self-conscious about being an outsider. Even so, eventually he asked his friend if he could go with her to church.

Churches reaching young adults like Nathan are seeing a growing number of new and renewed faith commitments among unchurched emerging adults. How are these bright-spot churches connecting with them, helping them come to faith in Christ, and seeing them stick? That's exactly what I wondered, and my investigation identified pathways—a sort of pattern of five practices that churches with emerging-adult conversions were implementing. This chapter explores "initiating," the first of these practices.

So how do unchurched young adults end up in a church—especially those who have grown up outside the church, steeped in North American society's negative or indifferent stereotypes of church and Christians? These outsiders or nones—people who identify with no religious background—are increasing. Pew Research estimates about 35 percent of millennials are nones.

And why do nones reject church? That's a great question since people have been telling us for years that young people don't like going to church. Sociologist Robert Putnam reported that nones purposefully reject the church due to its lack of Christian virtues and particularly because of its conservative views on sexuality, politics, and belief systems. Young people have a new moral sensibility and reject the church for what they perceive as immorality. David Kinnaman and Gabe Lyons write that many people outside the church accuse Christians and the church of being un-Christian due to judgmentalism, homophobia, right-leaning politics, hypocrisy, enclaving, and imposing their beliefs on others.

So young people that grow in their connection to and appreciation of church are all the more fascinating, as are the churches they are a part of.

How Did They Get Connected to Church?

Churches reaching and keeping young adults are rewriting the church narrative. Emerging adults connecting to these bright-spot churches for the first time or returning after a significant absence experience their churches as nonjudgmental. Like Maddy, they were surprised when they were first introduced to or reintroduced to church and did not feel judged. In Maddy's words, "It wasn't this stereotype that I had built. I felt like people were going to be judgmental. Because I didn't know much about things related to God, or I didn't know much about church, that was my fear. But once I went, everyone was welcoming, helpful and friendly."

Emerging adults whose expectations of judgment were overturned began to have a mind shift toward the church. One church dropout, who was confused about belief in Christ and described herself as a partier, explained her change in attitude: "I feel that my perception . . . is shifting. It's like I'm broken and confused, and all over the place, and I'm still there. And I don't feel judged." Young adults find that the scripts they had been given by society—through jokes, movies, television, and music—or believed about churches' judgmentalism were not true to their own experience. Their new churches served them by deconstructing their assumptions about church. Through experiencing church firsthand, they learn the stereotypes they believed about church aren't necessarily true.

New churches serve young adults by deconstructing their assumptions about church.

The unchurched emerging adults I studied followed one of three roads to church as part of their preconversion journey: they were (1) invited to church by friends under normal circumstances, (2) invited by friends while experiencing personal crisis or complexity, or (3) inspired by crisis or complexity to search—usually online—for help. Figure 2.1 illustrates these roads to church.

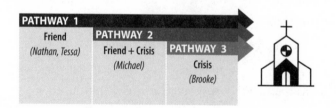

PATHWAY 1
Friend
(Nathan, Tessa)

PATHWAY 2
Friend + Crisis
(Michael)

PATHWAY 3
Crisis
(Brooke)

Figure 2.1. Initiate: three pathways to church as part of their preconversion journey

Tessa's story resonates with pathway one. She planned to party when she arrived as a freshman on campus. But instead, when an upperclassman invited her to church, she decided to check it out. That's when her journey toward faith in Christ launched. Michael's journey to church traveled along pathway two. When his new job turned out to be less than life-giving due to endless travel and little time for himself, a friend invited him to church and suggested he talk to the pastor. Brooke, reflecting pathway three—crisis—was tired of her alcohol addiction and looked online for a church to help her start over and leave her past behind. In crisis mode, her pathway started with a web search.

Unchurched young adults that connected to churches were most likely to connect initially through an invitation from a trusted or new friend. *Wait, you mean more programs, events, and citywide campaigns don't reach unchurched young people?* Yes, and not just in my study. The most effective outreach pattern observed by researchers George Barna and David Kinnaman, reported in their 2014 book, *Churchless*, was interpersonal relationships with unchurched people. These relationships trumped all other approaches to evangelism in our contemporary context, including social media. That's not to say a friends' invitation to a special event like InterVarsity's The Price of Life and conferences like Catalyst, One Thing, and Propel are not powerful tools impacting unchurched emerging adults. Events can be transformative if the key words in the previous sentence—*friend* and *invite*—are operating and in that order.

Poll research gathered by Barna and Kinnaman from a series of eighteen nationwide surveys between 2008 and 2014 with a total of 20,524 respondents revealed that the unchurched respond to the following outreach approaches:

- ▶ invitations to church from trusted friends
- ▶ an appealing event, such as a concert or seminar at a church
- ▶ ministries that regularly and effectively serve the poor
- ▶ mentoring and development opportunities for young people

There was declining interest in advertising attempts to reach unchurched people—including radio, TV, newspaper, billboards, and direct mailings.

Certainly the number one way unchurched young adults connect to church is through relationships. Either a friend invites them or they become so curious about a friend's faith that they ask their Christian friend if they can come with them to church. They make these requests after becoming increasingly intrigued by the church or the pastor due to conversations with friends. It's also important to note that young adults attend church for the first time accompanied by a friend or family member before committing to faith in Christ. They're a lot less likely to show up on their own.

All I Have to Do Is Ask?

Actually, there's a bit more to it than simply extending an invitation to church. Invitations people respond to don't come from just anyone; rather, unchurched people say they would be most likely to respond to invitations to church from good friends. Apart from the context of a close relationship with friends or family, unchurched people are not interested in coming to a church, small group, or "Bible thing."

And that's not all. Being *excited* about our faith—our relationship with Jesus—and about our church *and enthusiastically talking* about our faith, church, or pastor is a key factor in young people responding to invitations to church. If we aren't talking about our faith, church, or pastor to good friends in a way that's contagious and natural (not forced!) in our everyday conversations, close friends and family will be less likely to accept our invitations to church activities or services. Invitations most unchurched people say yes to are in the context of trusting relationships.

Drawing conclusions from Barna and Kinnaman's research and my own, I suggest that three significant steps your congregation can take to reach lost young people are, first, *initiate* relationships with unchurched emerging adults; second, enthusiastically *invite* friends to church services, church-bridging opportunities, and church activities; and third, scrutinize your church website through the lens of emerging adults. Let's begin to unpack these three suggestions.

Practice 1: Initiate

The word *initiate* best describes how church people cultivate close relationships with unchurched people: they have friendships with people who don't know Jesus! Bright-spot churches are exceptional at this.

Imagine, these churches are filled with church attenders who have deep, meaningful friendships with people outside the church. Not only do church attenders initiate relationships with unchurched people, their pastors model and encourage those relationships. Not surprisingly, some young people assume the front door to a church is closed and even locked. Close relationships with unchurched people are the crowbars that pry open the door of the church that appears to be shut tight.

Like Nathan, most unchurched emerging adults connect to church through friendship. A churched friend or family member invites an unchurched young adult to church or a church activity. That invitation is the catalyst for beginning a journey toward faith in Christ. Few unchurched guests attend church unaccompanied or uninvited; most are accompanied to church by a churched friend or family member.

This isn't to say that unchurched young adults never ask their Christian friends if they can come to church. Near the end of the summer sports season, Nathan initiated a connection by asking to visit his friends' church rather than waiting to receive an invitation, because his curiosity was awakened by his new teammates' enthusiasm for church and for their pastor. Emerging adults generally make these requests after becoming increasingly intrigued by the church or the pastor due to conversations with friends.

Genuine friendship. Of course, for relationships to be transformative and for invitations to be sincere, friendships need to be genuine. Nathan didn't feel that people were intentionally building a relationship with him to share their faith. He said, "I would have been very on guard if it felt like they were trying to convert me or something like that."

Campus ministers Doug Schaupp and Don Everts agree that honest and authentic friendships are important for college students on their journey to faith in Christ. In interviews with two hundred college students who came to faith in Christ while attending university, they found that trusting a Christian was the first step in students' journeys toward Jesus. Trust builds over time in the incubator of genuine friendship.

Trust builds over time in the incubator of genuine friendship.

Awakening curiosity. When people talk enthusiastically about their faith and their church in the context of genuine relationships, curiosity is often awakened. When a friendship is cultivated and growing, whether a new or renewed friendship, conversations are deep and trust is strong enough that often the unchurched friend says, as Nathan did, "Hey, can I go with you to church?" Curiosity is raised by the ways Christian friends care for unchurched friends and enthusiastically talk about their faith, their churches, and their pastors.

Connecting the dots. Having deep conversations with non-Christians is especially significant when Christians apply spiritual wisdom and understanding to their conversations. It's important to prayerfully consider topics to discuss, to genuinely be thoughtful and intentional in how we connect faith in Jesus to our own struggles and our dreams. We need to find ways to connect with unchurched friends through our common needs, concerns, struggles, and dreams to help awaken curiosity and connect the dots between their needs and faith in Jesus—and how the church fits into all that. Giving words to how we work through pain, loss, hurt, and rejection with God's help, and how we experience the presence of Christ, provokes curiosity and names for unchurched friends and family what they may be experiencing themselves.

Looking Closer

Let's back up a moment. We're assuming that church people have growing, healthy relationships with unchurched young adults. That's a big assumption that can't be taken for granted.

In my former work as a denominational evangelism director, I was continually reminded how church people are disconnected from relationships with unchurched people—and particularly unchurched young adults. My observations aren't limited to my own denomination. Among Christians in Protestant and evangelical churches, there is a general withdrawal from close relationships with the unchurched—and especially unchurched emerging adults. At a time when most social services—institutional, development, socialization, and care-taking support for children and adolescents—are withdrawn from young adults, the church also withdraws from engaging young adults and removes the scaffolding supporting young adult discipleship, which includes

▶ mentors

▶ community

▶ vocational counseling

▶ job training

▶ college funding

▶ life-partner guidance

▶ relocation assistance

▶ leadership development

▶ mental illness training and caregiving

▶ discipleship connected to developmental tasks and biblical moorings

Unfortunately, I agree with Robert Wuthnow, the message the church sends young people is *there's nothing here for you.*

Reduced, the evangelism problem is a culture problem: Most Christians do not have close personal relationships with unchurched people, especially young adults. Instead, they eat, work, and recreate with churched people. To see more faith commitments among young people, church people need to connect personally to unchurched young adults—both church dropouts and nones. Some churches need a culture shift. Does yours?

Belong Out There

Churchgoers need encouragement to live our faith beyond our own walls, where people live, work, and play. We also need to recognize that the places where we work and play are where God has released us into his mission to initiate relationships, build trust, and draw people toward Jesus. To live outside the church box (both church facilities and church relationships) is to become more biblical and more like Jesus. When we nurture unchurched friendships, as Nathan's former high school friend did by initiating lunch together, we follow Jesus in surrender to his commands to love our neighbor as ourselves, to make disciples, and to join Jesus in his mission of gospel proclamation and gospel restoration—restoring all that's broken in the world. We need unchurched friends.

When we nurture unchurched friendships, we follow Jesus in surrender to his commands to love our neighbor as ourselves, to make disciples, and to join Jesus in his mission of gospel proclamation and gospel restoration.

The problem is, a lot of our people are stuck when it comes to sharing their faith because they have trouble taking initiative with unchurched people, and they may have given up on friends, colleagues, relatives, or neighbors ever coming to faith in Christ. They express concern that they will be culturally insensitive or that young people aren't interested in relationships with older adults. We can help them initiate relationships with unchurched people by encouraging them in simple ways to "belong out there" and to be truly present in their neighborhoods and proximate to unchurched people by knowing and loving their neighbors well.

One simple way to belong out there and build connections with unchurched young adults is to join something. Megan became curious about church and God through playing board games with Christian friends. Katelyn, a bartender, had a returning customer who shared sermon messages with her. Adam connected to a Christian when he joined his college cross country team. Steve was invited to church by a friend from work.

Most people need help knowing how to connect with the unchurched. When training pastors and church leaders in outreach, I ask, "What do you enjoy? What are your passions, concerns, and interests? Do you care about the environment? Are you concerned for underresourced people in your city? Are you passionate about stopping human trafficking? Do you love to read, paint, surf, bike, or go to the theater? Join others who share your passions and interests. A thirtysomething year-old Anglican priest told me that he plays the bass and gathers with other musicians weekly to jam and build relationships.

Perhaps you have a family member who struggles with addiction. Celeste joined an agency that helps families struggling with addiction. One of her clients asked for additional resources, and Celeste gave her a book from a Christian perspective and explained it was a bit "Jesus-y" but a helpful resource. Celeste got a call from that client a few weeks later, who said, "I didn't know God was for people like me and my family." Several weeks passed and the client called again. This time she asked, "Celeste, I'd like to do that thing in the book."

"What thing?" Celeste asked. "You know, that thing where you ask Jesus to lead your life to help you have a relationship with God."

Celeste asked her when she wanted to do so, and her client responded, "I was thinking that on Thursday we could have coffee at ten. I'll stop by, and we can do it then."

I love this story because it illustrates not only how this client scheduled her own inauguration into God's kingdom but also because it illustrates the significance of "belonging out there."

When we join something, we gather with others that share our concerns, passions, and interests. In those spaces we connect to unchurched people and initiate relationships in which their curiosity is awakened.

Start Something

It can be tough to join something when you're commuting long distances, travel a lot for work, or can't make a time commitment. You'd love to coach a team, join a bridge club, be on the city planning commission, or volunteer at the homeless shelter, but your schedule is far too demanding. Starting something allows you to be in control of the schedule and to set the tone of the activity, event, or service opportunity. Because I could set the schedule, I started a neighborhood book club to get to know and love my neighbors. Over the next fourteen years, friendships formed, playdates happened, dinners were shared, barbecues were planned, Bible studies were launched, and faith deepened as we connected over good reads and shared life.

A faculty member who heard me speak on "starting something" began a Russian literature club at the local library to connect to people far from

God. A pastor started a bicycle group that road together and in which friends were formed. He became a good friend and pastor to several of the unchurched men as they went through the crises and chaos of life. Another millennial-age pastor connected to the recreation department in his city and started a weekly game night where he began to build into the lives of three young men.

Having trouble making friends in your community? Prayerfully start something, and ask God to bring young people who need him.

Imitate Jesus

Mission was the context Jesus intended for discipleship, and it involves both reaching the lost and restoring the broken. How can we imitate Jesus in discipleship if we are disconnected from people like Zacchaeus and the Samaritan woman in our immediate and surrounding contexts? The people Jesus deeply loved, cared for, healed, and proclaimed the good news to were not only the religious and the devout but also the poor, the marginalized, and those disconnected from mainstream religious life, much like the unchurched young adults of emerging generations. Jesus saw people as friends, not projects. When we imitate his posture toward those apart from God who need the Physician to heal them, we come to genuinely care and befriend folks far from God.

Churches that initiate are full of Christians who belong out there, who join something or start something, and who neighbor well. They are connecting and building bridges to unchurched people, including unchurched young adults. They're taking the first step—initiating—in serving the preconversion process of young adults.

⏎ CHAPTER REWIND

To reach young adults, encourage your church to initiate, develop, and deepen relationships with unchurched people, especially young adults far from God. Talk about faith in Jesus and church enthusiastically in the context of those relationships. Pray to build curiosity and influence.

STARTING THE CONVERSATION

▶ Do you have relationships with unchurched people, and are there any young people among them? How might you initiate or deepen relationships with emerging adults?

▶ Do you talk with unbelieving young people about your faith, your church, your pastor, or prayer enthusiastically and genuinely in thoughtful, intentional ways when appropriate and led by the Holy Spirit?

▶ Wait. No unchurched among your close friends? How can you belong out there or join something to begin to build relationships with people outside the church?

ACTION STEPS

Encourage relationship building. Consider how you can encourage your church or small group to initiate relationships with unchurched folks and become good friends with someone who is not a believer.

Pray for opportunities. Pray with your church or small group that God will direct and lead you to young people far from him. Then care for and befriend them for life.

Get out there. If you don't have any non-Christian friends or your small group or church friends don't, consider ways to belong out there, or join something and hold each other prayerfully accountable to follow through and connect relationally to unchurched people.

Take small steps. Consider ways this week you can create community with a non-Christian through sharing a meal or a cup of coffee and conversation.

3

Inviting

NO NEED TO BELIEVE TO COME TO CHURCH

People come to faith today—and have throughout history—through connection to a vibrant witnessing Christian community. They may take some steps toward Jesus outside of a faith community, but faith is nurtured and sustained in community.

As we build relationships with people and share our stories and our enthusiasm for Jesus and for our church, people are drawn to Christ. At some point, the young adults we initiate with will need to be invited into a faith community where they can make the rest of their journey toward faith in Christ. The following story of twenty-year-old Shea is a good example:

I was really broken, really hurting, and on Saturday night, my best friend Ariana invited me to a lecture. And there she asked me, "Do you want to go with me to church tomorrow morning?" I was like, sure, why not? I've nothing to lose. So, the next morning she drove me to church. It was an hour away from where we lived!

I just sat there and listened to the message. I felt something in my heart I couldn't explain. I just bawled my eyes out. In that moment, I felt like Christ was speaking directly to me, and the message was for me. It was called "The Way Out," and it was just very clear and very to the point, and it gave me action steps. It was like feeding your spirit, feeding your life with prayer, finding good community. There were literally action steps for a way out.

We didn't really talk about it that much on the way home, and I just bawled my eyes out for like weeks. I was like I think I want to go back. I'm the one who encouraged her, "We need to go back; we need to go back." I really wasn't sure what was going on in my heart. Like Jesus was there clearly pursuing me, and I just wasn't recognizing it because I didn't grow up in a church. I felt like I woke up a little more each day."

Emerging adults, just like Shea, initially connect to church through invitations made by close friends. Bright-spot churches enthusiastically invite family and friends to church. To reach emerging adults, the first and most significant practice your church can engage in is initiating relationships with unchurched people. The second is to be so enthusiastic about their faith and church that they invite friends to check out church too.

At some point, the young adults we initiate with will need to be invited into a faith community where they can make the rest of their journey toward faith in Christ.

Road to Church 1: Friends Extending Invitations—to What?

In chapter two I introduced the idea that there are three roads emerging adults follow on their way to church. Once they arrive at church, they follow one of three pathways to faith in Christ. We've spent a lot of time unpacking what the first path to church looks like because it's so significant in the lives of young adults: friends inviting unchurched friends to church.

So, what does an invitation look like? What exactly do you say? Twenty-year-old Megan invites her unchurched friends by saying, "Hey, come to church with me. You know, you don't have to believe anything to come. I always go, and it really helps me. There's always something I take away that speaks into my life. You don't even have to believe to belong there."

She adds, "Yeah, I just tell all my friends, 'You don't have to believe to come to our church. Just come. It's awesome. You may love it.'"

Pastors of bright-spot churches understand that the connection to the unchurched is through personal invitations by churched people. Peter Hong, the planting pastor of an urban multiethnic congregation in Chicago, New Community Logan Square, reported, "Eighty percent of folks come via personal invites by someone who's already a part of our church. This is research that we've done in the last fourteen years, and it's proven to be true over and over again." Pastors of churches reaching unchurched emerging adults catalyze the preconversion process by encouraging church attendees to invite their friends and family to church. Notice the key phrase in Pastor Peter's research: "personal invites." I cannot stress this enough: unchurched people respond to personal invitations of their friends, neighbors, and colleagues.

You may wonder, as I did, *Exactly what invitations do emerging adults respond to? What am I supposed to invite them to?* Pastors encourage their congregations to invite non-Christian friends and family to church events and activities hosted on-site and off, knowing that most emerging adults first connect to church through invitations to their main service. While some churches similar to Quest Church in Seattle often create innovative "portals," like the camping trip and the sports teams that Nathan connected to, the weekend worship service continues to be the main entrance for the unchurched invited by family and friends. Pastor Steve Wiens of Genesis Church in Minneapolis said,

> Most get invited by their friends to Sunday worship. That's the biggest front door. . . . We also have community groups, and a lot of those are intergenerational, and [include] people that are married or single. But it seems the biggest front door is still Sunday, for us. Lots and lots of visitors come.

Though some bright-spot churches try innovative ways to reach unchurched people, creating portals to connect with unchurched friends in places people frequent, it seems many pastors, like Pastor

Steve, find that the response is highest when folks are invited to the main weekend worship service.

You may be thinking, *Whoa, you mean young adults will simply show up at the church service when they're invited?* Yes and no. Remember, young people respond to invitations to church within the context of close relationships with friends or family. Interestingly, unchurched young adults sometimes ask to visit a friend's church rather than wait to receive an invitation. They make these requests after becoming increasingly intrigued by the church or the pastor due to interactions with friends. Young adults rarely show up at church alone; a friend or family member generally accompanies them.

The main point is that these bright-spot churches are filled with people who *invite* their *friends* to church. Young adults are no exception. Dena Davidson, campus life director of Thrive School at Bayside Church Granite Bay in Roseville, California, describes millennials as "great inviters." Alex Rahill, former lead pastor of LifeChurch Canton in Michigan, observes that some young adults are significantly persistent in repeatedly inviting friends to church. Craig Groeschel, lead pastor of Life.Church Oklahoma City, notes that people not only invite but also actively *bring* their unchurched and nominally churched friends with them to church.

The combined practices of *initiating* friendship and *inviting* her to church and to the Christian campus ministry played a huge role in Tessa coming to faith in Christ. She said,

> In college, freshman year, a lot of upperclassmen reached out to me and lived life with me, and I started to explore my faith more. It was a gradual progression of seeing the value of going to church, and CCFC [Cambridge Community Fellowship Church] was the first church I attended regularly. Through a series of conversations and a change of my heart, I realized it wouldn't make sense if it were just on my own, but that there was a higher being. I learned more about the story of Jesus, and it made a lot of sense to me. Also, a lot of people invited me to the Asian Christian fellowship, which

played a huge part. And obviously CCFC was the first church I went to. I started to check out CCFC probably because there was a huge group at Harvard that goes.

Note that Tessa said "a lot of people invited me" and "there was a huge group at Harvard that goes." A community of friends reached out to her with invitations.

In standout churches reaching young adults, members don't huddle up, view the church as a fortress to defend, or feel the unchurched are unwelcome. Churches reaching young adults do not partition themselves off from "the world." Instead they have deep and authentic relationships with their neighbors and those they sense are far from God. Churches effectively reaching young adults engage surrounding communities. The doors of these churches are wide open to guests—churched and unchurched people alike—and the church boundaries are porous, with unchurched people like Tessa and Shea and Nathan coming and going.

> *The doors of churches effectively reaching young adults are wide open to guests—churched and unchurched people alike—and the church boundaries are porous, with unchurched people coming and going.*

Road to Church 2: Helping in Crisis

A second road to church opens when an emerging adult with a Christian friend encounters a crisis or complexity. For some, like Chelsea, it's a crisis due to a moral failure or due to being the victim of a moral failure. Chelsea explained,

> I was nineteen. My friend invited me to a service, and one of our pastors gave a sermon that was so authentic. Even though I grew up in suburbia, we had a lot of secrets, and I had a hard story, so people always knew me for being the broken one and having all this hard stuff going on. When the pastor was speaking and telling his story, he also involved all these other people. I heard a girl talking

about how she had been raped. I thought, *Whoa, if they can be so vulnerable and open in front of these hundreds of people, this is something different. I want what they have.* Throughout the entire service, people were saying they were made clean in Christ. And I wanted to be made clean in Christ, 'cause I've had a lot of stuff happen to me.

Chelsea's friend pointed her to church and faith in Christ as a consolation and a solution for the immoral and destructive behaviors she had experienced. A bright-spot church encouraged her new faith commitment by identifying with her pain and her need for healing and cleansing. Christian Smith, the author of *The Darkside of Emerging Adulthood*, points to five moral failures in which young adults struggle the most during their progression. His research on the vulnerabilities of emerging adulthood from adolescence to adulthood identifies that some emerging adults are

- ▶ morally adrift and confused
- ▶ experiencing intoxication
- ▶ living the shadow-side of sexual liberation
- ▶ politically disengaged
- ▶ suffering from massive consumerism

If a young adult's moral compass points in a direction other than north, they will likely stumble over a tripwire in at least one of these and subsequently suffer. Note that pastors of bright-spot churches are aware of the social forces and cultural trends among young adults and their needs for healing, forgiveness, and freedom from addictions and the idols that ensnare them. Friends who point their friends in crisis, confusion, and complexity to faith, church, and pastors who can help are a significant route to church for unchurched emerging adult nones and dones.

Friends who point their friends in crisis, confusion, and complexity to faith, church, and pastors who can help are a significant route to church for unchurched emerging adults.

Road to Church 3: Searching Online for Help

Twenty-seven-year-old Brooke was prompted to visit a church by the statement she found on the church's homepage: "Know, Grow, and Go." She was captivated by the idea of "getting to know Jesus, to grow in your relationship with God, and to go out as a light and bring people to God." She also listened to two sermons online.

Brooke's first Sunday visit came as the church was starting a new series called, "The Purpose Driven Life: What on Earth Am I Here For?" She felt an immediate connection to the title:

> It was like I am supposed to be here because I was a mess. I was coming off of stripping for four years. I was coming off a lot of drugs, a lot of alcohol, a lot of broken relationships with my family, with my friends. I wanted to know what I was here for, who I was, and not try to find my identity in worldly things anymore.

Young adults are prompted by a crisis, a spiritual experience, or a relocation to look for nearby churches that may help. They often find churches by searching online. When Brooke was searching for a way out and a fresh start, that church website attracted her with its promise of purpose and hope because it appealed to her search for purpose and identity (characteristics of emerging adulthood, as you'll recall from chapter one). Brooke's story illustrates Jeffrey Arnett's proposal that emerging adulthood is

- ▶ an age of instability
- ▶ an age of self-focus
- ▶ an age of in-between-ness and transition
- ▶ an age of identity exploration
- ▶ an age of possibilities and opportunities

Brooke, struggling with common pitfalls for emerging adults, such as addiction, identified with the vision the website created for her. She recognized herself in its language. The church website gave shape and words to her identity exploration and her aspirations. Young adults search church websites for information to guide their decision on whether or not to visit. Church vision statements and sermon series titles particularly draw their attention.

After connection through friends—roads one and two—emerging adults connect to churches through church websites—road three. Bright-spot churches provide this step in young adults' preconversion process by creating inviting websites and social media that clearly appeal to emerging adults and connect to their dreams or ideas.

Kensington Commons's website (commons.church) is another example of how churches serve young people in their journey to church. Its website helps emerging adults imagine themselves at church and picture their future life there through the creative use of video, photography, and cultural cues. The video on the church homepage pans the sanctuary and flows into the hallways and coffee area, where emerging adults are laughing, drinking coffee, and having conversations. This is significant because one theme that emerged strongly in interviews with both pastors and young adults is that emerging adults connect to churches when they encounter others their age and in their stage of life that are on similar journeys. Although they appreciate intergenerational connections, they want to know there are other people like them.

Also prominently displayed on the home page are the church's vision ("Connect with Friends, Learn in Community, and Serve Where You Can") and values, which are essential parts of the church's vision of connecting to and serving the community. The site also includes several short videos telling the story of the church's planting and merger and introducing values and activities important to the church. In all these ways, Kensington Commons's website helps emerging adults explore whether they can identify with the church narrative before they even set foot in the building. No wonder Kensington Commons's experienced 92 reported conversions in 2015–2016 and 52 conversions in 2016–2017.

Pastors of bright-spot churches see unchurched emerging adults reach out to them through social media when they encounter complexity or crisis. For example, one pastor shared the following interaction:

I met a girl the other day who I never in a million years would have thought was interested in faith. She comes up to me in a coffee shop, with a tear in her eye, and she's like, "You probably don't even know me. I follow you on Instagram. I know your church has some cool people, I sort of know who you are. I'm, like, dying here, and I need someone to talk to. And I didn't know where else to go, and you seem like a safe person."

Church websites and social media can help churches reach and connect to emerging adults by giving them an inside look at the church before they take the risk of attending. Bright-spot churches facilitate a transformation process when they use their social media as a bridge to the broader culture and a means to make the foreign culture of church more familiar to those on the outside looking in through their open windows.

CHAPTER REWIND

To reach young adults, encourage your church to *initiate*, develop, and deepen relationships with unchurched people, especially young adults far from God. Talk about faith in Jesus and church enthusiastically in the context of those relationships, and *invite* unchurched friends to church. Then find some culturally savvy young adults to revamp your church webpages for those young adults on the outside peeking in.

STARTING THE CONVERSATION

- ▶ Do you talk with enthusiasm with unchurched friends about your faith and church? Why or why not?

- ▶ What need does an unchurched friend have that your church could meet?

- ▶ What are the portals at your church where unchurched people enter for the first time—especially young adults?

- ▶ In what ways does your church website appeal to unchurched young adults? In what ways may it be off-putting?

ACTION STEPS

Consider how you might naturally and occasionally begin to talk. Broach the subject of your faith or church with enthusiasm with unchurched friends. What would it look like to encourage others to do the same? *Ask questions to find out more about unchurched emerging adults.* Ask a focus group of unchurched young adults to view your church website and give you honest feedback. Better yet, invite young adults to design and maintain your church website with their own unchurched friends in mind.

4

Welcoming

OPEN THE DOOR AND SEE ALL THE PEOPLE

M addy, a twenty-seven-year-old kindergarten teacher, wasn't raised in church, but her engagement set her on a course to find a pastor to officiate her wedding. She wanted her wedding to feel magical and right for her, so she wanted someone she felt comfortable with. Since she didn't know any pastors, she began searching online. She found a promising candidate through a wedding website, and his calm and natural manner immediately made her feel comfortable.

Maddy left their first meeting with a strong sense that everything about the wedding would be okay—just what she needed. In fact, she found Pastor Todd Rodarmel so reassuring that she decided to visit his church the next day, in spite her fear of churches.

Nervous and a bit terrified that people would judge her for not knowing much of anything about God or church, Maddy dragged her unchurched mother to church with her. Then something unexpected happened: the scripts and stereotypes Maddy believed in began to crumble.

Once I went there, everyone was so welcoming and helpful and friendly, and it was so homey. The church they've built—it's amazing. It brought my mom and me both in. We were, like, with our mouths open. We were like, this feels really good and really natural. As far as his teaching, the first day was my first day of going to church, and he didn't lose me. I didn't know anything about the Bible. I had never looked inside of a Bible, I knew nothing, and he simplified everything. I didn't know any stories, and he made it seem like you didn't need to know all the stories in the Bible. I thought, going to church, *Oh, I need to know and read every single story in the Bible,* but it's not true. So that was my experience of how I came to my church, and that's how it all started. They were so friendly and welcoming, and they didn't put much pressure on me, which was what I was really nervous about. I didn't want them to force me into something I wasn't comfortable in yet. So, they were very natural, and I joined a city group that they started.

Maddy felt so comfortable and welcome—especially when she was greeted by several people after the service—that when a man standing at a table asked if she'd like to join a city group (a geographically focused small group), she decided to try it. He said it was a good way to meet people during the middle of the week, which appealed to Maddy because she lived some distance from the church.

Church felt natural, the teachings were easy to understand, and the sermon topics sparked Maddy's interest. But what drew her in even more was the passion she saw in the congregation's worship. "Seeing everyone so willing to show their passion with no shame, and they're here and in their zone—I wanted that too. Seeing everybody be themselves when they're worshiping, I wanted to be part of that as well." Passionate worship—people freely expressing themselves in worship—was attractive to Maddy.

Maddy also began serving in the church's children's ministry soon after she began attending. She'd been given a pamphlet that described places she could "belong" and where she could "find her place" and "help out." A couple of options strongly appealed to her, but working in children's ministry was the best fit for her schedule. Maddy described volunteering with kids as a natural fit, saying, "It was easy for me to work in the children's ministry because I already work with children and I love it. So I thought I could help there [and] give back to the community."

Among other benefits Maddy has received at her church are several friends, including members of her small group, people she serves with, and the woman who runs the children's ministry.

Asked what she likes about her church, Maddy said, "The sense of family and home and welcome-ness, that's what I love. That you don't feel like a bunch of strangers with everyone. You just feel like you are walking into a very great community. It's not a community of strangers. It's a community of friends and family, and you feel like you can be yourself."

Maddy began attending a small group and teaching in children's ministry within a few weeks of her first visit. The language of "finding a place to belong" appealed to her interests and aspirations, and it was important to her to be able to give back to a community where she belonged.

Churches that reach the unchurched are writing a new narrative for young adults. Young people who connect to these churches learn that they are valued and wanted. Some are drawn by the heartfelt worship of the congregation. There are opportunities for them to belong, serve, and grow, and though they are invited to participate, they don't feel pressure.

> *Young people who connect to inviting churches learn that they are valued and wanted. There are opportunities for them to belong, serve, and grow.*

How Friendly Is Your Church's Navigation System?

As we've seen, successfully inviting young adults to church requires a nuanced way of *initiating* (practice one, the most missional of the five practices) through cultivating genuine relationships, considering how faith and Christian community can address young adults' felt needs, and speaking enthusiastically about experiences of faith, church, or pastors. Churches that are good at connecting with unchurched emerging adults are filled with people who love Jesus and their church. They are excited and natural about sharing their faith and their church with others. They *invite* (practice two) unchurched friends and family to church because they want them to share those experiences.

I invite you to consider the practice of *inviting* in two ways, like two sides of a coin. Both ways are necessary to accomplish inviting. The first way a church is inviting is that they literally invite guests to church. And the second way a church is inviting is they provide an inviting church disposition toward unchurched people. Key characteristics of Christian communities that reach and keep young adults are *extending invitations* and *offering radical hospitality*. Churches that do these two things readily offer unchurched guests a welcoming "invitational culture."

The culture that guests are invited into really matters. I can't say that emphatically enough. Churches that reach emerging adults have a welcoming ethos—an inviting nature. But most of us think our churches already *are* welcoming. And, sure, our churches may seem welcoming to those who regularly worship with us, who in a sense *belong*. But are they really welcoming to guests? Are they hospitable to emerging adults and accepting of unchurched people as well as visitors, "others" unlike us churched people?

If most newcomers to our churches are entering through the "front door"—our weekend worship service—these services need to be *genuinely* welcoming to the unchurched. That means we need to be *intentional* about preparing for unchurched guests, creating inviting spaces for people who aren't familiar with typical church activities and traditions, and practicing radical hospitality in the context of our main church services.

If you want to know how welcoming your church is, try an experiment. Recruit a friend who attends a different church from you to buddy up and each go incognito to the other's church for a weekend service. Then swap stories of your experiences and how welcoming or not your churches were.

When I was interested in learning more about welcoming churches, I visited a number of churches on my own, without my husband and family. At one church a few people nodded at me, but no one spoke. At another church I wasn't seated by an usher, and when I tried to navigate on my own, several people told me, "Sorry, this seat is saved." When I eventually found somewhere to sit, no one around me said hello. No one had spoken to me—not one person in an hour and half had greeted me, asked my name, or introduced themselves.

I imagine the regular attendees of both of these churches saw themselves as friendly and their churches as welcoming. But that's not what I experienced as an outsider. Unfortunately, my other church visits made it clear that this wasn't an isolated case. That's why I'd encourage you to try something similar. If you don't feel welcome in a church despite already knowing your way around a worship service and despite having the emotional distance of knowing that you're conducting an experiment—what would the same experience be like for someone who's trying out church for the first time? What did you learn that will help improve your own church's friendliness?

Lest we dismiss the results of my experiment as an anomaly, let me describe my observations of a young adult's first few visits to church. James graduated from a college in Michigan and was hired by a large tech company in Kansas City. Our family knew James's family from our previous work in campus ministry, so we looked forward to his visit. He showed up unannounced one Sunday, and I recognized him as he took a seat toward the front of the auditorium. Someone was talking to me, and I was seated so far away that I was unable to greet James before the service began. I kept my eye on him, and I didn't see anyone greet him.

When the service ended, I tried to make my way quickly across the large sanctuary to James, but several people stopped me to say hello. James patiently stood waiting for me. Still no one spoke to him. No one introduced themselves. No one had a conversation with him. No one invited him to lunch. *Nada.* Unfortunately, this scenario was repeated for the next several weeks. This twenty-two-year-old hung in there for several more weeks, sitting in the same spot, surrounded by regular attenders, many of them my friends—and no one conversed with him.

You can imagine what happened next. Although my husband and I reached out to James, invited him to dinner, and included him in several events, it wasn't long before our church lost the opportunity to engage and incorporate a young adult into our community life.

James's story illustrates a cultural problem common to many American churches: we're not good at welcoming and incorporating guests. Like James, visitors are left alone to figure out how to "do church," and they either give up entirely or go someplace else. First-time visitors to a church need help navigating their experience—this includes answers to questions like *Now that I'm here, what do I do?* and *How do I connect with people and make friends?* But these and other uncertainties often go unaddressed.

Part of our problem is that we're not intentional about personal evangelism, inviting friends and family, and warmly welcoming and receiving guests into our churches. We don't have an outward focus on our guests and visitors, and we don't demonstrate a commitment to making them feel welcomed, accepted, and connected. Instead our focus is inward. Far from reaching out, we're often intimidated by guests.

Practicing Intentional Hospitality to the Unchurched

Churches that are effective in reaching unchurched people are radically welcoming and hospitable. They're not hit-and-miss; they help new folks feel welcome and comfortable in the main worship service even if they are generationally distanced. In the exceptional churches mentioned earlier, regulars are excited about inviting friends and family because they're confident that the people they invite will get a warm welcome and will have a good experience. So, what does that kind of place look like?

Here's how Maddy described the hospitality she experienced at church:

When you walk in, there's people outside [in the church foyer]. Everyone's talking with everybody; it's not just like they're in the corner waiting for service. Everyone's talking to everyone. Sometimes if you do go in and sit down on a bench or something, someone will come and say hello. Todd [her pastor] kind of makes his rounds and says hello. Outside they always have people with food. And then on the inside, when services are about to start, you have those greeters that are passing out pamphlets, which are super welcoming, kind of just letting you know what's going on this week in the community. As you sit down, you're sitting next to people, so you are communicating with them. Then after church people still kind of gather around as well. It's not just like you came and then you left.

Two other young adults described similar experiences at their churches. Shea said, "Everyone [is] saying, 'Hey, we're so happy to see you.' They're asking you how your day is. They're smiling at you. They're waving at you. 'It's nice to see you again.' If someone knows you, it's like, 'Hey, Shea!' They spot you from across the way and they're engaging you."

Garret said of his church, "It's so positive. They instill in your life. The second you walk through that door, everyone is just family. If no one knows who you are, everyone wants to know who you are. Like, 'Hey, who are you?' They're very welcoming, very kind—and not only that, the music that they play is very beautiful."

It's important also to note that emerging adults are not turned off by warm greetings from people outside their age group. Younger adults actually like and value older adults, and they appreciate cross-generational relationships. Pastors of churches reaching young adults are quick to explain that their churches are not millennial but inter-generational. Emerging adults in these churches are involved in small groups, activities, and ministries that are intergenerational rather than peer-oriented. And they say things like the following.

"Church feels accepting." Young adults experience pressure from the adults and institutions in their lives, so they avoid people and places that add to their stress. Unchurched emerging adults often expect churches to pressure them into religious beliefs or behaviors they're not interested in. Some regard churches as too morally restrictive; others view churches themselves as immoral and un-Christian. Many emerging adults expect churches to reject them due to their lack of belief or conformity to Christian expectations.

Churches that break the mold by defying these expectations are able to contribute to emerging adults' preconversion process. Churches with higher-than-average attendance of emerging adults are described by young people as welcoming, nonjudgmental, and not exclusive. One young adult noted that her church didn't exert pressure on her, such as by saying, "You're going to hell."

Churches with radically accepting cultures say things young adults don't expect to hear, like, "You don't have to believe to belong here," "You won't be judged or pressured here," "You are understood here," and "You don't have to be 'all in' to participate here." In these churches emerging adults feel welcome and comfortable whether they believe and act like Christians or not. They are comfortable attending church as people who don't necessarily "believe" and do not feel out of place or looked down on, regardless of how long they've attended without making a faith commitment.

They also experience church as a place where people are glad to see them. As Megan said, "It doesn't matter if you don't believe. You're still welcome here. It doesn't matter if you have no intent to believe. They're just genuinely happy that you're finding connection." Churches that send the message that newcomers are welcome and accepted no matter where they are in their spiritual journeys—approaching the starting line or halfway to the finish line—are both surprising and attractive to young adults.

"Church feels nonjudgmental." The unchurched and church-dropout emerging adults I interviewed expected churches to be judgmental and were surprised when they didn't feel disapproval in the churches they now attend. Maddy said, "I felt like people were going to be judgmental, that I didn't know much about things related to God, or I didn't know much about church. That was my fear. But everyone was welcoming, helpful, and friendly."

Young adults whose expectations of judgment were overturned began to change their opinions about church. Many of the emerging adults I interviewed found that the scripts they had believed about churches' judgmentalism were not true to their own experience. Their churches had served them by deconstructing those assumptions. Young people were forming new narratives about church based on their own positive nonjudgmental experiences.

Churches can make the preconversion process easier for unchurched young adults by helping them feel welcome and accepted—even when they lack biblical knowledge, think or act differently from Christians in the church, or deviate from the norms of church culture. And by accepting young adults where they're at and believing the best of them and for them, bright-spot churches envision a "believing" future that many emerging adults in time step into.

The emerging adults I interviewed described a particular church ethos that appears to lend itself to reaching, nurturing, and retaining them. The churches they felt drawn to and where their spiritual transformations occurred were places where they felt like part of a family, felt at home, and found friends.

"Church feels like family." Emerging adults experience a strong connection to their churches, which many describe as being like family. Brooke, a twenty-seven-year-old who had been attending church for three years when I interviewed her, felt this on her first visit. She said, "LifeChurch has a special way of connecting with people. When you walk in the door, you feel like its family." For Brooke, Maddy, and other emerging adults, a church that "feels like family" is a close community where people know each other's names and are intentional about getting to know and remembering newcomers.

Shea, who had been attending church for eight months when I interviewed her, also vividly described her experience of connection to her church: "You're never gonna be able to walk from point A to point B without at least three people saying hello to you, by name. If they don't know your name, they'll come up and ask you. People and the community there are very close-knit. They take the time to be super intentional about who you are, where you came from, and 'how can I serve you?'"

Church size doesn't necessarily impact the feelings of closeness and connection experienced by emerging adults. Shea, who attends one of the thirty Life.Church campuses, describes her ten-thousand-attendee superchurch as a close-knit community. This may seem surprising, considering it's a church that's part of a multisite replication model

looked upon by some as a McDonaldization of the church—with efficien-
cies that rapidly and predictably reproduced disciples by growing replica
churches using a tried method that works. A model that could feel disingenuous to young adults. But surprisingly that's not the case.

"Church feels like home." The former church dropouts and unchurched
young adults I spoke to now feel at home in their newfound churches. The

> *The word* home *clearly has positive connotations for emerging adults, conjuring up a place where they feel safe and don't experience much pressure.*

word *home* clearly has positive connotations for emerging adults, conjuring up a
place where they feel safe and don't experience much pressure. Interviewed after
ten months of attending church, Megan
said, "I walk in. . . . I feel safe. I feel like
it's home."

She also associated church with feel-
ing relaxed, which is apparent in the way she describes church to her
unchurched friends: "Even if you guys aren't looking to be involved with
God and Christ, it is still great to come and learn something and feel
more relaxed." In a high-stress North American culture, it's surprising
to hear a formerly unchurched Gen Z describe her church as relaxing.
The emerging adults I interviewed clearly felt comfortable in their
churches even before their faith was fully formed.

Michael described feeling "incredibly uncomfortable" on his rare visits to churches before he came to faith in Christ at Quest Church. I spoke
to Michael five years after he began attending church, and he said, "One
of my mentors, a guy I became very close with, once said the two places
he's most comfortable are in a weight room and in a church. I've gotten
to where I feel very similar. Now at church I very much feel at home."

When Maddy was asked what she loved about the church she'd been
attending for seven months, her response centered on the metaphor of
home. Maddy, Megan, and Michael are among those unchurched emerging adults that increase in religious belonging, behavior, and belief and
that experience spiritual transformation within churches that evoke a
similar sense of home and family.

"Church is where I find others on the journey." Churches enhance emerging adults' preconversion process by helping them connect to friends—especially friends who are on similar faith journeys. Garrett described the significance of his new church friends after attending church for five months: "I wake up, and I'm like, 'Yes! It's Sunday!' I get excited to go to church. I just have a lot of friends there, a lot of people that treat me like family." Similarly, Chelsea explained that she continues to attend Bayside Church because she recognizes other young adults at church, people she can identify with and potentially become friends with, and who will help her attain the social ethic to which she aspires. "I think that was my draw to stay. Seeing friends that I could actually relate to, not having to go to parties and all those kinds of things, like being able to actually have social outlets that were healthy for me."

Significantly, a welcoming church is a place to find friends to journey toward Jesus with that support particular moral aspirations. Many young adults start attending church because they want to adopt healthier or more stable lifestyle choices, especially in the wake of personal crises or when navigating complexities. Church provides a community of people who support their choices, provide alternatives to destructive behaviors, and offer friendships that help validate new commitments and beliefs. Emerging adults new to the church want to be among peers as they journey toward Christ. Bright-spot churches aid them on their way by helping them connect and form meaningful relationships with each other.

"Church is where I feel understood." Churches can encourage young adults in their faith progression by helping them to feel understood. Michael described his pastor as someone who understands millennials, knowing what drives them and the pressure they put on themselves. Like other young-adult interviewees, he appreciated when pastors spent a lot of time outside the church talking to emerging adults in order to understand their world. Pastors of such churches indicate that their churches understand the pressures emerging adults face as well as the corresponding temptations such as entitlement and consumerism. Young people appreciate

churches that know their struggles and help them to think biblically and apply Jesus' teachings, principles, and ethics to their everyday lives.

Zoe, who self-identified as gay, was raised in the Catholic Church but dropped out at eighteen. She learned about Community Church from a friend and initially attended out of curiosity, but she developed a sense of connection to the church because of her friendship with one of the pastors. Zoe and her senior associate pastor text and get together for tea whenever she has questions about her faith journey. Zoe said that part of their bond stems from shared experiences of gender discrimination. "Part of why I did connect with her is she is a woman, and I feel she could partly understand where I was coming from because I heard from her about her faith journey, and discrimination, and in her schooling and dealing with other people who don't think women should be pastors. I totally felt like she could understand."

Zoe's senior associate pastor didn't need to share Zoe's perspective on human sexuality in order to minister effectively to her. Zoe felt accepted and understood by her pastor. Churches and pastors serve emerging adults by communicating, "We understand you, we understand your struggles, we get what you're dealing with, and we're here to help you."

CHAPTER REWIND

Churches that are reaching emerging adults prepare the way for faith to take root by cultivating a radically welcoming, hospitable, and accepting culture—in short, by being ready for young adults when they arrive. When emerging adults encounter welcoming spaces, they linger long enough to explore Christianity and determine for themselves whether they find it credible. Churches with inclusive and supportive cultures—communities where young adults feel safe, comfortable, and understood—make it easier for young adults to deconstruct their faith barriers, hear and appreciate the gospel, and consider committing to faith in Christ.

What does radically hospitable and welcoming culture look like? For emerging adults a welcoming church is one where they feel accepted, at home, and part of a family, and where they can make friends with people like themselves who are on similar journeys. When they encounter invitational environments, emerging adults can imagine making a faith commitment without having their personal radar set off by negative stereotypes, hypocrisy, judgmentalism, and pressure to believe.

Here's the big idea: churches practicing invitational culture don't leave young adults alone to try to figure out how to navigate church culture and community; instead, they actively help them. Every member of a congregation can contribute to an invitational culture, and it can be as simple as keeping an eye out for newcomers and greeting them with a smile, initiating a conversation, remembering a young adult's name, or taking the initiative to introduce themselves. Bright-spot churches are truly welcoming, genuinely hospitable, inviting places, and unchurched emerging adults respond to their invitational culture.

STARTING THE CONVERSATION

- ▶ What's needed to establish an expectation that non-Christians are welcome at your church?

- ▶ How can you personally contribute to your church's hospitality and invitational culture?

- ▶ What are three steps your church could take to welcome emerging adults like family and make it a home for guests?

ACTION STEPS

Train your church. Create welcoming church environments for unchurched guests by encouraging regular church attenders not to ignore young adults at church but rather to welcome them and take the initiative to talk with them. Cultivate homelike and familial environments where young adults can feel welcome and find friends. Simple steps include reaching out and introducing yourselves,

smiling at one another and at guests, and lingering before and after
the worship service to talk with visitors. Train church attendees to
make it everyone's responsibility to be inviting and friendly, to learn
each other's names, and never to let a person walk through the
church doors without being warmly greeted.

Develop a metric. Measure your church's hospitality toward visitors.
Establish the means for evaluating whether non-Christians experience your church as friendly, welcoming, inviting, accepting, and
hospitable—something you can measure and be accountable to.
Your church can gain first-time visitors' insights by asking them to
fill out a short survey in the church bulletin to gather information
about their church experience, by sending visitors a short survey
monkey (surveymonkey.com), or by intentionally asking twenty-five
unchurched people to visit your church and report on their experiences using a questionnaire.

Be concrete and practical. Establish group ownership of a churchwide
vision to expect unchurched guests and warmly welcome them.
Begin by asking ministry teams to brainstorm three practical steps
your church could take to become more intentionally welcoming
and hospitable to unchurched visitors, especially young adults. Even
if you only have a few young adults in your church how might you
make them more visible to emerging adult visitors? Encourage every
ministry to strengthen its ability to welcome and to care for guests.

5

Changing

CREATING AN INVITATIONAL CULTURE

astors and church leaders have a huge influence on church culture. So does *anyone* participating up front in the weekend service. Their thought and attention to the design of the church service from the lens of the first-time visitor, especially from the perspective of an unchurched guest, will determine how comfortable people from outside the church feel when they come into our churches for the first time. We don't need to design a seeker service to help unchurched friends and family engage at church, but we do need to plan for, prepare for, and address our guests. Churches effective in engaging emerging adults expect and pray for unchurched guests to attend their worship services. As observed in chapter four, they don't ignore young adults or leave them to figure out how to navigate the church on their own. These congregations give new-comers personal attention, in part because their leaders have established the expectation that the church is a place for friends to meet Jesus.

Assume They're There

Making the effort to be more inviting to unchurched people makes sense only if you believe unchurched people actually are there to see what you're doing. The leaders of churches that are making inroads among unchurched emerging generations don't just wait for newcomers to arrive and then start trying to cater to them; they *assume* non-Christians are present in their worship services and act accordingly—even if at first none are attending. We create very hospitable churches by making small, welcoming changes.

We create very hospitable churches by making small, welcoming changes.

One way to prepare for unchurched young adults is to adjust our worship services to make it easier for unchurched visitors to understand what's going on, follow along, and feel included.

As they assume unchurched young adults are present, pastors and leaders adjust their announcements, worship leading, and preaching to accommodate a dual audience: people who know all about church and the Christian faith and people who don't. They constantly recalibrate their communications to target both churched and unchurched people. This process, called co-communicating, focuses on cultivating an inclusive church culture that presents faith as comprehensible and welcoming. By doing so, they're telling emerging adults and their friends that they're in a place that has something for them.

Set Expectations

Churches that assume unchurched visitors will come, that plan for their arrival, and that intentionally address their interests accomplish two things. First, they create an inclusive environment and send welcoming signals. Second, and just as important, they put regular attendees at ease about inviting friends and family. Most church folks are acutely aware that they have one shot at their church making a good impression on their friends. I often meet pastors, church leaders, and congregants who confide that they're uncomfortable inviting friends to church who don't know Jesus because their church isn't inviting.

Leaders of churches reaching emerging adults know that church is a place to bring friends who don't know Jesus, so they consider the needs of those who don't yet have a voice within the church as they design their worship services. In *Organic Outreach for Churches*, lead pastor and author Kevin Harney (Shoreline Community Church, Monterey, California), describes an approach to inclusivity called *two-degree vectoring.* He uses the image of a compass, explaining that due north represents caring for a church's existing congregation. He encourages every key church ministry to metaphorically push the needle two degrees off due north, directing some of their resources, time, and care toward those who are far from God.

I apply Harney's concept of two-degree vectoring to the church's metaphorical main entrance, through which unchurched young adults enter the church —the main weekend worship service. By tweaking the weekend service by a few degrees, churches become more inviting and attractive to young people who have little or no church background.

Church leaders can further shape their congregations' expectations by encouraging attendees to invite friends who don't attend church. Craig Sweeney, lead pastor of Bayside Citrus Heights in Citrus Heights, California, explained, "From the beginning, I emphasized inviting your friends. I create the expectation every week. I will talk about the friends who are going to come and the neighbors who are going to come. It builds an expectation in our people that we're going to talk about our faith with friends. We're going to invite people." Former lead pastor Alex Rahill of LifeChurch Canton, Canton, Michigan, prompts congregants to invite unchurched people who have not made commitments to Christ from varying spheres of their lives, especially every time a new sermon series begins.

Now Director of Church Planting for the Evangelical Covenant Church denomination, Rahill said,

> We are incredibly intentional about connecting to people who are far from God, inviting them into safe environments and explaining the full life God created everybody for, and there is no way to experience that life apart from life in Christ. When we do a new [sermon] series we do a postcard of the new series. . . . We hold these cards and consider who God has strategically put us in the midst of—a bunch of people who need him, are looking for him, and they don't know it, but you know it. God may be laying someone on your heart to invite, a friend, a relative. So, who are those friends

God has surrounded you with, who might be far from him and he wants you to be the conduit, he wants you to be the bridge?

If emerging adults receive a warm welcome when they first arrive at church, and if they're then encouraged to bring unchurched friends and family with them, they'll be able to recognize that church is a safe place to introduce friends to Jesus. And they'll do it! Lead Pastor Jeremy Duncan of Commons Church, Calgary, Alberta, said, "Somebody is resonating enough with the experiences that they're having at church that they're inviting people. And I think the big thing is that they feel comfortable to invite those people." Commons is an example of a church that expects unbelieving young adults to be present. And it saw a jump in attendance between a two-year period from an average of 327 attendees in 2016 to 786 attendees in 2018.

Unpack Christian-Speak

Next time you attend a worship service, listen carefully and flag any vocabulary and phrases that sound like words spoken and understood only by Christians. Paying attention to our language can make a big difference in how comfortable unchurched people feel at church. We can make our services more inclusive and hospitable by translating Christian symbols and churchy language as well as introduce elements of worship that may be unfamiliar to people who aren't used to the way churches do things. This can be as simple as explaining why we're doing what we do, tweaking our preaching to spend more time unpacking ideas that unchurched people may not have encountered before, and providing directions so visitors can find their way around the building. Insider language and jokes need to be explained or eliminated. All who speak and lead during a worship service should consider their communication in light of a simple question: Would my unchurched young-adult

Unpacking Christian-speak can be as simple as explaining why we're doing what we do, tweaking our preaching to spend more time unpacking ideas that unchurched people may not have encountered before.

neighbor, relative, or coworker understand what's being done and said? Would that person feel welcome while it's happening? Thinking along these lines helps us make a potentially awkward church experience enjoyable for our unchurched guests.

Let's start with church jargon. I'm sure you can think of many terms used at your church that are *only* used at church. Whether those terms are used by Christians of all denominational stripes, only by members of your denomination, or even only by people in your congregation, people who haven't traveled in Christian circles aren't using them, and visitors probably have no idea what they mean. Using insider language—words and expressions that won't make sense to someone who's new to an environment or conversation—can make them feel excluded. People who don't understand the specialized vocabulary feel like outsiders. And this is the opposite of welcoming and hospitable. In short, don't use insider language if you're trying to reach out.

Bright-spot churches extend hospitality to guests by going out of their way to use language that everyone in the room—including people who are there for the first time—can understand. Leaders of these churches know this can be a challenge. As Senior Pastor Larry Kim of Cambridge Community Fellowship Church (CFCC) in Cambridge, Massachusetts, explained, "Being able to preach as if there are people who have no faith background was an adjustment for me. I try to do as much explaining as I can—that's not something I used to do five years ago. It's an awareness for me that we have more and more people coming with no faith background and don't know what I'm talking about." Pastor Kim assumes that non-Christians are present in his church's worship services, so he takes a few small steps to help his preaching make sense to people with little or no faith background. Like other pastors I spoke to, he avoids a churchy vocabulary, explains biblical or theological terms, and tries to use language that's familiar to unchurched listeners.

Pastor Andrew Mook of Sanctuary Church in Providence, Rhode Island, is another example of a lead pastor who carefully plans how to speak inclusively. He recognizes that, for some guests, church is an alien environment, so he prefaces many of his comments in an effort to make Christianity understandable and plausible for those who aren't familiar with church culture. By doing so, he functions as a cultural informant for newcomers, shedding light on the cultural norms of Christian worshipers and helping make known the unknown.

Pastors like Andrew take time in worship services and small group settings to explain concepts and cultural texts that may be foreign to young people who are unchurched or church dropouts. For example, Pastor Mook takes care to explain why Christians study an ancient book. As he does so, he not only introduces the Bible but also begins to build credibility for the Christian faith:

> Some of you may feel like, what does this archaic book say to us? Look, most people believe that there's something beyond their five senses. They have some sense of spirituality, some sense of love and beauty. If I told you that there was this collection of stories that people for thousands of years have turned to for inspiration, and it's a story in which a lot of other people are exploring their spirituality beyond their five senses, and this is their account, and their doubts and their questions of making sense of how to communicate this understanding of who God may or may not be—wouldn't it be worth exploring something like that?

The pastors I interviewed believe that avoiding or explaining insider language helps churched emerging adults feel comfortable inviting people to church because they know their unchurched friends won't get lost in a sea of Christian jargon when the pastor stands up to talk. They encourage worship leaders to pay attention to anything that sounds like Christian-speak and to be intentional about avoiding or unpacking words, phrases, acronyms, and labels that have an insider feel.

Make a Big Impact with Small Changes

In their book on leading change, *Switch: How to Change When Change Is Hard*, brothers Chip Heath and Dan Heath explain how a few simple changes can have an enormous impact. This approach, which when combined with what they define as "shrinking the change" or providing immediate payoff, reassures participants that continuing efforts are worthwhile and the task itself is doable.

I imagine in many North American churches we need to "shrink the change" by making small changes in the way our church communicates in public spaces, like our main worship service. The goal of this change is to become more inclusive and welcoming to guests in the hope that (1) our church members and attenders risk inviting their unchurched friends to church, and (2) unchurched guests, especially emerging adults, will feel comfortable enough to hang around and learn more about the Christian faith and community. We "shrink the change" for unchurched guests by tweaking our communication to be clearer and more understandable for guests, which will go a long way toward helping young adults and their friends stick around long enough to feel a sense of belonging.

Instill Awareness of Unchurched Guests

The church leaders featured in this book understand that an invitational culture helps non-Christians become familiar with the Christian worldview, appreciate the credibility of the Christian faith and the Bible, and feel included in the family of God—which create a path to belief. Pastors and staff of churches reaching unchurched young adults actively cultivate an awareness of pre-Christians—including unchurched friends and family who may be present at any given service—within their congregations. How? By starting a conversation. Church leaders encourage congregants to invite their friends and raise awareness of pre-Christians' presence by initiating dialogue with church members and attendees about their unchurched friends and family. By discussing the significance of the presence of people that may be far from God at church and stressing the importance of unbelievers' need for spiritual transformation, pastors can launch a churchwide conversation.

Pastors and church leaders of churches effectively reaching unchurched emerging adults encourage congregants to let them know when their friends are present, often via text message or social media. Some young adults even tell their pastor or church staff member what they hope their unchurched friends will hear during their visit. For example, a young adult planning to bring a friend to church may reach out on social media to ask her pastor to define faith, present an opportunity to come to a deeper understanding of faith in Christ, or invite a faith commitment. Young adults may also ask pastors to repeat certain teachings or illustrations they've used in the past so that that their unchurched friends can hear them.

Pastor Mook observed, "I get emails all the time, like 'Hey, can you give that whole breakdown you gave of why we worship this week, 'cause I'm bringing four friends.'" The expectation, excitement, and enthusiasm for unchurched guests expressed in these kinds of conversations are fueled and propelled by pastors who make themselves accessible to emerging adults through social media and face-to-face communication, and they keep the conversation going by expressing interest in friends as well as friends of friends.

Schedule Meetups with Unchurched Friends

The church leaders I spoke to not only make sure they're accessible to their congregants by text and email, they also let church attendees know they're available to reach out and meet with unchurched young adults to help them take steps toward trusting and following Christ. A churched young adult may send her pastor a text message saying, "Hey, someone came to our community group this week. Can one of you reach out and have coffee with him?" A lead pastor or other church staff member will then arrange a meeting with the unchurched friend, either at the church or in a more neutral space, such as a coffee shop or on a college campus.

Pastor Larry Kim described the process of keeping the church cognizant of the presence of unbelievers through conversation and personal pastoral follow-up.

We hear, "Did you know so-and-so is actually not a believer?" And then we try to connect with that person. . . . I usually try to connect with every single one of those people. I reach out to them, and I say, "Hey, I want to connect with you." They come and meet in my office, and I say, "It's so great having you here in the community, and people love you. What is your story? What brought you here?" It's actually the people who come to the church who have no faith background, they have the best stories.

Church leaders make it very clear that they're available and eager to meet with their congregants' unchurched friends and family members, and to provide pastoral care to those who don't yet have a Christian faith. By doing so, pastors help the members of their congregations influence their friends toward trusting and following Christ.

Make Calls to Faith and Calls to Mission

Churches reaching emerging adults intentionally create spaces for unchurched people to respond to God. This often involves providing explicit opportunities to make new faith commitments in the main worship services and in small group settings. In both large and small group contexts, speakers and leaders give calls to faith and calls to join God in his mission to reach and restore the world. Lead pastors at these churches value evangelism enough to set the expectation that guests will be given regular opportunities to make faith commitments, respond to calls to mission, and commit to applying what they learn in a sermon to their lives.

At the churches I studied, invitations to faith in Christ are incorporated into weekend worship services with varying frequency, ranging from weekly, to every time Communion is celebrated (according to the church or denomination's tradition), to a few times a year at designated times in the church calendar. At one end of the spectrum, Pastor Craig Groeschel issues a weekly invitation as part of a general emphasis on the idea that the church exists for the world—that is, for those outside the church. He said,

If I'm not doing an invitation, I'm sending a message that we're not evangelistic. So we do it every service. It's just woven into our culture; it's what we do. We invite people, we bring people, we teach publicly on evangelism, and we tell stories. Vision drifts and values leak—so we have to say it over and over and over and over again.

Lead Pastor John Teter of Fountain of Life Church in Long Beach, California, takes a different approach, focusing on three seasons in the life of the church when he finds it natural to emphasize evangelism: leading up to Christmas, leading up to Easter, and leading up to the start of fall.

Regular invitations to take steps toward faith in Christ are part of bright-spot churches' culture and are not deterrents to extending invitations to friends. Church people, aware that calls to faith are regularly incorporated into their church services, bring their friends in the hope they will be prompted to make new faith commitments.

Among many of these churches, calls to faith in Christ are not extended in isolation. Often dual calls are made: invitations to make a first-time faith commitment or to renew a faith commitment in Christ, and invitations to follow Jesus more deeply by committing to some aspect of his mission to reach and heal and bless the world.

Effective churches cultivate expectancy by establishing an understanding that the unchurched are welcome, expected, prepared for, and addressed. People know what to expect when they take the risk of bringing their friends to church, and this gives them confidence to extend invitations.

Small Group Calls to Faith

Churches reaching young adults also encourage a culture in which they make first-time commitments to faith in small group settings. Many of the emerging adults I talked to told stories about the significance of their small group in their journey to faith in Christ; they recalled when their small group prayed for them to know Jesus personally or offered healing or prophetic prayer. Remember Maddy's story at the beginning of chapter four? Her small group was instrumental in her spiritual journey. Asked how she came to faith in Christ, she said, "When they [her small group members] prayed for me aloud, they did this thing where they all go into a circle and prayed for me, and I think that was the eye-opener for me." When asked what approach best described her coming to faith in Christ, Maddy said, "They welcomed me into church, and they prayed for me."

Like Maddy, Garrett described his experience of coming to faith in Christ in the context of a small group of youth leaders who prayed with him. "I felt like it was prayer and caring. They all prophesied over me, actually. They all cared for me and started speaking into my destiny and who I am and my identity, and they all prayed over me. And from that point, people kept on giving me prayer and kept on loving me. And I feel like that was a big, big thing for me."

As these examples illustrate, community groups play key roles in the spiritual awakening of young adults. These experiences will be unpacked in greater detail in chapter six. Here, however, the significance of the small group leader's role must be emphasized as a key factor in young-adult dones and nones coming to faith in Christ. Pastoral staff and small group leaders are comfortable leading young adults to faith in Christ by calling them to commitment and by praying for and with unchurched young adults.

CHAPTER REWIND

Pastors and leaders set the stage for an invitational culture by leading the whole church to prepare for visiting unchurched emerging adults. They influence church participants to assume that people who don't follow after Jesus Christ are present. These leaders encourage their congregations to invite unchurched family and friends to worship services, church events, and activities. Extending invitations to church is a key missional invitational practice of churches that are helping young adults awaken spiritually.

Of course, once an invitation is extended, the church culture that awaits the invitee really matters. That culture must be invit-

The message needs to be loud and clear: church is as much for our unchurched guests as it is for Christians.

ing. An invitational culture develops when regular attendees know that unchurched family and friends are welcome and expected. The message needs to be loud and clear: church is as much for our unchurched guests as it is for Christians. Church members need to hear and talk about how guests and friends can become Jesus' followers.

Furthermore, unchurched young adults shouldn't be expected to decipher unfamiliar churchy terms, which make them feel they may not belong in church. Tweaking church communication and making small changes to the main worship service to be more inclusive help alleviate the anxiety and pressure most young adults expect to experience when they visit. Unbelieving young people should be actively welcomed, accepted, spoken to, and given regular opportunities in various contexts to respond to invitations into God's family. With practice, these aspects of invitational culture become part of the natural rhythm of church life.

STARTING THE CONVERSATION

▶ Is your church a safe space for Christians to invite their non-believing friends? What adjustments does your church need to make in worship and in community groups to communicate to church attendees to help them believe and feel that it's safe to invite their unchurched friends?

▶ Where can you begin to set expectations that your church is a welcome environment for young adults and their friends?

▶ Is there any church chatter going back and forth among pastors, staff, and people about their unchurched friends and visitors? How could you start and maintain that conversation?

ACTION STEPS

Listen like an outsider. Reflect on the language being used in your weekend worship service. What churchy words, phrases, and ideas do you notice? If you wanted to communicate similar things without using insider language, what terms would you omit and add? How would you explain unfamiliar terms and concepts to an audience of unchurched young adults?

Emphasize inviting. Encourage members of your congregation to invite close friends to church. Send the message loud and clear that church is a place for unchurched people and a place where friends meet Jesus. Repetition is one of the keys to whether church folks begin to extend invitations. People need to be reminded repeatedly of the church's vision until they act on it.

Make it explicit. Establish a culture of calls to faith (directed to unchurched people) and calls to commitment (directed to Christians who could go deeper with God's mission to reach and heal the world). Create opportunities in the weekend worship service for people who don't fully believe that Jesus is Messiah, the Savior of the world, to respond to calls to faith in Christ and for Christians to respond to calls to commit by specifically encouraging next steps based on the message.

Train the callers. Train preaching staff and small group leaders how to give calls to faith. InterVarsity Christian Fellowship has excellent training materials for training university students on large and small group calls to faith.

6

Including

We first met Brooke in chapter two, where we heard her story of addiction, online stripping, and broken relationships. Yet she was developing an interest in knowing and following Jesus. Brooke experienced some Christian influences through her boyfriend's family and relocating gave her a chance to start down a new path and discover a sense of meaningful purpose and identity. As we saw, Brooke started looking at the websites of churches in her new town and was attracted by the message (in her own words) "Know, grow, and go" on a particular church's homepage.

The full invitation on the church website reads, "At LifeChurch, it's our desire for everyone to come to Know Jesus, Grow in meaningful relationships with Him and with others, and to Go serve others in order to make a lasting impact on our world. We invite you to visit us and see what we're all about!" That invitation appealed to Brooke.

It's worth noting here that the Christian language on the website didn't turn her off—rather, it was straightforward, understandable and helped her find words for the stirrings and longings she was experiencing in her search for a fresh start. So she emailed the church's pastor of connections, saying, "I'm moving in from another state. I don't know anything about this God thing, but I do want to help, so where can I go, how can I serve, and what can I do to help?"

Brooke's email received an immediate response. The pastor of connections' willingness to meet with Brooke and her boyfriend right away and his enthusiasm about connecting Brooke to God and to service were very inviting and inclusive. Here's what he wrote:

> Let me introduce myself in return. My role is to help you get connected to LifeChurch, and in the process more connected to God. I am very excited for you, in what God is doing in your spiritual journey! I suggest we connect by phone, or I would be happy to meet up with you both for coffee if you prefer that. I have a number of ideas for you to be involved in what God is doing at Life-Church; you can join us in this great journey to know Him more. Send me a phone number or let me know if you prefer to meet. I look forward to talking with you in more detail!

Not only did an associate pastor respond promptly to Brooke's email, he also followed up on her inquiry with a face-to-face introduction and a plan for her first visit. On the very next Sunday, Brooke and her boyfriend received an in-person meeting, a tour of the church, and arrangements to have lunch with another young couple.

Brooke was also asked how she'd like to get involved with the church, and she was invited to come back the next week for Starting Point, which she describes as a group for people who want to know how to "put their relationship with God into practice." The invitation to Starting Point gave Brooke a place to belong to the church and to begin building relationships with people who would support her spiritual journey. By responding to her immediately and quickly offering opportunities to get involved, the church did a great deal to jumpstart their emerging faith journeys and to encourage Brooke's choice to be active in her new church.

From Church to Faith Through Compelling Community

Once they're in the door, how do young adults get from church to faith? One common route is through compelling community. The most striking

characteristic of the churches I studied is how quickly they include newcomers to their community. They excel at the *including*. These churches
begin assimilating emerging adults into the life of the church on day one.

How do they get young people not only to come but also to stay? First,
as we've already seen, they go out of their way to make visitors feel welcome, both by providing environments that are friendly, safe, and orderly,
and by clearly communicating where to go, what to do, and what's going
on, being sure to use language first-timers can understand.

Then, as Brooke's story shows, they go out of their way to include
unchurched young adults in the church's activities in meaningful ways,
especially by helping them find places where they can develop a sense of
belonging before they commit to embracing Christian beliefs. For these
churches, inclusion is an invitational practice: they include unchurched
newcomers before they believe and, in doing so, collaborate with the
Holy Spirit to help them come to belief.

The young adults I talked to who recently came to faith in Christ
connected to meaningful community immediately or soon after they
began attending church. Nathan, for example, described how his community group was foundational to his coming to faith in Christ:

> I started coming in August, and the community groups were just
> starting up in September. I was hearing about them having a
> brunch, and I just decided to tag along with my friend. I would say
> that the community groups are really the heart of what kept me
> going, the people there and the connections I formed. For me,
> becoming a Christian was a process or journey over time, especially
> over the first year in community group. I was meeting people, I was
> learning more, how people live in the faith.

When emerging adults join small groups, organic gatherings of friends,
or young-adult programs early in their church experience, they gain a
place to ask questions, familiarize themselves with Scripture, examine
and reconsider their preconceptions about God and the church, and get
to know what Christianity looks like and means. Inclusion in a church

community keeps them from becoming isolated, encourages their curiosity, exposes them to examples of Christian faith and life, and helps them explore faith in Christ as a serious option. In effect, inclusive communities provide companions for unchurched young adults who find themselves traversing unfamiliar territory. Faithful friends who listen to their stories, help show the way forward, and generally walk alongside them are tremendous gifts to young adults experiencing spiritual awakening.

Making Friends to Journey With

Christian communities such as small groups can be sources of acceptance, support, love, and optimism. They can also be places to make friends. Emerging adults need to know peers on similar spiritual journeys not only for the sake of companionship—*I see people who can journey alongside me*—but also to confirm the legitimacy of new faith experiences—*I find people who validate my faith exploration.* Compelling Christian community allows emerging adults to make friends who validate their burgeoning faith and give credibility to their Christian experience. Having friends to journey with is a kind of stamp of approval communicating that the Christian experience they're having is okay, it's real, it's valid, and other people like them are connecting to church, faith, community, and Jesus.

Having friends to journey with is a kind of stamp of approval communicating that the Christian experience they're having is okay, it's real, it's valid.

Why do North American emerging adults need friends to validate their religious exploration? Partly because they won't find much validation in the broader culture. Indifference toward the church is on the rise. George Barna and David Kinnaman reported that while more than half of unchurched Americans say their faith is very important to them, still nearly half of unchurched Americans see no value in attending church. Young adults in particular are indifferent toward religion.

In the conclusion of his book *The Rise of the Nones,* James White wrote that Americans "may not be losing our belief in God, but we are losing our religion. While we may not be turning into atheists, we seem quite content to accept the idea of faith being privately engaging but culturally irrelevant. And yes, this is because of the process of secularization." White concluded that their indifference is due to religion's irrelevancy to life. Connecting to a Christian community provides both a supportive group, credibility, and exposes the relevancy of Christian faith to life needed for young North Americans to continue their journeys toward faith in Christ.

Further, as many cultural observers have noted, Americans have become increasingly skeptical of institutions—including churches—in recent decades. Researchers David Kinnaman and Gabe Lyons, for example, found that unchurched young adults age sixteen to twenty-nine view Christians and churches as sheltered, judgmental, overly political, anti-gay, hypocritical, and paranoid about "saving the lost." Further research suggests that many twentysomething dones dropped out of church because they perceived it as overprotective, shallow, antiscience, repressive, exclusive, and doubtless. It's not surprising, therefore, that the most robust recent study on the religious lives of emerging adults, the National Study of Youth and Religion, found that most Americans between eighteen and twenty-three don't feel comfortable or have a sense of belonging in church.

In many respects, then, the big picture looks bleak. Yet the churches I looked at are doing a great job of drawing young adults into Christian faith and practice, despite the cultural headwinds. As we're beginning to see, this seems to have a lot to do with Christian community. To most of us, this seems intuitive, but social science research can shed further light on why Christian friendships play such an important role in young adults' spiritual journeys. Sociologists know that community is a powerful agent for social transformation. Again, this is a pretty basic concept: the people around us affect how we think and act. Sociologists have observed that people generally change only when they experience pressure—and significant personal relationships are one important source of this pressure.

All humans, Christians very much included, rely on moral communities—communities of people who hold to similar beliefs and practices to help them sustain those beliefs and practices. Research on Christian students in university contexts helps illustrate this point, showing how like-minded Christian community strengthens religious faith and helps it survive and thrive in secularizing contexts.

Young adults exploring Christianity are helped along by religious friends who encourage them to increase in their religious participation and progress in their spiritual journeys. Christian community can give young adults confidence and conviction that exploring Christianity is a worthwhile pursuit, even if they face pressure or ridicule from skeptical peers. So, the sooner we connect unchurched young adults to people who can validate their religious exploration, the more likely they'll stick around long enough to really try out Christian faith.

Using Superglue

Relationships foster a strong sense of group identity and bond individuals to communities, so young adults need relational ties in order to connect to a church and feel that they're a part of something. Becoming part of a community is an important aspect of young-adult identity formation, and it plays an important role in motivating young adults to linger in a church long enough to figure out if it's a good fit for them.

The term *social capital* has a diverse range of meanings across different disciplines. Here, I simply use it to mean "relationships that bring people benefits" for when we belong to a network of relationships or to a group, we accrue benefits from that group or those relationships. These benefits are social capital.

Bonding social capital is a type of social capital that relates to connections within a group. It exists in strong relationships among similar people who share something significant in common, such as family, close friends, and neighbors. Robert Putnam calls bonding social capital social "superglue" because it creates strong adherence to a social group. I suggest that making friends at church provides the superglue—the emotional support and the strong connections—that helps young adults stick around long enough to decide if they want to become long-term members. Connecting to social environments like small groups provides a space for them to make decisions about giving church a chance and committing to faith in Christ. The new friends and relationships—the inclusive community—are the superglue, and the social space or small group is a laboratory for testing the Christian faith.

Megan's description of her small group illustrates the role of bonding in a young adult's faith journey. Notice her emphasis on table fellowship—or, to use noninsider language, eating together. Activities like eating together that are naturally associated with home and family—two important aspects of an invitational culture, as we saw in chapter four—help young adults feel warmly welcome and connected or bonded to a group. Megan said,

> The small group was really important to me in coming to faith because it wasn't [as if] we all showed up with our Bibles, and "Okay, everybody, let's study hard right now." We made it a point to always have a meal or snacks, because we felt it was a great way to bond. Come to the table. And we'd chat, and catch up, and ask, "How was your week?" "What's going on in your life?" And then go into discussing the sermon.

Emerging adults often describe shared food, meaningful conversation, Bible or sermon study, and challenging discussions as important aspects of their church communities. They may meet more than once a week: young adults who are beginning to connect to church often talk about meeting regularly, sometimes daily, with their church friends or community members to share meals, go to movies, play sports, or otherwise hang out and do life together. Some share housing with friends from their church and participate in ministries together. Some even work together

Activities naturally associated with home and family help young adults feel warmly welcome and connected or bonded to a group.

and network to offer members of their community vocational opportunities in their companies, schools, and nonprofits.

Creating Compelling Community

Let's pause and take a closer look at Christian community. What type of Christian community will help sustain young adults moving toward trusting and following Jesus? Belonging is certainly a key factor in keeping them around long enough to begin to explore Christian faith, but a community that draws young adults toward faith in Christ needs to do more than just provide a safe place to belong.

Unchurched emerging adults need compelling Christian community. By *compelling* I mean powerfully engaging and influential—the kind of community that not only grabs and keeps a person's attention but also inspires them to change and grow. It's community that takes us somewhere—for our purposes, toward Jesus. For unchurched young adults, a compelling community challenges their beliefs, behaviors, allegiances, and idols. Moreover, it encourages them to move toward alternatives, propelling them forward in a journey toward faith commitment.

In a compelling Christian community, faith is discussed robustly and in ways that help young adults connect the dots between their intellect, emotions, and will, challenging them to move toward surrender to Christ in all these areas. Compelling communities focus on the importance and relevance of Jesus Christ and his mission to bring God's reign to all the earth. Their members strive to bring honor and glory to the Father in all they do, and they pray for people to enter God's kingdom and receive his gift of salvation. Communities like these exert a powerful influence on young adults' lives, capturing their imagination and their allegiance.

Compelling community is also a space where young adults have a strong sense of feeling loved. They are attracted to churches where they experience Christian love through their community. Kara Powell, Jake Mulder, and Brad Griffin, in their book *Growing Young*, on helping churches grow younger, refer to the significance of a "warm community."

Where young people find a church and stick to it, warm community fuels their spiritual connectedness.

Are the small groups at your church ready to receive young people? Are they compelling? Remember, the church has something unique to offer emerging adults—something that goes beyond group bonding, as important as that is. The "Christian-ness" of Christian community matters, because in this context unchurched young adults engage in a process of faith exploration, deconstruction, new behaviors, and reconstruction.

Compelling community is a space where young adults have a strong sense of feeling loved.

Let me be clear: Christian faith isn't a requirement for participation in small groups at the churches I studied. On the contrary, many young adults with little or no faith background come to these groups to ask questions, find answers, and discuss issues without feeling stupid, judged, or pressured. At the same time, they're using the opportunity to observe the Christians around them—to see how they behave and how they respond to life, each other, and the biblical narrative. Again, I reiterate that small Christian communities give unbelieving newcomers a laboratory for exploring Christian faith and questioning their assumptions.

Blowing Up False Narratives

With all the church stereotypes people are exposed to through the media, movies, social media, and literature, emerging adults especially grow up bombarded with negative messages about religion and religious institutions. The emerging adults I talked to explained that participating in small groups helped unravel some of their negative stereotypes about church, Christians, and Christianity. In particular, the experience of being accepted, affirmed, cared for, and encouraged by people in their church led them to see Christians as smart, genuine, and approachable rather than ignorant, hypocritical, and judgmental. Attending church and finding authentic Christian community helped to dispel the suspicion and skepticism that characterizes many unchurched people's attitudes about religion. The replacement of old, off-putting beliefs with positive associations and relationships allows unchurched young adults to make progress toward embracing Christian faith and identity.

Building Something Else

Reconstruction is the word I use for finding an alternative church story for a false stereotype that's been exposed. When people reconstruct or rebuild their understanding of something (such as the church as God's faithful community), they insert another option or a different belief in the place of a former belief or falsehood. In community, unchurched dones and nones begin to reconstruct their understanding of Christian faith and community—this time in a healthy, biblical way. They learn about God's big story—creation, fall, redemption, mission, and consummation—and how Jesus fits into the picture. They come to understand the cost of their redemption and what Jesus accomplished on the cross. They grow to know how deeply God loves them.

It's important to note that this process of learning and reconstruction isn't about accumulating abstract knowledge of Christian doctrine. It's about helping unchurched people get to know the God their community worships—the God they're considering committing their lives to. With a better sense of what Christian faith is all about, they'll be equipped to appreciate the ways they're experiencing God through their new community and church.

If we want to have a committed relationship with someone (that is, God), we need to know something about him and his story (that is, the biblical narrative). Young adults need both knowledge of and experience of God. On the one hand, we can't just stick people in a theology class and expect them to come out Christian; they have to meet God. On the other hand, we can't just send people off to hang out with their friends and call it discipleship; they have to know God. This interplay between knowledge and experience, a really passionate, vibrant experience of God, is significant to genuine conversion.

Encouraging New Behaviors

Participating in Christian community gives unchurched people opportunities to participate in Christian behaviors or enactments—that is, to do what Christians do, act like Christians act. For example, when attending small groups, unchurched emerging adults hear the Bible read and may read along or even read it out loud. They get the chance to worship and pray in an intimate small group context. A number of the young adults I interviewed said it was in their small groups that they first learned to pray—and especially to pray aloud. Sometimes they joined with their small groups to volunteer in the church or the broader community.

We will pick up this theme again in chapter seven. For now, it's important to note that healthy communities do not *coerce* anyone to perform Christian enactments. The point isn't to get newcomers to play along in order to avoid awkwardness, much less to compel anyone to fake a spiritual experience. The point is to give people space to respond to God. For someone with little in the way of Christian background or experience, this inevitably involves trying new things. So unchurched emerging adults engage in new behaviors that the Christian community also engages in when they participate in compelling Christian activity.

Boosting Conversations and Mentoring

Small groups provide a context for emerging adults to receive casual but intentional group mentoring. As political scientist Robert Putnam wrote in his book *Our Kids: The American Dream in Crisis*, mentors other than immediate family often help young people reach their full potential. Leadership expert Sharon Daloz Parks also recognizes the benefits of "mentoring communities," which she believes provide the most powerful form of mentoring for emerging adults. A mentoring community offers hospitality, challenging questions, and "access to worthy dreams of self and world." Compelling community is where the unchurched are challenged through meaningful conversations and the mentoring community to consider a new identity that includes following Jesus as well as future opportunities and possibilities.

Parks wrote that young adults need both a place of belonging that provides support and "forward movement toward fulfilling purpose." When a Christian community is healthy, it beautifully fulfills this dual role for unchurched young adults by providing, on the one hand, a support system in which to explore faith, and, on the other hand, encouragement, tools, and direction to help them achieve their purposes in life by contributing to God's world and mission. We can see both of these dynamics—affirmation and direction—at play in Garrett's description of his small group:

> They were all very strong in God and they're all supportive. It didn't matter what my past was; they accepted me for who I am and saw the positive things in me, and I really feel like they've surrounded me with a lot of love. They taught me basically how to love, just love on everyone. They showed me the way, so it's been really good. They're just there for community, actually caring, like a family.

Garrett's community met many of the needs commonly experienced during emerging adulthood, a period in which young adults are trying to figure out who they are in a world that feels both unstable and full of possibilities. By showering Garrett with love, acceptance, and positive Christian messages, teaching him to love, and showing him "the way," the members of his small group provided mentoring and guidance that contributed to his transformation. When it fulfills these functions, a small group can serve as a dynamic and compelling mentoring community for emerging adults, propelling them toward discovery and faith in Christ.

When it provides love, acceptance, and positive Christian messages, a small group can serve as a dynamic and compelling mentoring community for emerging adults.

Reaching Moral Aspirations

The young adults I interviewed spoke about church as a source of healthy relationships and support for healthy behaviors. Compelling Christian community creates a supportive environment for young adults who are trying to practice healthy behaviors and work toward new ethical standards. Brooke, for example, described how her church provides alternatives to the self-destructive behaviors she wanted to move away from, such as clubbing, partying, and excessive drinking:

> Saturday nights are important because when you have a group at church, we're able to say, "Hey, let's all go grab dinner afterwards." So then you're expanding your community and you're building relationships. A lot of people struggle with Saturday nights by going out with friends that maybe aren't the healthiest for them. So, after Saturday night service, we always play volleyball.

Young adults often aspire to live out moral convictions but find themselves unable to attain those goals on their own. When the church as a mentoring community surrounds them with love and holds them accountable to their aspirations, they begin to experience progress in this area. This growth helps them trust that God is able to deliver them from the snares and temptations that prevent them from reaching their goals.

Experiencing God

In the context of close community, young adults begin to experience God for themselves, many for the first time. Simply put, as they participate in acts of faith like reading the Bible, worship, and prayer, they encounter God. Perhaps the most significant thing churches can do to help unchurched emerging adults become new creatures in Christ is to give them opportunities to encounter God firsthand. Emerging adults are attracted to churches that offer them intimacy with God and provide space for emotional religious experience.

The young adults in this study observed that they began to awaken spiritually in the context of Christian community. God started doing something within them, and their lives began to change. Shea put it like this:

> Finding a Life Group was a big thing for me. Finding that community. Meeting girls my age who were struggling and were honest with each other. They didn't even know me, and it was like they

loved me and cared about me, and they were interested in who I was and what was going on in my life and what was God doing in my life. So that drew me in. My first time I went to this Life Group, I was like, "This is it! This is what I've been looking for." Some people say when they meet Christ it's like overnight, but for me it was gradual. Then I started serving, and that was around my baptism as well.

Shea's story illustrates how inclusion in Christian community can facilitate a young adult's conversion. Genuine, caring friendships in the context of compelling Christian community drew her toward Christ and a new beginning in life. Shea was baptized three months after her first visit to Life.Church Broken Arrow.

Including is the third invitational practice of giving unchurched young adults the chance to experience compelling community. Including involves inviting unchurched young adults into spaces within the church where they are welcomed, included, and given clear signs of what to do next. Like physical signs, the first three practices (initiating, inviting, including) provide clarity for guests about what to do next and provide next steps for Christians seeking to share their faith with unchurched friends and family. Churches influencing unchurched emerging adults go the extra mile and warmly welcome people as if into their own home, and then they extend invitations into Christian community where people can belong, such as, "Here is a small group for you; this activity is your next step."

CHAPTER REWIND

Churches collaborate with God and participate in emerging adults' preconversion process by giving them an experience of compelling Christian community. Community, whether experienced in young-adult programming, small groups, or more organically, is where emerging adults (1) meet companions for their faith journey, (2) find friends to validate their faith and provide legitimacy for their Christian experience, (3) ask faith questions and find answers without feeling judged or pressured, (4) experience the deconstruction of their stereotypes and perceptions of Christians and church, (5) begin to experience God at work in their lives, (6) are challenged through meaningful conversations and supported by a mentoring Christian community as they practice new beliefs and behaviors aligned with their aspirations and identity formation, and (7) begin to understand what the church and Christian discipleship look like.

STARTING THE CONVERSATION

▶ How could your ministry teams better plan and pray as they consider how to serve unchurched young adults? Is this conversation already happening among your ministry leaders? If not, how could you start the conversation with them?

▶ How will you communicate your vision to include unchurched young adults in your church? What response do you expect to receive from your staff or congregation, and how will you proactively engage those responses?

ACTION STEPS

There are a lot of ways to address inclusion, depending on the church, parachurch, or missional community. If you have a young-adult group or ministry, naturally that is the first place to connect visiting emerging adults, but not every church or parachurch has that. The following suggestions apply whether you connect unchurched emerging adult guests to age-specific or to intergenerational groups. *Become an inclusive community.* Commit as a group or ministry to becoming more inviting and open to emerging adult guests and pray together for God's help to be a community that welcomes and accepts dones and nones. Encourage your church, ministry, small group, or Christian community to become welcoming and inclusive. Pray together that God will help you express inclusion in tangible, intentional ways to newcomers and for opportunities to invite emerging adult guests to your community. Whether you are a pastor or small group leader, consider opening your small group(s), church community, or ministry to guests and first-time visitors. What would be most challenging about letting people join who are new to the church or group? What will motivate your group to be open to visitors?

Don't wait—connect! Connect emerging adults to community and small groups immediately. Provide opportunities for newcomers to connect to small groups or other kinds of intimate community that meet regularly without a wait time. When you meet them for the first time, that's the time to invite them. Extend an invitation to a compelling community that's meeting during the next week. Don't let any grass grow under your feet. And don't worry that you're being pushy. Your invitation will go a long way to help young adults feel accepted and valued.

7

Involving

CONTRIBUTING BEFORE COMMITTING

During my conversation with Garrett about his college years, he spoke of a defining experience. He and his girlfriend lived together for three years. He remembered her shouting at him in an argument, "F– you! I never loved you." And she moved out. Garrett's night was restless and unsettled. During that time of naked vulnerability and utter helplessness, he sensed God's presence—his reality. As if he were staring God in the face as one to another, he asked God to forgive him for "all the stuff" he'd done.

Garrett then questioned his experience. He asked, "God, was that really you, or did I imagine things? Give me a sign if my experience was real. God, please give me a sign." Later in the day, a high school friend texted him and asked if they could meet up. Over coffee, Garrett shared what had happened and his sadness. After taking it in and allowing a silence to hold the weight of Garrett's words, his friend said, "God wants you. He's chasing you, Garrett. He loves you."

As he told me this, Garrett's wry smile reflected the words he spoke: "That friend also said, 'Garrett, you will be an amazing leader one day.'" Perhaps not surprisingly, this friend was a youth pastor. And he invited Garrett to visit the high school youth group. He said Garrett's past didn't matter, and he envisioned Garrett's future: "I know you are going to be a leader."

Describing his first visit to church the following Sunday, Garrett said, "The moment I walked in the doors of the youth ministry, I felt the Holy Spirit. And I felt impacted."

The community of youth group leaders at Garret's friend's church embraced him. He recounted how they accepted him and profoundly communicated their support:

> My friend (Caleb) showed me the way and his whole community house—his wife and Tim and Jacob and Roberto and a lot of friends from church. They are all strong with God and supportive, and it didn't matter what my past was. They accepted me for who I am, saw positive things in me, and surrounded me with a lot of love, talking to me positively about my sports and my job.

Garrett's new friends took a personal interest in him and in his interests. Although there was a lot of God talk, it wasn't all about God and Jesus. They cared about Garrett and the things he cared about and was involved with. Their commitment to God was attractive to him, as was their positive outlook toward him, his circumstances, and his future.

When Garrett was asked, "Which evangelism approaches best describe your own coming to faith in Christ?" he described his new community of Caleb's youth-group leaders, how they cared for him, prayed for him to receive Christ, prophesied over him. He said they "spoke into my destiny, and they all prayed over me, and that was a big thing for me." Garrett had attended church for four months when I interviewed him and now lives in the community house with his friend Caleb, Caleb's wife, and several youth leaders. He described the dynamic way the group of Christian leaders embrace and continue to care for him:

> We have Bible study nights and leader nights, and we work together about things we learn from God. They all add into me and fill me with stuff and bring me up to a higher level. They taught me how to love on everyone, and they are there for me for community, caring for me like a family.

Garrett found a family, a Christian community within the church, that embraced him and took him in, accepted then nurtured him with generosity and kindness. That community of youth workers also challenged him to be open to learning with others about discipleship. They believed in him and for him until he believed in himself and in God. Family, community, acceptance, generosity, kindness, challenge, knowledge, community, positive encouragement, and prayer were all important dimensions of his spiritual journey toward faith in Christ.

Let's look at Garrett's story more closely. His spiritual narrative illustrates four invitational practices:

- *Initiate.* His old high school friend initiated a renewed relationship by texting Garrett and meeting with him four to five years out of high school.
- *Invite.* That high school friend, now a youth pastor, invited Garrett to help at youth group with him.
- *Include.* The youth pastor then included Garrett in compelling Christian community by inviting him not only to hang out with the church youth group but also to join the youth workers in their discipleship group meetings.
- *Involve.* Once Garrett responded to his friend's invitation and showed up at youth group, the youth pastor continued to invite Garrett to get involved at church by participating weekly as a youth leader.

Becoming a youth leader connected Garrett to more emerging adult friends who love and serve Jesus at church and who befriended, prayed for, and spoke truth to him. They envisioned a future in which he had a positive and meaningful impact on the world in the context of church. As discussed in chapter three, all are components of compelling Christian community. And each of the four practices were a significant step in Garrett's preconversion pathway.

Contributing before committing. *Involve,* the fourth invitational practice of churches that has a positive effect on emerging adult nones and dones, is illustrated by Garrett's faith story. It's noticeable that churches influencing young adult conversions consistently ask emerging adults, Gen Z and millennials to get involved at church even *before they make faith commitments.* Did you catch that? Reaching young adults combines the two practices of including and involving *before* they commit to trusting and following Christ. This pattern emerges again and again in the stories of young adults spiritually transformed through the agency of the local church. Seeing a significant change in the lives of secularized young people usually requires giving those folks a pathway and the means to be involved at church.

> *Reaching young adults combines the two practices of including and involving before they commit to trusting and following Christ.*

Contributing leads to meaning, significance, and identity. What does it look like for emerging adult dones and nones to be involved in church? Do they have to be connected to a cause or a social justice issue? Not necessarily. In his book *The Rise of the Nones,* James Emery White suggests that the most effective way to reach nones is by connecting them to a cause and by doing good "before them, and with them, good that will open their ears and hearts to the message of the gospel." Although my research doesn't suggest that connecting to a cause is essential, White may be on to an important evangelism strategy. I agree that doing good is very significant in reaching young adults, but what reaches young people is giving them an opportunity to contribute, not necessarily to join a cause.

Young adults I communicated with characterize their involvement as giving to their church community. Their contributions needed to be meaningful to them and others in the church. And they needed to see that their contributions made a difference. When church people notice and comment on their contributions, young adults find greater meaning in their involvement and also feel valued by the church community, which add to their feelings of significance, value, and belonging to the church.

Pitching in is an important factor in a young adults' developing identity as they explore meaning and find significance and purpose in the

world. Emerging adults need opportunities to explore their identity
before making commitments. Giving them opportunities to serve and
contribute offers them occasion to explore and the space to experiment
with finding meaning and purpose in God's family, his worshiping and
witnessing community—his church. Involving unchurched emerging
adults is a necessary stop on the road to faith in Christ.

Contributing leads to bonding, belonging, and responsibility. Think about
this: People contribute to where they belong. Actually, contributing is key
to bonding to a community. By contributing, people feel they have
ownership of and responsibility for a community. Notice how Maddy, a
purely unchurched none who had attended church for only eight months
when she and I talked, as you will recall, described her connection to her
new church: "It was easy for me to work in the children's ministry because
I already work with children and I love it, so I thought I could help there
as well give back to the community." Maddy revealed her new attachment
to her community and the growing sense she had of her own responsibility to contribute—or as she said, "give back" to her new community. Contributing not only bonded Maddy to her church; it also created an
increasing sense of her ownership toward her church. Maddy wants to
help, and she views her work in the children's ministry as helping and
giving back.

Here's another way to identify what's happening when churches
implement the invitational practice of involving. When emerging adults
contribute to their community, a two-way exchange occurs. Young adults
like Maddy develop healthy attachment and belonging through serving
their community. Furthermore, belonging to a community is expressed
through contributing, so a continuous circle of involvement and attachment, contribution and belonging is perpetuated.

Are You Sure About This?

Sometimes churches are hesitant to ask visitors and newer people to
contribute or serve at church before they've made a commitment to
belong. Some are reluctant because, out of a desire to practice hospitality,

they don't want to place expectations on guests. Naturally they want people to feel like guests and to not be bothered by serving in childcare, teaching Sunday school, directing visitors, and the many roles that make a church system run smoothly. They say, "We want our visitors to feel welcome, with everything taken care of for them. Young couples need a place where they don't have to do anything for their children and know that the church has that covered." *But is that what newcomers really want?*

Some churches are hesitant to recruit visitors because they fear placing people with little, no, or an unknown faith background in roles of influence. Out of a desire to protect, a desire to defend the faith, and an impulse to ward off cultural contamination—to say it rather strongly—they don't recruit unknown volunteers.

And many church cultures consider ministry positions and opportunities to be only for those who have attended church for a lengthy period, gone through membership classes, and earned the right to serve. Only then are people recruited to serve.

All three of these church cultural scenarios are at cross-purposes with helping young adult newcomers cultivate a sense of belonging through contributing. Moreover, as was important in Garrett's and Maddy's case, involvement—specifically serving—is essential to how emerging adults commit to trusting and following Jesus through the support of effective churches. *No getting around it, young adults' church involvement usually looks like serving.*

What Do You Mean by Serving?

We've observed that, in effective churches, emerging adults begin volunteering very soon after they begin attending. In some cases, like Garrett's, the portal to church is service.

Garrett was helping with youth group, which eventually led to attending the main worship service. Emerging adults identify those early experiences with serving as significant steps in their faith journeys.

In effective churches, emerging adults begin volunteering very soon after they begin attending.

First, let's address the idea of involvement and the word *serving*. Pastors of effective churches and formerly unchurched young adults recognize that what significantly impacted their journey toward faith in Christ was indeed serving in the church. In the cases represented in this research, young adults served in their churches, including in significant roles where they interacted with youth and children. A few even taught during their first year of church attendance. Let's drill down and get a feel for what that means. (Note that I'm reporting my research, not necessarily supporting this practice.)

What were formerly unchurched emerging adults doing in their churches? They were coleading small group Bible studies, serving as volunteers in kids' ministry, teaching Sunday school, helping with youth group, feeding underresourced people, running the sound, lights, and visual needs of their church service as tech crews, participating on church vision committees, serving as greeters, ushers, prayer team coordinators, and more. Time after time, young adults and pastors mentioned their service to a church and the positive impact serving had on them. For them, serving meant contributing and helping and even leading in their church's ministries, programs, activities, and mission.

Effective churches are finding ways to welcome unchurched young adults into ministry roles while they are en route to understanding the Christian faith and figuring out what it means to trust in Jesus and follow him. Admittedly, this powerful step in a young adult's journey can be a challenge for churches, especially those that view church ministry as falling within the purview of those who are church members. Traditional church membership often includes training on church polity or spiritual formation, and it typically requires a profession of faith in Christ. It's not surprising, then, that many churches assume ministry should be left in the hands of faithful attendees who have proven themselves by demonstrating orthodoxy and orthopraxy over time and through appropriate processes.

If you're feeling disconnected with what you're reading, that's understandable. Nonetheless, I hope you'll take these findings seriously:

churches highly effective at reaching unchurched pre-Christians are enthusiastically encouraging young adults to get involved in ministry before they fully understand Christianity and make faith commitments.

Cctt does this well)

Safeguards

Did the churches I studied build in safeguards to preserve the integrity of Christian teaching and protect the church—especially young and vulnerable attendees—from the potential negative consequences of allowing relative newcomers to fill ministry roles of prominence and impact? Yes, safeguards clearly were on these churches' radar screens. I saw four main types of safeguards in place: supervision, limiting spiritual influence, training, and follow-up and accountability.

Supervision. Clear supervision safeguarded church dogma, Christian faith, and moral influence. Young adults were not left alone to figure out or carry out ministry. They were surrounded by mature Christians who carefully, intentionally, and enthusiastically supervised and worked alongside them. For instance, Katelyn began attending church one August, shortly after leaving her bartending job. By February she was serving on her church's vision board alongside church staff and leaders. She longed to see other young adults become Jesus-followers. So she approached her new mentor, and together the two of them began a small group for young-adult women, which they led together. Throughout the process of becoming involved, contributing, serving, and eventually coleading, Katelyn was supervised through the process of inviting friends and other young-adult newcomers, selecting curriculum, preparing lessons, and leading weekly debriefings of the small group sessions.

Limiting spiritual influence. Limitations were set on the influence formerly unchurched young adults had on those they ministered among. When they were working among children or youth, they were carefully supervised and never left alone. Fellow Christian leaders co-led or worked alongside them, guiding and debriefing the process.

Training as an integral part of serving. Young adults were given curriculum and training. Supervisors met with them on a regular and continuous basis to introduce, review, and debrief lessons and activities. So not only did a more mature Christian work alongside them, they also met together for mentoring and follow-up to debrief the ministry activity, event, small group, or classroom experience.

Are the Five Practices Unique to Reaching Young Adults?

Will the five practices work for other populations? Yes. Churches doing an outstanding job of reaching and keeping unchurched emerging adults are not necessarily young-adult churches or millennial or Gen Z churches. Repeatedly, pastors reaching emerging adults say their churches are intergenerational, particularly in urban contexts; many are also multiethnic churches. But they never say they are intentionally young-adult churches. As they reach emerging adults, they are reaching everyone!

Initiating relationships with unchurched people, inviting them to church spaces and contexts, including them in compelling Christian community, connecting them to small groups, getting them involved in places of meaningful contributing and serving—these practices are what churches do to reach their unchurched friends and family. And this is definitely working with the younger generation.

I attended my daughter's church plant and was surprised to recognize a previous neighbor—a boomer—from the suburb where our family used to live. When the service concluded, we greeted one another, and I asked him how he was getting along; I knew he and his wife had divorced a few years back, and both had moved away after selling their home. After we talked for a while, I asked how he got connected with that church plant and how long he had been coming. He told me a young tech guy from his office attended the church and had invited him. This was his second week. He extended his arms and said, "Beth, it's been great seeing you again. Hey, I got to run and fill these carafes with coffee." Whoa! A young adult had initiated a relationship with an older unchurched adult, invited him to church, and involved him in pitching in to help. It was week two—only the second time this man had visited the church—and he was already serving and contributing.

That church understood that people, and especially unchurched people, want to contribute, and that that's how people begin to belong—through their contributions and involvement. That's what retains people, keeps them coming back, and is a significant practice in their spiritual journey toward faith in Christ.

Unchurched young adults need to be thoughtfully placed in a ministry of limited spiritual influence, trained, and followed-up on. That means they aren't going to preach, lead worship, or be the sole teacher in a Sunday school class or small group—any place where they may have unlimited spiritual influence. Yet when they are guided toward places of meaningful service and contribution, emerging adults will begin to bond, gain a sense of responsibility and ownership toward their new church, and through their contribution they grow in their sense of belonging to the church community and make progress toward faith in Christ.

Are there any moral failures among the emerging adults given opportunities to serve at their new churches? Yes, in my study one young adult was removed from leadership in the youth group due to her destructive behavior outside of church. That removal process included a restorative element that the church initiated. Although she was removed from ministry, she wasn't left alone to navigate the guilt, shame, and brokenness. She received counseling and was invited to live with another staff member.

That young person is now growing in her commitment to sobriety and in her ability to steer clear of destructive behaviors. The church's parents and students are aware of the issues this young person struggles with and that she's walking on a path toward health and wholeness within the loving care of the church community. Her latest email to me shows her tremendous growth in Christ.

Hi Beth,

Thank you so much for reaching out! I absolutely love hearing that my experience can be a tool for others to grow in understanding my generation of humans! Any way that I can help you in getting this out there please let me know—my life has really gone forward for the better in so many new ways.

The Lord has really blessed me with an incredible husband. We are expecting our first child the end of March this year. I hope things are going well for you and would love to hear more about how your research has helped to educate others.

Serving—combined with affirming, caring, and prayerful relationships that affirm identity and purpose in life—powerfully combine to play a significant role in the faith journeys of young adults. This can propel them from meandering to becoming open and actively investigating, trusting, and following Jesus.

Service: An Inroad to Faith Commitment

Pastors of bright-spot churches are aware of the importance of service in emerging adults' faith journeys. They recognize that serving often leads to new faith commitments and for some is a major approach in reaching emerging adults. For instance, Pastor Will Barnett, colead pastor of Highrock Covenant Church in Acton, Massachusetts, identified service as a significant influence on young adults' journey to faith in Jesus.

We want to invite everyone to serve, even if they don't fully identify as a Christian. In fact, that's one of the ways of learning the culture and learning who Jesus is, through invitations to serve. Actually, for a number of them, it's still a question for me where they are at spiritually with Jesus. A number of them serve in our Kids Rock ministry, our hospitality ministry, or some other ministry. We've had some who were really wrestling with their faith, but they're serving on the worship team. In terms of leadership, I'm more careful about who we select as our leaders and want them to be in a more established place in their faith.

As pastors of bright-spot churches affirm that contributing to the church community through service is a significant means of outreach, they're also observing a newer phenomenon: emerging adults can contribute to the effectiveness of evangelism.

For a while, evangelism leaders and scholars have recognized the profound impact of community on faith formation. Pastor Craig Groeschel, founder and pastor of the largest and fastest growing church in America, with a regular attendance of 100,000, asserts that giving younger generations ways to serve is just as consequential as providing compelling community. He said,

Pastors of bright-spot churches are aware of the importance of service in emerging adults' faith journeys.

> I used to think, and I still do, that getting young adults connected relationally really matters. But I think that getting them contributing matters even more. That generation wants to make a difference more than they want to make a living. If the church isn't missional or serving in the community or making a difference, that's a real turn-off. If the church is missional and making a difference, that's a plus. If there's a place they can use their gifts and help make a difference, that's a plus. If they can lead it, that's a hundred times better—if they can be in charge of something.

The stories of young adults and pastors match. Emerging adults who begin serving within a few weeks or months of attending their new churches seem to make new faith commitments more quickly than those who don't become involved in contributing, serving, or leading.

Rather than worrying about whether or not these young adults are "saved" before they serve, bright-spot churches are concerned that young adults are open to Jesus becoming the center of their lives. Their hope is that young adults move in the same direction as Jesus, as expressed through the mission of the church. Churches engaging young adults seem most focused on how to swiftly get newcomers moving toward and along with Jesus on his mission.

CHAPTER REWIND

Emerging adults want to become involved in something bigger than themselves. Though many emerging adults, especially eighteen- to twenty-three-year-olds, want to make the world a better place, only a small minority find a way and the will to do so. Churches reaching emerging adults are helping them make meaningful contributions while also reaching their aspirations.

For example, Garrett recognized that his contribution and service at Mountainview was valued and welcomed. He experienced being known, affirmed, prayed for, and loved by those he served alongside. Shea, who attends Pastor Groeschel's church, said, "I think everyone wants to be part of something. And so, when someone is, like, 'Come with me to be a part of this—serve with me in high school ministry,' you are more inclined to do it. You're like, I was just waiting for someone to ask me to be a part of something, instead of 'Hey, I'll meet you at church.'"

In their own words, young adults need an opportunity to "give back" to their community in order to experience a strong sense of belonging, to take responsibility for their community and in doing so become attuned to their own spiritual journey. I suggest that they also are better prepared to make faith commitments.

STARTING THE CONVERSATION

▶ Are there arenas where contributing in a significant way helped you take more ownership in a community?

▶ What current opportunities does your church provide for unchurched people, especially young adults, to be involved or to contribute in meaningful ways?

▶ Take ninety seconds to generate a short list of church ministry areas and activities where unchurched people can begin serving before they fully commit to faith.

▶ How will your church ensure formerly unchurched volunteers receive biblical input, guidance, and supervision?

ACTION STEPS

Examine the options. Evaluate the service opportunities available to young adults in your church. Are emerging adults—including those with little Christian education or background—able to contribute in ways that are meaningful to them? Do they have places to give back to their community and make a difference?

Design new volunteer opportunities. Kindle church leaders' interest in imagining volunteer positions that would be a good fit for unchurched emerging adults and newcomers. Create places and openings where young adults who don't know Jesus can get involved and contribute to your church community.

Build pathways to service. Create clear, simple steps to help pre-Christians and new Christians connect with entry-level service opportunities, especially ones in which young adult newcomers feel they can make the world a better place.

Supervise and protect. Ensure the safety and integrity of your church's ministry by supervising newcomers and young Christians who contribute to the church. Keep them from having much spiritual influence on others, and mentor them toward maturity.

Shorten the distance. Look for ways to reduce the amount of time that passes between when individuals are invited to church, when they first visit, and when they're given opportunities to contribute and serve. Encourage young adults with more experience in the church to invite their friends to serve alongside them when appropriate.

8

Investing

THE CHURCH IS HERE FOR YOU

*I know that my church is growing me into a strong disciple and
leader so I can bring others to Christ—because they are already doing
it. So, for me, I'm sticking with it, even though it's hard to be held
accountable. It's hard to be transparent and to accept truth. But they
do it in the most loving way possible and grow you into a leader.*

BROOKE, AGE 27

As emerging adults begin to contribute to their churches, their
churches reciprocate and invest in the growth and leadership
development of those emerging adults. If young adults aren't already on
a church's investment radar, they will be when they begin to serve.
Churches that are inviting to unchurched young adults provide them
with places of meaningful inclusion and involvement, and—pivotally—
invest in them before they convert. A church's investment sends a powerful message to emerging adults.

"We Are Here for You!"

Churches positively affecting emerging adults *invest* in them in surprising ways. They show young adults that they are here for them by providing mentoring and leadership development, including developing young people who don't know Jesus yet and who may still be considered visitors— people hanging around the fringes of the church, not at the center.

As emerging adults begin to contribute to their churches, their churches reciprocate and invest in the growth and leadership development of those emerging adults.

Emerging adults often unconsciously absorb the message, "There's nothing here for you," from churches. Rightly or wrongly, they get this impression either from the church's silence on issues important to them or from the lack of attention given to the presence of young adults in church—especially single young adults, who make up most of Generation Z and a little more than half of millennials.

During a recent young adult ministry consultation, emerging adult ministry leaders from various locations in the United States agreed that a failure to address young adult concerns in church allows a loud silence to speak on behalf of the church. When it comes to topics such as race, ethnicity, gender, and political struggles—including significant social issues involving economic and educational disparity, white supremacy, mass incarceration, mistreatment of immigrants, police shootings, violence against black youth, and human trafficking—silence is understood to mean "we don't care." Silence feels inhospitable, disingenuous, and un-Christian to emerging adults whose worlds are saturated with social travesties and inequities. When the church doesn't address the things they see happening in the world around them, they find little reason to attend such an antiquated institution.

Churches that draw the interest of young adults share a profoundly simple quality: they are there for young adults. But *how* are they there for them? They not only address the concerns of young adults. By verbally acknowledging those concerns in worship services and by taking time for

lament and repentance over injustices and social ills, they provide pathways for personal growth and leadership development. And they promote young adults' aspirations and help them cultivate their identity.

I was taken with these churches through the stories young adults
shared with me. Each story young adults shared with me was unique, but
they all shared a common denominator: churches that are truly there for
emerging adults *invest* in them in particular and powerful ways.

Bright-Spot Churches Care

Many young adults first come to church in a time of crisis. Some are overwhelmed by the consequences of destructive choices and behaviors.
Some are suffering the effects of drug abuse or other addiction. Some
have been badly hurt by others. Emerging adults experiencing any combination of these challenges need care from the church community.

When Sydney accepted some friends' invitation to visit their small
group Bible study, her life felt out of control. She'd partied heavily during college, drinking every weekend and smoking pot a couple times a
week. Then her sister ended up in a mental health facility on a suicide
watch. Sydney partied harder to anesthetize herself. At one party, a
man took advantage of her vulnerability in order to abuse her. This
experience left Sydney feeling ripped apart emotionally; she felt
"gross," and her self-esteem was shattered. She also abused herself
through self-harm.

Sydney needed the care of a Christian community to help her walk
through the fear, sadness, and loss she was experiencing. She had grown
up unchurched—her divorced parents were both nonreligious—and
she'd stayed away from church most of her life, thinking it was "weird."
But when she visited her friends' small group, she was drawn to the leaders and other participants because they didn't judge her. They let her
explore faith in Christ at her own pace, all the while helping her to see
herself as God sees her.

Sydney's small group leader eventually asked her if she wanted to
"accept Christ." She wasn't ready the first time. The leader determined

that Sydney just needed to understand Christian faith from the inside. So she invited her to colead a small group Bible study together, and Sydney came. She recalls that the second time she was asked if she would like to accept Christ, she had a better understanding of the gospel. She willingly prayed to receive him, and eleven months later she was baptized.

Sydney's story illustrates how young adults need care and patience from the faith communities that embrace them. She needed a safe place to be loved by friends and to spend time in God's Word so she could learn the central truths about God and the healing he offers. Sydney's small group leader invested in her by spending time with her one-on-one and inviting her to colead a Bible study, even though she hadn't made a faith commitment. Sydney says the members of her small group and her small group leader led her on her faith journey and helped her prepare to commit. Asked about the benefits of being a Christian, she pointed to a community of people who were there for her, providing accountability, working together through struggles with sin, and connecting on a deep level.

In Sydney's story, we see both an individual leader and a small group offering care to a young adult who was struggling with abuse and self-harm. We observe the church in action: offering friendship and belonging, patiently extending love and care, modeling Christ's character, and repairing brokenness by offering acceptance. Sydney's small group expressed Christ's love to her and thereby supported the development of her Christian identity by giving her an experience of what it's like—in her own words—"to be seen as God sees you."

Unchurched emerging adults arrive at churches in need of care and openheartedness. They may be suffering trauma from physical or sexual abuse inflicted on them by strangers, significant others, or family members. Or they may find themselves unhappy for other reasons. If they can't find a job to support themselves after countless attempts, they may feel in limbo. If they miss the close-knit community

Unchurched emerging adults arrive at churches in need of care and openheartedness.

they used to have in college, trade school, sports, or gaming, or they long to share mutual care and companionship with a partner, they may be lonely. They may feel flat-out miserable due to jobs that are boring or stressful, coworkers they don't have anything in common with, room-mates they don't identify with, or a lack of opportunity to meet people their own age. For these and other reasons, emerging adults need care that includes understanding, acceptance, patience, love, support, and guidance.

Bright-Spot Churches Invest in Mentoring

One brilliant way bright-spot churches stand out is by providing deep care through mentoring. Emerging adults appreciate it when people fur-ther along in life's journey take the time to invest in them and share their experience and wisdom within the context of mutually respectful and engaging relationships. And it's not just millennials who appreciate men-toring. When five thousand Gen Zs were polled and asked what benefits were most important to them, they responded that health care (37.7 per-cent) and mentorship (33.3 percent) were the two most important.

It's not solely within the reality-TV world of music and fashion that young adults find mentoring. According to a national Add Health study, one out of seven respondents age eighteen to twenty-six reported they had benefited from a significant relationship with a nonparental adult that had lasted an average of nine to ten years. The report concluded,

> These findings suggest a broad and multifaceted impact of mentor-ing relationships on adolescent health. Mentoring relationships may foster positive development and health among young people through several mechanisms, including the provision of social sup-port, role modeling, opportunities to develop new skills, and advo-cacy. Nonparent adults who function as mentors may serve as crucial educators and support figures, promoting learning and competence, providing exposure to positive social norms, increas-ing a sense of efficacy and mattering, and helping youth realize their full potential.

More recently, Fuller Theological Seminary's High School Transition Project found that contact from at least one supportive adult from their congregation (who didn't know them primarily through youth ministry) meant that during their first semester of their freshman year of college, the students continued in their faith. The report noted, "Hearing from an adult from their home church—whether via text, email, phone or something you've perhaps heard of called the US Postal Service—seems to help students take their faith to college with them. In fact, that ongoing contact still makes a difference three years later."

As a result of their findings, Kara Powell and Chap Clark recommend mentoring as a strategy for helping young people continue in faith after high school. After Powell's second study, she and coauthors Jake Mulder and Brad Griffin encouraged churches to give every young person a team of at least five supportive adults to provide an "ecosystem of discipleship for each young person within their church's influences."

So, what exactly is mentoring? Looking across disciplines, fields, and organizations that use the term *mentoring*, a group of scholars identified three core dimensions of mentorship: (1) the mentor has greater experience, knowledge, or wisdom than the mentee; (2) the mentor offers guidance to foster the mentee's development and growth; and (3) the mentor and mentee are connected by an emotional bond that includes trust. I use the word *mentoring* to describe relationships with these three dimensions—greater experience and wisdom of the mentor, mentor provides guidance to foster growth, and mutual trust between mentor and mentee—as well as two additional elements discussed below. When I write about mentoring in churches that are attracting and holding on to young adults, these are the kinds of relationships I have in mind.

In conversations and interviews, I've heard young people talk about how their relationships with people in their church help them to grow, to become leaders, or to develop moral integrity. This fourth dimension of mentoring—helping young people reach their aspirations—is prevalent in *youth mentoring*:

The mentor is ordinarily several years older, a person of greater experience and seniority in the world the young mentee is entering. The person acts as a teacher, sponsor, counselor, developer of skills and intellect, host, guide, exemplar, and *one who supports and facilitates the realization of the young mentee's dream.*

Finally, a fifth dimension of mentoring is accountability. For many of the emerging adults I talked with, mentoring—and especially mentoring that included accountability—was an important step along their journey to faith. For some, it was the decisive step.

Mentoring looks different from relationship to relationship. But whether it involves regularly meeting one-one-one with a more mature Christian (a lead pastor, church staff member, small group leader, etc.) or a small group mentoring community, in most cases mentoring includes most of these five dimensions.

The Timeliness and Frequency of Mentoring

Young adults in my study commented on the short time between beginning to attend church and entering healthy, meaningful relationships with supportive Christian adults in the congregation. Their church began to invest in them through meaningful mentoring relationships within weeks or months of their first visit. The degree of trust created through these relationships within a short period of time was striking.

Michael's relationship with Peter Hong, lead pastor of New Community, is an example of timely, empathetic mentoring that was simultaneously caring and challenging. Michael grew up unchurched and skeptical because a church had turned its back on his mother when she became pregnant in high school. Imagine the script Michael believed about church: *Church is not for people like my mom and me. Church is judgmental. Church lacks generosity, grace, acceptance.* Because the church rejected his mother, he in turn rejected the church. But when Michael hit a crisis and couldn't take the disappointment and pain of his life anymore, Pastor Peter didn't hesitate to reach out and offer empathy and mentoring to him.

Here is Michael's story.

After I graduated from college, a management consulting firm recruited me. I started working, and my hours were miserable. I didn't like what I was doing, traveling every single week, gone from home four nights a week. I got to the point of feeling I couldn't handle what I was doing anymore.

Lauren, my wife—we were still dating at the time—had been going to New Community. I finally said I would go with her. I have this memory of driving home from work one night. We left at 10 p.m., and it was dark and raining. I was just trying to figure my life out. I experienced a ton of physical pain driving home, and emotional pain, and I started bawling as I was driving, thinking, *I can't handle this anymore.*

Then I had the strongest urge to talk to this guy, Peter, who I had seen speak at church a few times. He is a charismatic, wonderful speaker. I thought, *I just have to speak to him. Maybe there is something more to this than I originally thought.*

So, a week later, there was a dessert night. Lauren and I went and stayed late to chat with Peter. Peter and I decided to have coffee soon after—I think less than a week later. We probably had a three-hour conversation. I told him a lot about my past, being raised by my single mother, and how I was born with a hip disease—I had eight surgeries before I was six weeks old. Which is something that I still struggle with today. I still experience a ton of hip and back issues.

I'll always vividly remember my first conversation with Peter, where he cut to the heart of the matter pretty quickly and said, "Michael, you are worthy. It's nothing that you can actually earn; it's something that you are given: salvation, acceptance by God, and peace through Jesus Christ." I had never heard that before, and it was at a time when I really needed to hear it.

Pastor Peter continued to meet with Michael once a month for coffee. Michael had questions about faith, God, and Jesus. They discussed books like *Mere Christianity*. Peter guided their discussions and gave Michael time to process what he was hearing and learning. Michael said that after six months, Pastor Peter challenged him, saying,

> "You know, Michael, you can ask all the questions you want to, but more than anything else, the only evidence in time that you should need is personal experience and personal transformation." And Peter said God has done so much work in him—that he is such a different person than when he started, and he still continues to grow—that there doesn't need to be more evidence than that for him. That was a really powerful statement and something that stuck with me. I think that's a pretty good summary of where I was when I first started pursuing Jesus, or felt like he was pursuing me, and I was finally acknowledging it.

Pastor Peter's relationship with Michael demonstrates elements of mentoring, including listening, expressing acceptance and care, building trust, offering wisdom, and sometimes challenging the mentee to take the next step (accountability!).

Mentoring relationships follow different formats. Mentors and mentees may meet as often as once a week or as infrequently as once every six weeks. Continuity, care, and trust are the glue that bonds mentor and mentee. And let's not forget timeliness; we observed Pastor Peter connecting to Michael, an unchurched guest, soon after his first visit.

The Mentoring Community and Identity Formation

Does mentoring have to take place one-on-one? Not necessarily. In fact, it can be healthier for young people to be mentored in community because they're less likely to be susceptible to any negative influence, biases, or vulnerabilities of a single mentor. Small groups, missional communities, and church and parachurch ministries can function as mentoring communities.

Intentional mentoring communities are highly influential in prompting young adults to grow in competencies, develop critical-thinking skills and a sense of responsibility, and foster strong and cohesive identity formation. In the United States, young adults generally make big decisions—such as about choice of school, college major, career, housing, and marriage—independently, during a period of decreasing support and input from family members and other adults due to physical and emotional distance. The absence of family and caring adults leaves emerging adults unsupported by those who love them or a supportive Christian or moral community. As a result, young adults are often making their most critical life decisions informed solely or primarily by their self-selected peers.

That's why mentoring communities are crucial during young people's decision-making years. Mentoring communities provide space where young adults can strive for their ideals and begin to imagine their future lives. Christian communities help young adults discern how they fit into God's world and mission to reach and restore broken individuals and communities, bless the world, and cause it to flourish. In this way churches can be positive influences for identity formation.

Some effective churches invest in intentional living (residential) and learning communities—often called discipleship communities—for young adults. These vary from an informal community to one guided by regulations or commitments, requiring a formal application process that includes a written contract.

Inviting emerging adults to live with church staff members and pastors and to work alongside church members in work and ministry gives them opportunities to observe Christians who are further along in their spiritual journeys and to learn how Christians live out their faith every day. These relationships provide numerous occasions for emerging adults to receive care and mentoring, to be held accountable, and to envision their future as Christ followers.

Participation in mentoring communities helps young adults find meaning and purpose within a community and to find their place in the world. Sharon Parks's assessment is that emerging adults without mentoring communities are more likely to remain stressed and distracted from the matters that are most worthwhile.

Bright-Spot Churches Invest in Leadership Development

As Brooke's comment at the beginning of this chapter demonstrates, many young adults consider themselves to be leaders. And they learn leadership language and identity from their churches—that is, the church introduces them to the idea that they are leaders. In many instances the church uses *leadership* as the frame for mentoring and maturing as disciples but also for assuming roles that assert influence on others.

Chelsea (age twenty-five), a former church dropout, had attended church and followed Jesus for less than two years when she and I sat down to talk about her faith journey. She described what she does as a leadership intern at her church, including this: "I always try to make sure I lead with authenticity and rawness." Clearly, Chelsea understands that leaders need to be transparent, honest, and real. She recognizes that her church is growing her into a disciple and a church ministry leader. She also knows her church loves her—and this nurturing message is helping her flourish.

Shea also sees that her church is developing her for leadership. She's been attending church for about eight months, and at age twenty she already has a forty-hour-a-week position as a church leadership intern. Shea describes her leadership trajectory this way: "I'm in a pipeline for a staff role." It's significant that she exhibits character qualities that churches find attractive and fitting for potential leadership—passionate spirituality, humility, a servant heart, and a love for the church. She said,

> The Life Kids team coordinator . . . brought up the LXP [an internship program called Leadership Experience or LXP] position. I was just on fire. I was very hungry. I wanted more of church. I was always at church. I just wanted more responsibility. I wanted to help. I just really had, and I still do, a heart to serve. And so, she mentioned the LXP opportunity to me and I was like, I don't know if I'm equipped for that. I'm very new to my faith. Are you sure? And she's like, "I brought it up to you. We can see you potentially being on staff." And that just empowered me. It made me want to step up even more.

Shea's church envisions an attractive future for her that appeals to her own aspirations. She's excited about her new faith in Christ, her church, and her future as a result of how her church is investing in her and giving her a new script about her identity—at a time when her identity exploration is at its height.

A Magnetic Field: Churches Investing in Emerging Adults

When emerging adults become involved in their churches and begin to serve, their churches reciprocate and give back. When young adults serve, they are in turn supervised, trained, mentored, developed as leaders, and appreciated. They're invited to coffee, lunch, meetings, committees, conferences, training events, and retreats. And they collect relationships! They grow relational connections and networks through the people who supervise them, their fellow volunteers and leaders, and the participants they serve. All these investments and relationships make effective churches increasingly attractive to emerging adults. In countless and measurable ways, young adults receive huge dividends from their churches.

> *When young adults serve, they are in turn supervised, trained, mentored, developed as leaders, and appreciated.*

A former bartender, Katelyn, who we met earlier, had been attending church for a few weeks when she signed up for a series of three classes designed to help attendees get to know the church better, identity their spiritual gifts, and find a place to connect and serve at church. These courses put Katelyn on track to an invitation into church leadership. She said, "I went to Best of Life, on finding your spiritual gifts. One of mine is leadership and [a staff member] reached out to me and said, 'We're coming up with a new leadership group, and you would be great at it!' That is how I got super involved in the church."

That "new leadership group" was a leadership board tasked with creating the future vision for the church. In addition to serving on that board,

Katelyn joined her church mentor in cofounding and coleading a small group Bible study for young-adult women.

When I asked Katelyn what helped her grow in her faith as a new Christian, she replied,

> The accountability and me being more involved in this church and also getting more connected with like-minded people like this Bible study, which has only been going for two weeks and we've already grown. And being involved in leadership and hearing the behind-the-scenes of the church and meeting different people from there to get involved in different areas like Bridge [another ministry in which Katelyn serves].

She put her finger on several ways her church is investing in her. They affirm her as a leader, acknowledge she has leadership potential, and give her opportunities for leadership development. She also believes she is growing, and that's an important trigger for emerging adults. Over and over, they say their churches help them grow, and that's attractive to them. Investment in young adults encourages them to come to faith in Christ and to stick with church.

All these elements in Katelyn's story—identifying and using her spiritual gifts, leadership development, a place to serve, and new Christian relationships —are helping her grow as a new Christian and deepening her faith and her commitment to church. The numerous ways the church is investing in Kaitlyn act like a magnetic field pulling her forward.

Churches that invest in young adults become even more attractive to unchurched emerging adults who receive benefits—the social capital discussed earlier—from their church communities: care, mentoring, the ability to reach aspirations, accountability, relationships, and leadership development.

CHAPTER REWIND

> The theme distilled in all these stories includes: when emerging adults are *included* in Christian community, *involved* in service or

leadership, and *invested* in (via care, mentoring, or leadership development) *immediately* (within weeks or a few months of their initial church visit), their preconversion process is not only propelled but accelerated.

In of all these stories emerging adults were invited to belong to church before they believed in Christ. Belonging to church gave them opportunities to try on Christian roles like church attender, community member, small group participant, volunteer, leader, and mentee before they committed to trust and follow Christ Jesus. As the church *invests* in young adults who become involved and find meaningful places of service or leadership, those young adults receive more and more benefit, and their churches become more and more attractive. So the five invitational practices combined are a transformative pathway to new life in Christ (see fig. 0.1).

Once young adults connect to church, the three elements of community (*inclusion*), serving (*involvement*), and care or mentoring (*investment*) are powerful catalysts for new birth, preparing young people to be lit by the regenerating work of the Holy Spirit.

STARTING THE CONVERSATION

▶ What are the prerequisites for investing in the emerging adults in your congregation? How could those prerequisites be adjusted to allow for unchurched young adults also to receive relational and leadership development?

▶ How is your church regularly investing in emerging adults? What opportunities do formerly unchurched individuals have to grow at your church?

▶ What would care, mentorship, and leadership development of young adults look like in your church?

ACTION STEPS

Develop mentoring resources. Find or develop a curriculum for working with young adults that includes discipleship and leadership development. Create a repository for curricula and books for young-adult discipling and mentoring.

Identify mentors. Locate trustworthy adults and mature young adults who can guide emerging adults through discipleship and leadership development issues. Look for missional mentors who are committed to the integration of evangelism and discipleship and who demonstrate love for people who aren't yet committed to Christ.

Train mentors in the mentoring curriculum. Instill a vision for mentors in which evangelism is considered incomplete until new disciples are deeply rooted in Christ, connected to a vibrant and compelling church community, attentive to God's Spirit, growing in spiritual disciplines, reproducing disciples, and releasing them into mission.

Identify mentees. Attempt to invite young adults into mentoring relationships and mentoring communities soon after their first church visit.

Cultivate leadership development. Gather and assess resources for the leadership development of young adults. Assess the need for curricula, hands-on experiences, service and leadership opportunities, internships, funding, and parachurch partnerships. Plan a leadership-development pipeline for the young people in your church. Create leadership opportunities for emerging adults, and lay out a pathway for developing as leaders and accessing these opportunities.

Create leadership internships for young adults to help them reach their leadership aspirations. Encourage young adults to apply for leadership internships. Goals for leadership interns may include

- ▶ recognizing the importance of God's mission to the world

- ▶ understanding the church's role in God's mission

- ▶ developing a strong ecclesiological vision for the significance of the church in the life of the believing community

- ▶ identifying interns' individual and communal callings to contribute to God's mission

9

Leading

WHAT'S A LEADER TO DO?

B rooke's honesty is refreshing:

I have a full book of every message I've listened to. I really like to go back and revisit them, because when you listen to the message, you start to feel convicted about certain areas in your life, and they give you appropriate tools that help you to put these things into practice—these convictions that you're feeling—and to take baby steps into the next part of your faith.

I wasn't a Christ-follower when I got here. I was living with my boyfriend—having sex with my boyfriend—and I didn't know any different. That's what I've done in every relationship that I had prior. To me it was, you live together, you see if it's going to work out, you have an escape hatch if it doesn't. The messages really convicted me to say, "Maybe this is not how it's supposed to go."

Brooke clearly arrived at church with values that differed from traditional Christian norms, but within a short time her assumptions were challenged by her pastor's messages. Rather than balking, she seriously considered accepting a standard of behavior alien to her experience. Her pastor presented a new possibility, and she wasn't necessarily opposed to it. He made it clear that no conversation topic is off the table, acting as a much-needed trail guide in the early stages of her faith journey.

It's often the lead pastors, ministry staff, and lay leaders at bright-spot churches that track the spiritual progress of young adults who are moving toward Jesus, and they provide help where needed. How do these pastors and ministry staff do it? How do they invest in young adults who don't know Jesus and lead their churches by example to do the same?

In bright-spot churches, pastors play a key role in facilitating young-adult faith commitments primarily by establishing an evangelistic ethos and an invitational culture in their churches, and secondarily by being personally accessible to young adults through relationships and mentoring. You'll notice that this is a two-way street: these pastors are helping their congregation reach out to unchurched young adults, and they are helping young adults move toward the church. They act as trailblazers for congregations who are reaching and keeping emerging adults and as guides for emerging adults on a journey toward finding identity in Christ Jesus.

The bright-spot churches in this study prioritize reaching out to non-Christians, and they prioritize accessibility to young adults. In the words of Pastor Alex Rahill, formerly senior pastor at LifeChurch Canton, Michigan, "One of our core values has been that we're unapologetically biased toward reaching the next generations. . . . We want to hand off to the next generation. To do that you have to get them in your doors; you have to reach them for Christ." His passion is typical of pastoral leaders who emphasize ministry to emerging adults.

> *We want to hand off to the next generation. To do that you have to get them in your doors.*
> Pastor Alex Rahill

In this chapter we'll consider what it looks like for pastors to make reaching unchurched young adults a priority for themselves and their churches. Let's start by looking at evangelism, a topic that most evangelical churches are familiar with and value—at least in principle.

Evangelism: Better Than Its Reputation

Let's just put it out there: the word *evangelism* is usually a turnoff—and not only to non-Christians. I've taught classes on evangelism to undergraduate and graduate students at three Christian colleges, and I've seen firsthand just how strong the negative connotations are, particularly among young people. Reactions can be especially strong in churches that embrace a missional identity and emphasize impacting communities and culture through proximity, hospitality, and incarnational presence. All in all, evangelism is a concept in dire need of deconstruction.

Here's the thing: The issue is *not* that believers and students don't want to see their friends, family, neighbors, and coworkers experience new birth in Christ. The issue is what evangelism has often looked like: door-to-door visits, preachers on street corners, religious billboards and bus ministries, stadium campaigns, and radio and television evangelists. These are images that emerging adults (and, yes, lots of boomers) instinctively react against. And they do so with good reason: offensive, impersonal, businesslike, and consumeristic delivery strategies for a supposedly life-giving and life-transforming experience with a personal God. Not only do we need to deconstruct the idea of evangelism, we also need to do the hard work of introducing a new imaginative framework for what evangelism can mean, something that can replace old models and images that no longer communicate well. That's what I saw happening at the bright-spot churches I studied.

Pastors of the bright-spot churches I studied shared a commitment to making evangelism one of their churches' top priorities. They emphasize evangelism frequently and openly, and they talk about evangelism in unique ways. I heard phrases like "helping people take a step closer to Jesus," "helping people find their way back to God," "reaching people far from God," and "a new beginning" among others, but whatever their vocabulary, they talk about it a lot. Most approach evangelism primarily through relationship building and friendship and secondarily through addressing tangible needs in their community. And they go out of their way to get their congregations excited about participating. Whether they use the exact "e"-word or not, they emphasize evangelism frequently, and they integrate evangelism into as many ministry areas as possible.

You may be wondering, if churches need to prioritize evangelism, does that mean their pastors need to be great evangelists? True, churches whose lead pastors are evangelists are usually evangelistic churches. But is there any hope for churches led by people who don't necessarily have evangelistic gifting? The short answer is *yes!*

In my experience, churches that want to reach and keep unchurched young adults need strong evangelism leadership more than they need an evangelist as their leader. After all, *evangelists* in the traditional sense aren't necessarily great leaders; many are far more comfortable going off to do outreach in person than doing the long, slow work of developing strategies and designing processes. Shifting a church's culture to become more evangelistically focused requires, among other things, casting a vision, building a coalition, and developing systems. Above all, it requires *commitment.*

Getting the Congregation Up to Speed

An essential part of building an evangelistic church culture is getting the congregation onboard. Existing church members need to be persuaded that evangelism is important, and they need to be educated about what that means.

When it comes to evangelism training, pastors have many options available to them. It's still possible to find excellent formal evangelism classes or conferences not unlike one from "back in the day." Training resources I highly recommend are Organic Outreach International, the Amplify Conference, and the Church Evangelism Institute, especially joining a cohort of church pastors and leaders committed to growing in evangelism leadership.

Some churches in my study include material on evangelism in general courses introducing the church, while others focus on teaching apologetics or sharing your spiritual biography (your personal journey to faith in Christ). I was somewhat surprised to find that most of the bright-spot churches I looked at didn't have much formal evangelism training. Only a few of the pastors were aware of *any* formal training in evangelism taking place in their church, though some recalled programs, such as *Becoming a*

Contagious Christian, being used within the past five or ten years. Where it did exist, the training was diverse and wasn't based on a comprehensive program or curriculum.

Pastor John Teter, founding and senior minister at Fountain of Life Covenant Church in Los Angeles, is perhaps the most systematic in his approach to educating his congregation about evangelism. His process focuses on building relationships and helping non-Christians look at their lives from a spiritual perspective. It also includes a strong emphasis on prayer.

> First, we help people become friends. Then we give them four main questions to ask as a spiritual inventory. I say, "You're the detective." We always ask people (1) what's their church experience, and then listen to what they say; (2) have they had any miracles or supernatural events in their life? Hear what they have to say. Then, (3), what are the questions they have about God and the Bible? Listen to what they say. (4) Then, what is a real, personal, current prayer need? So we try to really break it down where people can ask those things. . . . And we see the Holy Spirit act! He oftentimes does far more than we could hope.

While Pastor Teter described equipping his congregants with explicit strategies and resources for relational evangelism, most of the pastors I spoke to were more focused on encouraging church members to serve unchurched people and to invite them to church. Differences in context may play an important role here. Pastor Daniel Hill, senior pastor of River City Community Church in Chicago, for example, moved from a suburban church to an urban one, and he found that his new congregants didn't need help building relationships with non-Christians.

> Here in the city, people are surrounded by non-Christian everything. They don't need to be intentional to enter non-Christian environments—they're in non-Christian environments all the time. What I think is most critical is that they're growing in confidence, in vibrancy around their own faith, and they just by definition become lights. So I think context matters. When I was at

Willow Creek [a megachurch in the Chicago suburbs], you had to
urge people to get out of their Christian cocoon. In our context,
most of our millennials are just saturated with non-Christian environments, and so the most important thing is to get them as whole
as possible and thinking in terms of holistic Christian ways, and
then trusting that evangelism flows from that fairly naturally.

A lack of formal training opportunities need not mean that a church
or its pastor doesn't believe in evangelism or doesn't think relationships
with non-Christians are important. In fact, most bright-spot churches—
churches that stand out precisely because of their effectiveness at reaching out to emerging adults and bringing them into Christian
community—do not offer formal evangelism training on a regular basis.
I *did* see the pastors of these churches integrate a commitment to evangelism into the regular life of the church.

Making Evangelism Normal

Pastors of bright-sport churches have a vision for evangelism, and they
make sure their congregation knows it. That vision appears prominently in worship services, communicated through public announcements, stories of people coming to faith, and preaching on the value of
evangelism. The message is crystal clear: evangelism is a priority, and
the pastors expect their congregations to do the same. At the same time,
they cultivate an environment in which evangelism and its fruit—
including spiritual conversations outside the church and the presence
of non-Christians inside the church—are regarded as normal and
familiar. Pastors of bright-spot churches intentionally demystify evangelism for their congregations as a crucial part of communicating their
evangelistic vision.

As we'll see repeatedly in this and the following sections, the process
of normalizing evangelism varies widely from church to church. Pastor
Craig Sweeny focuses on encouraging conversations that are explicitly
about faith, creating a sense of expectancy in his congregation. Here's
how he describes his message:

We expect God's going to bring these opportunities to us. In past churches, we talked about sharing our faith in the context of maybe once a year. What we did here is say, "Sharing your faith is a regular part of your life. You may have three, four, five opportunities in a week." And then we show them what that looks like; we talk about how it's not all in one conversation, but it's one conversation at a time—maybe only ten minutes here and another thirty minutes there. So we break it down and help demystify what it is to share your faith and point to Christ. I think there is an equipping aspect to that. People recognize "I can do this!"

Pastor Sweeny works to build energy and positive expectations by helping his congregants imagine initiating spiritual conversations on an almost daily basis. In this framework, evangelism isn't mysterious and scary; it's normal.

Pastor Alex Rahill described telling members of LifeChurch Canton that evangelism is easy if they practice "prayer, care, and share."

We help people understand that when you pray, you are helping someone take one step closer to Christ. We constantly use that language. When you care for them in Jesus' name, you are helping someone experience the love of God, and that is bringing them one step closer to Christ. When you share, you are helping people. You're giving them an opportunity to invite Christ into their life. So we tell people to do those three things regularly.

In this framework, congregants are encouraged to engage in a range of specific evangelistic practices, all of which are both doable and meaningful.

Some pastors and churches use the idea and language of mission to communicate an evangelistic vision to emerging adults. Lead Associate Pastor Aaron Cho of Quest Church, Seattle, Washington, asks key questions to help the congregation see themselves as part of God's mission to the world: "What does it mean to be a good neighbor? How do we serve our neighborhood? How do we be light and salt in Seattle? Those are things that are evangelistic." Pastor Cho's church may not use the word *evangelism* much, but it does communicate a vision for a life that draws others to faith.

Creating Opportunities

When building a culture of evangelism, consistency is key. Prioritizing evangelism well means prioritizing evangelism year-round. And effective evangelism leaders create opportunities to place a special emphasis on evangelism at certain points in the calendar. The pastors I interviewed described a few different approaches: Some churches follow the church calendar, focusing on evangelism in the weeks leading up to Christmas and Easter and encouraging congregants to invite unchurched friends and family to special activities, events, and services. Others focus on evangelism in the context of Communion services.

Some churches use the launch of a new sermon series as an opportunity to remind their members to invite unchurched family, friends, and neighbors to church. This can be an occasion for significant spiritual and practical preparation. In the weeks leading up to the launch of a series, these churches strongly encourage congregants to pray for the non-Christians in their lives and to invite them to the series. They may also invest significant effort in producing print and electronic invitations that their members can use as evangelism resources. Pastor Rahill described both of these processes, beginning with a prompt to help listeners notice the unchurched people in their lives.

Who are your relatives? Do you have family members? Acquaintances? Who is your barista? Where do you go to the gym? These are not accidental relationships. Who are the people you play soccer with? . . . God put you there because he wants you to minister into people's lives and care for them. We help people understand the implications that the Holy Spirit is working in, through,

Some churches use the launch of a new sermon series as an opportunity to remind their members to invite unchurched family, friends, and neighbors to church.

and around us, and we pray for God to give us opportunity to invite these people. Our postcards become invitation cards to a new series, and that's why I'm a big advocate of regular, frequent series.

Later in this chapter, we'll learn more about the use of sermon series as an outreach tool.

What If It Works?

Effective evangelism leaders expect their congregants to build friendships with non-Christians, engage in spiritual conversations with non-Christians, and invite non-Christians to church—but it doesn't stop there. They also expect non-Christians to *be* at church. After all, if we expect evangelism to happen, we also have to expect it to work! This requires further expectation-setting. The pastors I interviewed took care to communicate an expectation that their church is a place where non-Christians are welcomed, received, and included, and where they can ultimately come to faith in Christ.

We've already explored the importance of *invitation* and *inclusion*, but it deserves to be repeated: pastors of bright-spot churches cultivate a culture of invitation and do everything they can to include newcomers in the life of the church. Notice that this can serve two purposes: it prepares the church to receive newcomers who respond to evangelistic outreach, and it makes it easier for members of the congregation to extend invitations. Church attendees will be far more motivated to practice evangelism if they can imagine their unchurched friends and family feeling comfortable in church and benefiting from what is communicated there.

Cultivating an invitational church culture also encourages churchgoers to tell their pastors about friends and family who are far from God—especially those who may be visiting or planning to visit the church. Pastors and ministry staff in bright-spot churches regularly initiate conversations about the non-Christians in their congregants' lives, discussing the importance of sharing God's love and further normalizing evangelism.

Talking to Non-Christians

The pastors I interviewed recognized that non-Christians were present for their sermons, and they often went out of their way to talk to them. Pastor Peter Hong described pausing to speak to non-Christians during his sermons: "I specifically and directly address non-Christians. I will say, 'For those of you that don't know if you're a Christian,' or I'll say, 'If you're asking questions about this,' or 'You know, if you're not sure about . . .' So I'm regularly referencing, regularly talking as if they're in the audience. Our church folks catch on to that."

Pastor Hong is conscious of the need to give unchurched visitors language for what they're experiencing in church. And the Christians in the audience also notice this. When pastors make an effort to speak in a way that makes sense to newcomers, regular attenders learn that they can trust their pastors to talk to their own non-Christian friends too.

Pastors of churches that are effectively reaching emerging adults make calls to faith a regular part of their work to bring people to Christ. They often include some kind of invitation to respond to Christ in their weekly services. Exactly what these invitations are can vary widely, often reflecting different understandings of what "responding to Christ" will look like or involve. Some pastors emphasize a single point of decision and commitment. Pastor Larry Kim, for example, says in his sermons that every Christian makes a decision, that many people have made this decision, and that it's the best decision they ever made. On the other end of the spectrum, Senior Associate Pastor Brynn Harrington at High Rock North Shore explained that she and other pastors in her church network encourage church attendees to make small, incremental commitments to Christ. "We talk a lot about how faith is a process for everyone. We are all on a journey. It's bit by bit, and it's little decision after little decision. That has started to come up in every sermon that we preach. How do you follow Jesus in the small things, not just in the big one-time decisions?"

Calls to faith in bright-spot churches range from explicit and laser-focused to subtle and suggestive. Not surprisingly, explicit invitations lend themselves to immediate response and therefore tend to reflect an emphasis on conversion as an experience that occurs at a particular moment in time. For example, megachurch pastor Craig Groeschel described closing every sermon with what he calls a "direct ask": "If you want to turn from your sins, surrender your life to Jesus, invite him to be your Savior and Lord, lift your hands right now." While he noted that he doesn't assume everyone who responds will "populate heaven," he does believe it's important to count weekly responses in order to measure and track new faith commitments.

All the bright-spot churches made calls to faith in the main worship services. Craig Groeschel's, Alex Rahill's, and Craig Sweeny's direct and even quantitative approach to evangelism from the pulpit represents pastors on one pole along a spectrum among the pastors I spoke to—weekly calling for precise, clear decisions.

Pastor Aaron Cho expressed a very different perspective when he explained that his church doesn't emphasize praying "the sinner's prayer" or "raising your hand if you want to receive Christ," nor does it measure evangelism results. Instead, Quest Church in Seattle emphasizes the relational dynamic in evangelism, picturing it primarily as "conversations with people on the journey" toward faith in Christ. Notably, Cho commented that while conversion can be a "moment in time" experience, most of the unchurched people he observes in his church are working through a process of conversion.

Pastor Cho's church and others are intentional about inviting newcomers to faith but tend to take a more flexible approach to expressing the invitation, integrating it into their preaching on various topics. Pastor Daniel Hill, for example, described shifting from moralistic to Christ-centered preaching under the influence of well-known pastor and writer Tim Keller. In every message Pastor Daniel includes a natural invitation to respond to the gospel.

> I've definitely been influenced by Keller's stuff, that every sermon should have a natural gospel presentation and even a call to the gospel. I would hope there is never a sermon where I am not clearly

stating what the gospel is and inviting people to respond to that. So it's not always in the "give your life to Christ right now" way. The whole service is built around it, but it's always in the sermon that if you've not responded to this gospel message, you should. I try to do that every single week.

Other pastors expressed a similar desire to provoke response but allowed for diversity in both invitations and responses. Colead Pastor Will Barnett, High Rock Acton, for example, includes a call to respond to the topic of the message every time he preaches. He explained that a response to the good news of God may look different in each case.

Every sermon is preaching the gospel in some way. The gospel is all the good news of the things God is to us and the relationship we can have with him. It doesn't only have one articulation. Every sermon is an articulation of God's grace, and there are different ways to respond. It can be with an invitation to why we're praying in response to this message, for you to pray and have the conversation you need to have with God. It can be the invitation to "Hey, I'm going to be journeying with those who are exploring faith." I call it the First Steps of Faith group. "If you want to become a part of that with me, join me on a journey where we can ask questions together."

Aaron Cho reflected on how invitations to faith at Quest Church can flow naturally from the circumstances of an individual service, a sense of the Spirit's leading, and a pastor's individual style.

We say, "Hey, if you're new here and you've never had Communion, and you don't know who Christ is"—and the language that we use changes depending on whoever is facilitating the elements. If we feel like the Word had a natural flow connection and an evangelistic bent, then toward the end of the sermon as the preacher feels led, they'll say, "If you are new here at Quest and God is tugging at your heart and you've never done this, but you believe God is stirring your heart, then we want to welcome you to a space to respond to God."

We've done [calls to faith in Christ] both in the context of a sermon and more so in the context of an introduction to communion.

Uniting all these approaches is the pastors' awareness that non-Christians are listening to their sermons, they choose to speak directly to those people, and they desire to help unchurched young adults move toward a relationship with Christ. In all these ways, pastors of bright-spot churches help inspire and develop a culture of evangelism through their preaching.

Leading by Example

The pastors of the bright-spot churches I interviewed had high expectations for evangelism by their congregants, but they didn't ask congregants to do anything they weren't willing to do themselves. In fact, one of the most important elements of their evangelism leadership was the personal example they set. While many admitted that they didn't get to spend as much time with non-Christians as they'd like, they did describe spending as much time as possible having meaningful conversations with non-Christians, building relationships and having significant conversations in which they hoped to have opportunity to share Christ.

Pastor Larry Kim at Cambridge Community Fellowship Church shared a story that reflects many of the themes we're looking at throughout this book:

There are some young guys that hang out in the parking lot in the back of church. Around midnight or so, I just approached them and introduced myself. I invited them back into church, and just hung out with them. I think I talked about music with them, and probably about drugs, you know, because I think they were doing drugs. Then I explained who I was. I explained a little about who Jesus is, and then I invited them to come to church on a regular basis. And they came. They just started coming to church. They didn't do, like, a Jesus prayer or anything. But they're now a part of the church, and they come regularly on Wednesdays and do Bible study with us.

Pastors like Larry Kim don't just talk about the importance of having relationships with non-Christians; they actually *have* relationships with non-Christians. They model initiating conversations, extending invitations to church, and helping newcomers connect to Christian community. They also keep these relationships going. The pastors I interviewed described meeting regularly—often once a month or every six weeks—with emerging adults who aren't fully embedded in the life of the church and have no history of meaningful contact with other churches.

Personal engagement in evangelism and relationship building is important for pastors not only because it sets a good example, but also because pastors are uniquely situated to serve as points of connection between the church and the rest of the world. Pastor John Smith, senior pastor at Crossroads Church in Loveland, Colorado, at the time of our interview, described his approach to personal evangelism this way: "I make friends with people. I care about people. I listen to their story, and I look for inroads to eventually tell the person what I do. [I hope] that they understand I actually care about people."

And he is on to something: young adults both inside and outside the church notice when pastors have relationships with non-Christians. The emerging adults I interviewed were very aware that their pastors prioritize evangelism, have unchurched friends, and genuinely care for non-Christians rather than treating them like projects. Michael, for instance, stressed the significance his pastor Peter Hong puts on understanding people's struggles in coming to faith in Christ.

> One of the things heavily encouraged and prioritized at church is building relationships with non-Christians. The bigger part is really getting to know what the needs are of others, you know, non-Christians— what their sticking points are, why they haven't come to faith, and just what they struggle with in general. It's so easy to project on them what you think it is they need, when you may have no idea.

Michael's observation captures many of the themes that will emerge in the next section of this chapter, which looks at how pastors and ministry leaders of bright-spot churches turn evangelistic passion into effective action plans.

Leading by Being Accessible

If you want to get to know people, it helps to be around them. This may sound simple, but ask yourself this: how many unchurched young adults have you seen hanging out in your church offices lately? Pastors of bright-spot churches recognize the importance of putting themselves in physical proximity to the people they want to reach. They usually spend significant time—at least a few hours a week—at coffee shops or other places where emerging adults gather. They sometimes meet with young adults by appointment, but sometimes they just go about their work in a place where emerging adults can see and become comfortable with them.

Most conversations between pastors and emerging adults happen outside of church buildings. When pastors go out of their way to be in places comfortable to those they're reaching out to, it communicates something important about their intentions. It also puts them in a position where they can easily listen, learn, and begin building bridges between those in the Christian culture and secular young adults.

Now, let's be clear. While it would be nice if we could reach young adults just by showing up in their space (passion + proximity = new church members!), it's not that easy. Connecting with unchurched emerging adults takes effort, and it takes a profound openness to listen, to learn, and to look at familiar things through new lenses.

Making Connections

When the pastors I talked with meet with unchurched young adults, they do so with a couple of purposes in mind. The first goal is to help non-Christians make progress toward a faith commitment and to help new Christians continue to grow in faith and discipleship. This probably comes naturally to most pastors, but it's worth pausing to note its importance. For dones, personal relationships with pastors and ministry staff give them an experience with faith and religion that contrasts with disappointing past experiences. And for nones, receiving personal attention from a pastor can be a source of amazement.

For nones, receiving personal attention from a pastor can be a source of amazement.

Michael's vivid narration of his initial connection with Pastor Peter Hong illustrates this kind of positive response to a pastor's efforts.

When I first started going to New Community, the biggest pull for me was Peter. I felt an urgency to speak with him, to listen to what he was saying, and to build a relationship. It was beautiful that he actually spent the time of a massive church to build a relationship with me. That meant a great deal to me. I still see him as a big mentor of mine. I think that was my immediate attraction to [the church].

As important as the spiritual nurture of individual young adults is, it's also important to realize that every conversation with unchurched young adults is an opportunity to learn about their world. In a way, it's a research opportunity—not in the sense that the people we're relating to are test subjects, but in the sense that they have a lot to teach us if we're paying attention.

Pastors who want to reach unchurched young adults need to recognize that they'll have to bridge significant cultural divides—divides between generations as well as between the Protestant evangelical church culture and the world as the unchurched experience it. They also need to acknowledge that the barriers we encounter aren't *just* a matter of unfamiliarity. Distrust, suspicion, and misplaced assumptions also come into play.

Let's be honest. Just as Christians do not appreciate certain things in the broader culture around them, we need to remember that many non-Christians are equally apprehensive about us. Church dropouts in particular may be wary of church and Christians because they are influenced by negative stereotypes and often by painful personal experiences. Empathetic pastors and other church leaders can build and repair bridges to emerging adults who are disillusioned with the church, and they need to be honest with themselves about the reasons behind that disillusionment. We'll address this shortly, but first let's look at some of the basics of crosscultural understanding as they apply to unchurched young adults.

Pastors of bright-spot churches *get* emerging adults, yet their understanding generally doesn't come naturally. They work hard to develop cultural fluency. They deliberately educate themselves by reading about and interpreting pop culture, identifying cultural heroes and idols, exposing themselves to art and media consumed by young adults, and learning how young adults prefer to communicate. Above all, they recognize the importance of genuinely listening to young adults in order to understand their experiences and challenges, learn about their perspectives, and improve their ability to communicate with and care for them.

Emerging adults see and appreciate these efforts. One student described a pastor this way:

> He does a great deal of actually listening. He does a lot of his work in coffee shops, does a lot of sit-ins and interviews to understand what the issues really are, and doesn't project things that he thinks we might be struggling with. He does his best to understand what drives us. He definitely understands his audience; his audience is very young and full of students from the different universities. He understands the pressures we put on ourselves.

Pastors like this make sure they're being informed by emerging adults and exposing themselves to this group's concerns and needs. Even pastors of very large churches can take steps to ensure that they're regularly hearing from young adults, such as by making sure they ask younger staff members for their ideas and opinions. Pastor Alex Rahill, for example, color-codes his weekly schedule to ensure he meets with an emerging adult at least once a week and Senior Pastor Ray Johnston at Bayside Church Granite Bay regularly includes young adults in staff meetings.

Pastors who gain cultural fluency are equipped to engage in a two-way translation process. On the one hand, they can act as cultural informants to unchurched young adults, making foreign aspects of Christian belief and practice more familiar. In the process these conversations give pastors insight into how unchurched young adults perceive God, faith, and the world, leaving them better equipped to translate the world and perspectives of young adults to their older congregants. Pastors who consistently practice openness and empathy with unchurched young adults are able to function as intermediaries or go-betweens who bridge the cultural divide, connecting young nones and dones to the Christian church subculture.

The Pastor As Go-Between

Pastors are often the ones who help unchurched emerging adults navigate church culture. The process often begins when a pastor invites a young adult to join a Christian community, such as a small group. Such in-between spaces where two-way translation can take place are vital to showing the way to unchurched emerging adults. In this way, pastors negotiate an understanding between non-Christians and the Christian community by creating a social space in which unchurched young adults can learn more about Christian faith. This often involves introducing dones and nones to people their own age and to leaders who work with emerging adult cohorts.

One pastor, for example, had interactions with the wife of one of his congregants who seldom attended Sunday worship service. She had described her experience visiting a church women's group as being like "hearing a foreign language." So he tried a different approach, inviting her to a small group book study. He said,

> She responded to my invitation to be part of a first-steps of faith group where we read through N. T. Wright's *Simply Christian* book and just talked about it with actually no pressure for her to believe any of it, but just as a way for her to explore this foreign language and get to know it. We met over a period of time, and I'd say, "What

are your questions, and let's talk about them." My approach was to not have the answers but to say, "This is how I understood this," and let her ask her questions and try to clarify. In reference to the women's group, she even told me, "The way these people talk is so foreign to me. I don't talk about God or religion like this."

Later this young woman mentioned that through their book study, "I went from the outside looking in at this thing that just felt very foreign to now I'm on the inside, trying to make sense of what's happening." Pastors of bright-spot churches make an effort to build relational connections with non-Christians and extend invitations into safe and welcoming communities, such as small groups, book discussions, and even Bible studies. Safe communal spaces provide time and opportunities for pastors to translate the gospel to nones and dones in the context of developing and deepening relationships.

The Significance of Sermons

While young adults often experience significant spiritual progress in small groups, we also need to acknowledge the importance of sermons. One striking—and perhaps surprising—finding from my interviews of previously unchurched young adults is that listening to preaching was a major contributor to their journey to faith and early Christian growth. Maddy and Garrett, for example, both affirmed the importance of Lead Pastor Todd Rodarmel's (Mountain View Church, San Juan Capistrano, California) preaching in their new faith commitments. In fact, they both mentioned the same sermon. Garret described Pastor Rodarmel's style in general, and this sermon in particular, like this:

He relates to life a lot. He pulls things in from Scripture that lead into other things, and it just leaves a big impact. The other day he was preaching on how God should be the center of everything you do. Not your wife. Not your kids. I mean, those can be number one, number two, but God's the center of everything you do. And he's really good at relating to me.

Maddy referred to the same message when she was asked to explain what it means to "commit your life to Christ." Her answer: "making God and Jesus the one thing, the center." Maddy said this center was what she had been searching for. She returned to this sermon later in our conversation when I asked if she felt a sense of belonging in her new church. She replied, "Yes! A person can belong [here] if Jesus is their center. The only really important thing is making Jesus and God the center of your life."

Pastor Todd is adept at translating the language of his Christian community to young adults with little or no Christian background. Pastors like him explain the gospel to young adults in ways they can understand and apply to their own experiences. And they help translate in the other direction too, helping longtime church people accept and receive unchurched emerging adults into the community.

Preaching Their Language

Many of the young adults I spoke to told me that they love their pastors' preaching. Asked what they liked about it, they used terms like *not preachy*, *down to earth*, *genuine*, *real*, and *relevant*. They generally interpreted their pastors and church ministry staff as personable and laid-back, and they appreciated clear communication with practical implications. Just as importantly, these young adults were clear on what their pastors were *not* like: "super opinionated," "trying to convert you or change you," "shoving information at you" or "telling you a bunch of rules." This list of negative characteristics is very revealing: the young adults I spoke to understood that they would respond poorly to pastors and sermons that failed to respect their intelligence and abilities.

When I spoke to these young adults' pastors, it became apparent that the positive reaction to their preaching was far from coincidental. These pastors were intentional about designing sermons to connect with emerging-adult congregants and their unchurched friends, and they were conscious of the fact that they didn't have much time to make a good impression. As Lead Pastor Bill Johnson at Cornerstone Church of Boston said, "We only get one shot with the unchurched. If we haven't landed the message to touch their heart or intrigue them to hang around a little bit longer, they are gone."

These pastors described a variety of ways they fine-tuned both the style and the content of their preaching to appeal to young and non-Christian audiences. They described actively looking for opportunities to draw connections to young adults' lives, especially through storytelling. They also stressed the importance of being willing to address hard questions—including hard questions about Christianity and the church.

Yet these pastors' personal styles and methods varied considerably. There was as an almost even number of those who preferred expository preaching and of those who prefer a topical approach—and many blended the two. Approximately a third followed a liturgical calendar. Their emphases on simplicity versus intellectualism also varied, with pastors working near university campuses leaning toward more sophisticated presentations. Only one pastor took a more dialogical (or Socratic) approach to preaching.

The Importance of Being Real

As we consider how pastors can tailor the style and content of their communication to better connect with unchurched emerging adults, it's essential to realize that no one can fake relatability to emerging adults—or anyone else. They know when someone is putting on a show. Though emerging adults can be surprisingly accepting of imperfection, they are intensely intolerant of hypocrisy and insincerity.

Pastors of bright-spot churches make a commitment to transparency. Senior pastor and founder of Genesis Church, Robbinsdale, Minnesota, Steve Wiens put it this way: "What you see is what you get with me. I'm not a pastor who is a different guy on stage than I am out to coffee or out to beer. I try to be myself. I'm pretty transparent about my flaws, and I think that makes me approachable. The millennials I've met with and talked to are untrusting of leadership in general and untrusting of a slick package."

Emerging adults I spoke with also had this understanding. Daniel, for example, commented on the impact of his pastor's (former Lead Pastor

John Smith at Crossroads Church, Loveland, Colorado) transparent
manner in the pulpit.

> I love that his message and delivery are practical. I love that he's
> honest and he shares lots of stories about himself and his reactions
> to certain events and communication with people. Or [he shares]
> even the things he thinks or his initial reactions, and how he works
> through them and realizes, "Yeah, this isn't something I should be
> doing; this is what I should be doing." Then he explains how he
> corrects himself. So he is leading by example. He has a lot of humil-
> ity; it also shows that no one's perfect. He is setting the example
> that I think is very important and very impactful.

The value emerging adults place on authenticity extends to their perceptions of other aspects of a church service. As Senior Pastor Edrin Williams of Sanctuary Covenant Church, North Minneapolis, put it, "Young
adults value authentic discipleship more than they value huge productions.
Most young adults aren't looking for lights or a projection show—they're
looking for genuine faith. They want to know that the person doing the
teaching in a church is real, knowledgeable, and genuine in their faith, not
just putting on a nice show on Sundays." Emerging adults generally feel
more at ease in worship services that feel less canned and more honest.

One assumption underlying the previous comments is that church
leaders must convince emerging adults of their trustworthiness. Millennials in particular tend to be suspicious of anything that evokes their
dislike of prepackaged institutionalism, inauthenticity, or corruption.
Senior Pastor Craig Groeschel of Life.Church reflected on the importance of consciously breaking down suspicions and biases against large
churches in particular.

> I try to bring the real me to the message. Like, I'm writing on racism,
> and I'm forcing myself to tell a moment when I had a racist response.
> I don't want to do that, but if I don't bring transparency to it, then we
> don't have anything. And so I've forced myself to be more vulnerable
> than I normally would be. Millennials are looking more for authentic

experience than for a produced experience. I think that authenticity from the leaders matters more than you could imagine, and even transparency. I think they're coming in, some of them, with a little bit of natural skepticism against big and organized [religion]. And that's kind of what we are—big and organized—and so there might even be a bias. So we have to break through that natural bias quickly.

Senior Associate Pastor Brynn Harrington at High Rock North Shore too noted the need to build a foundation of trust that extends beyond church activities and beyond the pastoral staff. She and the other pastors at her church don't do evangelism training but instead focus on challenging congregants to earn recognition as good and trustworthy members of their communities.

> We [seek to] earn trust in the community by being people who are trustworthy, authentic, welcoming, and hospitable, and who are not afraid of saying that we're Christians. So people can see, "Oh, these are loving people. They're serving the community. They're doing good things that I can get on board with. Oh, and they are all Christians." Somehow it becomes a little bit more viable.

Pastors of bright-spot churches realize that unchurched emerging adults rarely have warm feelings toward organized religion in general and Christianity in particular, and that one of the essential tasks of evangelism is to earn the credibility needed to challenge their assumptions about the church and the Christian faith. If churches or pastors smack of self-righteousness, arrogance, hypocrisy, or immorality, emerging adults walk out and don't come back. But when their search for relational wholeness and community brings them to the door of a church where the pastors and the culture are sincere, transparent, and genuinely good, they'll take time to linger, explore, and respond.

Facing the Tough Questions

A sincere appeal to young adults includes a good-faith effort to engage with the issues that affect them. The emerging adults I interviewed agreed that their pastors are able to address local and global events as well as the problems, struggles, and temptations that emerging adults face in their everyday lives. Michael, for example, said this about his pastor's preaching:

> He's great at focusing on who our gods really are. What we're worshiping in terms of success, money, our pride, and doing a great job. Even relationships are a great topic, obviously for millennials, and finding our worth in girlfriends, boyfriends, marriage, having to have someone, not being alone. He focuses on the hot issues a lot and does a great job, I think, taking them head-on and not walking around the difficult conversations.

Some pastors make strategic use of sermon series to address the questions, concerns, and needs of unchurched young adults. Their goal is to make it easy for congregants to get their friends interested and to invite them to church. Former Lead Pastor of Life Community Church, Roseville, California, Chuck Wysong, for example, recalled launching a sermon series called "Fighting for Relationships," which he said appealed to non-Christians who deeply value their relationships. The series included four sermons, the first three prepared non-Christians for the final sermon on how to have a vital relationship with God.

Pastors of churches that are effectively engaging young adults give themselves permission to explore and address topics that matter to that age group, even when that involves hard questions and contentious issues. These topics often transcend individual concerns to include broad economic, social, and political injustices—such as poverty, racism, violence, and consumerism—as well as specific issues like police brutality, homelessness, human trafficking, and corruption. Pastor John Teter said his preaching fit British theologian John Stott's analogy: preaching with a Bible in one hand and a newspaper in the other.

Churches may worry about addressing tough questions and thorny subject matter, but refusing to do so comes at a cost. Dominique Gilliard, an ordained minister, the director of Racial Righteousness and Reconciliation for his denomination, and the author of *Rethinking Incarceration: Advocating for Justice That Restores,* believes that young adults care about Jesus and justice but don't believe the church cares. "Church hasn't been a place where young adults have been able to have real conversations about their concerns about racism and incarceration, and they're frustrated by the church's silence in the face of problems that are traumatizing them and people they care about." Gilliard says that young adults

> *Churches may worry about addressing tough questions and thorny subject matter, but refusing to do so comes at a cost.*

> want to respond with faith to the concerns that polarize our nation. Christian young adults yearn for a Christocentric way to respond to social injustice and their Christian identity must mark and inform how they respond. Young adults want to know how to share the good news in that framework. They need to be discipled in these spaces where the church is often quiet.

His argument is that the church's silence on events and topics that concern emerging adults drives many of them to drop out of church at the very time when it could be helping them respond to these issues as people of faith.

Pastor Peter Hong of New Community Church in Chicago listed young adults' desire to "advance the cause" of a better society as one of the top-three reasons that his church is seeing new faith commitments among young adults.

> Passion for the poor and racial justice are actually evangelistic tools for folks not churched and who don't know Jesus. But in their hearts, they know that it is a good thing and there is something deep in all of us that wants to make a difference in the world and make an impact in the world where flourishing can happen. A group of people living their lives beyond four walls of the church and genuinely caring for the least of these is attractive. A lot of them grew up in churches where issues of race and poverty were not talked about. . . . We regularly talk about them.

Churches committed to racial righteousness and reconciliation and justice are attractive to young adults who want to make a difference in the world. While they may not personally serve in a ministry to the poor or marginalized, they want to be affiliated with churches that do.

Pastor Edrin Williams believes the church has an opportunity to help young adults make the connection between the justice causes they're passionate about and their day-to-day faith. He notes that young adults often have "a bifurcation where they hold their faith in one hand with Bible study and prayer, but causes are held in the other hand. We need to help young adults see the two go hand in hand." He sees a twofold challenge: helping young adults understand and practice missional discipleship and helping them avoid the burnout that often follows when social concern crowds out personal devotion and spiritual growth. Churches that address what it means to live as disciples of Jesus in a world of complex societal challenges can attract and nourish young adults who are drawn to these issues.

The Elephant in the Room

So churches that want to reach and keep emerging adults need to talk about big problems. But what happens when the church or Christianity is itself the problem?

Simply put, churches need to talk about that too.

The pastors I interviewed weren't afraid to critique Christian culture and institutions in their sermons. While that may seem surprising, it appears sensible and even necessary in light of the need to build credibility and address the deeply felt concerns of wary observers. A number of pastors commented on the need to speak with humility, transparency, and vulnerability, and several described using self-deprecating humor in their communication for this purpose.

When asked if he could pinpoint anything he thought his church was doing differently from others that contributed to its impact on emerging adults, Pastor Barnett highlighted the use of sermon series to connect to people who dislike and distrust the church.

In our preaching we try to address contemporary questions and cynicisms about the church and make it a safe place for questions. For example, we all [churches in the High Rock network] did some version of a preaching series over Lent called, "Forgive Us: The Separation of Church and Hate," where we identified major historic sins of the church and repented of them. We talked about judgmentalism and about political posturing and how the church has played into that. We had a sermon on "Sins Against Thinkers." We discussed how we often alienate scientists and have the wrong posture toward thinking folks. . . . We did a sermon on sins against the LGBT community; we actually didn't advance a theological position, but just said this is the way the church has had the wrong posture. We did [a sermon on] sins against the hurting, where we focused on mental illness. So, a series like that, I feel, actually validates a lot of the questions asked by people on the outside of the church or who've been hurt by the church. It validates their criticism. I think that's actually a really different posture, that we're not trying to defend the church in a sense and can be honest and authentic.

CHAPTER REWIND

It's impossible to overstate the importance of pastors in building and maintaining an evangelistic church culture. They often play a key role in young adults' perseverance in their faith journeys. While they don't have to be gifted evangelists themselves, pastors who want to reach unchurched emerging adults have to lead evangelism well by communicating their vision consistently and with excellence, becoming students of culture, serving as translators and cultural brokers between the churched and the unchurched, and cultivating transparency and trustworthiness throughout their personal and corporate identities.

STARTING THE CONVERSATION

▶ Are you keeping informed by emerging adults? When was the last time you had a conversation with an emerging adult? What movies, music, and podcasts popular among young adults will you absorb in order to inform your communication with them?

▶ What would it take for you to be off-site a few hours a week, working from a venue at the same time every day to develop relationships with young adults outside the church and to mentor those attending your church? Do you need to propose a reworked schedule that allows you time to connect and invest in reaching, mentoring, and developing young adults?

▶ What is your church doing about social injustice and racial righteousness? Do young people know about these ministries, and are they invited to the table? Are they empowered to connect to causes that they are passionate about?

▶ What priority does your church place on evangelism? Among the top-ten priorities of your church, what number would you give it?

▶ How are you modeling evangelism, inviting, and inclusion for your congregation? How much time do you give weekly to practicing personal evangelism? To leading evangelism?

ACTION STEPS

Make it personal. Cultivate a personal passion for those far from God by spending time with them in conversations. Deepen your relationships with people outside the church and pray for them.

Rewrite your job description. Add to your pastors' and pastoral staff's job descriptions time spent with emerging adults in emerging-adult venues and staying on top of cultural trends among emerging adults for the purpose of greater ministry to them.

Practice. Cultivate your personal evangelism skills through practice by having spiritual conversations with non-Christians.

Prioritize evangelism. Make evangelism your own priority and one of the top three or four priorities of your church. Whatever word your church uses for evangelism, make sure life transformations through faith commitments to Christ is the priority.

Get others involved. Inspire your ministry staff, church leaders, and laity to commit to evangelistic mission. Equip them to pray, to care for their non-Christian friends, and to share their faith in Christ naturally with their friends and family.

Keep it up. Make a plan for how you'll accomplish this objective to reproduce evangelistic passion and practice in your congregation.

Learn from the best. Listen to and analyze sermons by pastors of churches that attract and retain emerging adults, drawing large numbers of emerging adults. What illustrations and stories do they use to communicate biblical truth to that age group? How do they use humor? How do they communicate humility to their congregation?

10

Attracting

CONNECTING EVANGELISM, DISCIPLESHIP, AND MISSION

You don't have to be absolutely Christian to go. That initially really grabs people.
Then once they're hooked in a small group, if you can get them there,
that's what makes them stay. The biggest part is how inviting and accepting
and laid-back the church is. People aren't really expecting that when they come.

CHELSEA, AGE 25

Here's where we've traveled thus far in taking a good look at what's happening in a number of churches where emerging adults are coming to faith in Christ and are being incorporated into the life of the church. It's clear that standout churches *incorporate young adults before they make full faith commitments.* Young adults aren't hanging around the church wondering what to do next. Bright-spot churches intentionally welcome emerging adults and help them navigate church culture to feel at home. Non-Christians and formerly unchurched young people are becoming *embedded* in the life of the church through community, service, and mentorship.

Young adult non-Christians are active in small groups and are involved in service opportunities and ministry. Pastors, church staff, and lay leaders are investing time and energy to train and disciple these young people. In return, these emerging adults are participating in churches and behaving like Christians before they make faith commitments. By *behaving* I mean they are practicing Christian enactments like prayer, worship, Scripture reading, and service. *They belong and behave before they believe and commit.*

Churches that affirm the discipleship practices of young adults who have not yet committed to Christ give them space and opportunity to explore and experiment with Christian identity—to try it on and to see if it fits. Churches serving emerging adults' maturation and identity exploration encourage them to consider Christianity as a viable identity commitment and a place to serve the world, enhancing their religious identity commitments in the context of supportive community.

So where are we headed next? This chapter will show how the five invitational practices are not only an approach to evangelism but also a retention tool: young adults are active in the church as they are in the process of being evangelized. What's more, they attract and evangelize more emerging adults. Finally, the five practices function as a discipleship wheel: young adults find that the same processes that drew them to church and faith also help them grow in discipleship. As they experience transforming community, they become curious about faith in Christ and begin to serve in ways they believe make a difference. In doing so, they grow toward Christ and begin to follow him in mission. As they follow Christ, they experience his love, healing, and grace.

Meanwhile, others—church leaders and members—invest in unchurched emerging adults as they continue to grow more deeply rooted in Christ, transforming into his image and making

> *The five practices are not only an approach to evangelism but also a retention tool: young adults are active in the church as they are in the process of being evangelized.*

new commitments. In turn they initiate and invite friends and family to journey with them. So the five practices are all part of a wheel—that is, evangelism, retention, discipleship, and multiplication keep rolling on, resulting in disciples that make disciples.

Figure 10.1. Five practices of churches reaching emerging adults

The Road to Retention—Not "All-In" Is Okay

The spiritual stories of young adults reveal that they need safe places where they can explore Jesus, God, faith, and discipleship without feeling pressured to convert or to accept everything. By providing emerging adults with a safe space to explore—a sort of spiritual sandbox—churches actually retain them.

The emphasis isn't on giving their whole life to Christ, although those opportunities are made available on a regular cycle in the life of the church, whether in the main worship services or in small groups. Without being pressured, young adults are allowed a space where they can wrestle with questions and faith issues—a space to investigate belonging, behavior, belief, and identity.

Perhaps there is a generational difference in evangelism. Bright-spot churches realize that young-adult barriers include fearing pressure and being judged. And that's the intriguing distinctive feature about these churches: although they have high expectations that everyone is welcome and encouraged to become involved, they send a message that church is a safe place to get involved and to explore without having to commit fully. Many young adults are retained at church before they're evangelized; others are retained simultaneously as they are being evangelized, as evidenced in stories like Michael's.

As someone who never felt comfortable speaking about my faith in any kind of church before—and even with any type of Christian—New Community was a very easy way for someone who didn't have faith to go to the church and not feel out of place or threatened or looked down upon for at least not having made a decision or understanding what a decision is. I felt very, very welcome from day one, which was big for me, to keep me coming back.

Pastor Barnett's story shows his desire for his church to be a safe place for people on their exploration.

[A regular visitor] doesn't have to check . . . questions at the door to identity with having a faith in God—those can be part of her journey. She still doesn't believe all of it. We were talking about the resurrection and whether she believes in a literal resurrection, and she told me, "I feel like maybe metaphorically I can get that, but I still don't buy it yet." But she feels safe and enough a part of the community that she feels like she can keep exploring those questions. I think she's identified with God and Jesus in significant ways; she identifies with being a part of the community, and there is some sort of faith seeking and understanding. For me, her journey is what I want our church to be doing regularly. You can belong and start to serve and live as a Christian, even while asking questions about belief. It doesn't have to be a linear process.

Bright-spot churches have high expectations that pre-Christian young adults will "jump in" without being "all-in."

The Wheel of Evangelism and Retention

The interesting thing about the five practices as a wheel of evangelism—*initiate, invite, include, involve, invest*—is that it's also a wheel of retention. Independently and collectively, these scenarios are building blocks that support a strong frame, sort of a scaffolding for building a strong, cohesive identity and commitment to Christ.

Remarkably, the strategies churches use for reaching young adults are comparable to their strategies for keeping emerging adults. When pastors were asked for their church retention strategies—*How do you keep and incorporate emerging adults into the life of the church?*—their responses were akin to the same strategies they use to reach or evangelize young adults. Reaching and retaining strategies are one and the same, simplifying what is often a complex process into a two-for-one strategy: what evangelizes young adults retains them, and what retains young adults evangelizes them.

Five overlapping strategies for keeping young adults in church and helping them to become active in church were identified by pastors of bright-spot churches.

1. Relationships and community. Not surprisingly, pastors mention connecting young adults to relationships or community as their church's number-one strategy for keeping emerging adults. Brynn Harrington, senior associate pastor of Highrock North Shore in Salem, Massachusetts, estimates 80 percent of the attendees at Highrock are in small groups, and that's what retains them. "Millennials need to be a part of something bigger than themselves," she said. "We encourage them to be a part of a life group, so they are in relationship with people every week." She added that when visitors get connected to small groups, they stick. Engaging in small groups encourages a strong sense of belonging to a church. And a strong sense of belonging contributes to churches' ability to retain emerging adults. It's a no-brainer; by enhancing relationships and community, attachment to the church is enhanced.

2. Serving. Key to getting emerging adults to continue with church is getting them to serve. Craig Groeschel, pastor of Life.Church, says, "Relationships are important, but serving is the anchor." All but two emerging adults in my study were serving in a church. The two that weren't serving were also the two who were least connected and attending church the least, though this may be due to their challenging circumstances.

3. Relationships and serving in combo. Bayside, a thriving church in Granite Bay, California, of about eighteen thousand attendees, uses two methods to retain emerging adults. First, the church focuses its energy on connecting newcomers to relationships with people who know Christ. Dena Davidson, Bayside Granite's campus life director of Thrive School (a discipleship, internship, and academic partnership between Southeastern University and select churches), says the church forecasts that young adults who attend church for several weeks without making friendships will drop out of church. Dena describes Bayside's strategy:

> Everything we do is to help them form friendships and relationships with other people who know Christ. Something one of our senior pastors says is "We want to help everyone at Bayside make several friends who will lead them closer to Christ." And that's definitely a huge part of our approach with millennials. We use the phrase "Come, be known in the community." That's the first part. It is connecting them to relationships.

First, Bayside seeks to connect every emerging adult with *seven* strong Christian friends who will journey with them toward Christ, helping them stay tethered to church and faith in Christ. Second, Bayside staff recruit teens and twentysomethings to volunteer and serve. Routinely the church offers leadership opportunities to young adults. It also isn't unusual for young adults to supervise ministries. Dena amplifies this part of Bayside's retention strategy:

> There's a few on-ramps in our church to get anyone volunteering, but mostly it's just our youth staff going after people and saying, "Come, greet at middle school ministry. Come, volunteer in high school ministry." I would say the dominant force behind that is the youth staff seeing a young person and saying, "Hey, come, be on my team."

No matter the depth of an emerging adult's commitment to Jesus, Bayside finds ways for that person to connect to meaningful service. Youth staff are not bashful about approaching young adults to ask them to help out.

4. Biblical teaching and relationships. Pastors point to a combination of strong biblical teaching and relationships as the reason young adults stay. For example, Lead Pastor Jeremy Duncan at Commons Church in

Calgary, Alberta, described his church's twofold retention approach: "Connect with Friends and Learn in Community." Commons Church first seeks to provide emerging adults with strong biblical and intellectual teaching. Second, it connects people to one another through small groups and activities. Activities designed to help young adults connect include the DinnerPartyNetwork, where newcomers meet friends and are funneled to HomeChurch to find a home group. About 250 young adults are connected to small groups.

5. *Community, God's mission, and mentoring.* Yet another powerful combination for retention is compelling community, connecting to God's mission to the broader community and the world, and mentoring. Quest Church in Seattle seeks to keep emerging adults from feeling isolated by connecting them to community. They believe community is a safe place where young adults can wrestle with tough questions, share their faith struggles, and receive encouragement and prayer from the group. This model assumes smaller church communities like small groups are loving, caring, and empathetic.

Emerging adults also are expected to serve God's mission at Quest. Through serving, they learn to live as disciples and become active contributors to their church and the wider community. Quest Church is all about being a good neighbor to their immediate neighborhood as well as to the city of Seattle. The church also values being a good global neighbor. Ministries young adults participate in at Quest include homelessness and hunger, immigration and refugee advocacy, racial justice and reconciliation, global presence and development. The webpage dedicated to global and local ministries reads:

Global + Local + Glocal

You're invited to be part of the life-changing, soul-enriching, kingdom-focused work of discipleship that is Glocal Ministries— local and global acts of justice, compassion, advocacy and presence. Following Christ's call, these commitments are central to the life of our church; learn more how you can #GetGlocal.

At Quest, associate pastor of community life and formation Aaron Cho tracks young adults' spiritual progress and provides them with pastoral care and mentoring. He describes the processes working together as three pathways converging in faith in Christ.

> For us and for me, the process has always been getting young adults into community. I oversee our community life groups, our C Plays [sports groups], and so they are plugged in to other people of faith when they connect to life and C groups.
>
> Acts 2:42 and other passages are an anchor for our community groups and for how Quest started as a church plant. I find that a part of the evangelism process and of getting on that journey is this: Are there others here who are with me? That question is often asked. Is this spiritual journey isolated and alone? They feel alone in it.
>
> I think things begin to happen when we do things together in community. Questions are asked; questions are answered. Sometimes questions are asked, and questions aren't answered. I think the miracle is people are not opting to leave. They're opting to stay, and they're still wrestling with unanswered questions. They're still on this journey. God is doing something in you, and you're still staying and sticking with it. So, getting them plugged into the life of the church through small groups is the main way [to keep young adults] and obviously serving. When they get to the point of serving on a team, that's where something happens, whether it's psychologically or spiritually, where now they've bought in and they are now [saying], "I want to invest in the life of the church." At that point, folks more or less become active in professing faith and walking like disciples of Jesus.
>
> The ones on the edge may have only gotten into a small group or C group, and then the other part is working with me. I meet with them maybe once a month or every six weeks, checking in on all things related to their lives, all things spiritually, talking about questions they may have. These may even be with young adults that only show up to Quest once every two to three weeks, so you don't even see them every Sunday.

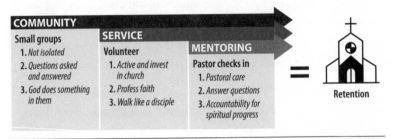

Figure 10.2. Community, service, and mentoring lead to retention

> I would say there are three main ways to interface. I see them active on Sunday morning at worship; I'm meeting with them one on one, just a pastor care meeting or to get to know them; and they're getting plugged into small groups. Those are the ways that I feel they're getting plugged into the life of the church.

The three processes of community, serving, and mentoring work together to retain emerging adults at this multiethnic urban church focused on God's mission to the poor and marginalized (see fig. 10.2).

All of these retention strategies emphasize the importance of connecting emerging adults to community soon after they arrive on the church's doorstep. Three of these strategies pinpoint serving as a grip for firmly holding on to young adults: community, service, and mentoring.

Why Young Adults Say They Stick

Perhaps you, like me, want to hear what young adults find so attractive about church. I asked some what motivated them to get up on Sunday mornings and go to church. Their responses varied from commonly repeated themes like (1) the strong sense of community and connection, (2) challenges and opportunities to grow, (3) inspiring sermons, (4) church relevancy, (5) and feeling welcomed and loved. Shea's response included more than feeling welcomed and loved.

> I was constantly being kept in communication throughout the week. When I got involved, and I wanted to be part of something, and everyone welcomed that. And I started inviting people on Facebook,

and they were constantly speaking life into me. People [from Life. Church] were texting me throughout the week and giving me an appreciation gift—giving me more responsibility. It constantly built me up and makes me feel valued and important and known.

Shea's church *saw* her. She felt known by her church. Often church people assume newcomers want anonymity, but that's not necessarily true and needs to be tested. From what we know about emerging adults, many crave community and being known. Life.Church demonstrated Shea's value to them by giving her a strong sense of being known and recognized and valued by the church—even though she was nineteen when she started attending, and she didn't even live in the same community. In fact, she drove an hour to get to church. Still the church reached out to her and included her, making it a safe place for her to get involved.

Like Shea, emerging adults recognize their churches are giving them opportunities. Interestingly, in Shea's first church visit of another church, she was left to navigate on her own. She said, "No one was showing me how it worked." She felt out of place, but at Life.Church, she experiences the opposite. She receives attention and appreciation and is growing in her identity as a Christian and as a leader. In turn, her appreciation for her church increases.

Previously unchurched emerging adults name a lot of reasons that motivate them to stay at their church of choice. As they talk about what they like about their church, their descriptions include "I'm growing into a strong disciple," "church is inviting," "church is welcoming," "church is exciting," "church understands millennials' challenges and struggles," and "Jesus calls us to commit to church."

Katelyn's response is typical: "I love Pastor Chuck's way of how he presents the message in genuine relevant ways. It's like you're having a conversation with him. Then also growing relationships and the genuine feel of the church. I'm not just a seat to get in the door."

Clearly, emerging adults stay because they like the invitational ethos of their churches and what their churches offer them. But what is it about these churches that helps emerging adults grow as people and become Christians?

The Most Important Way Churches Help Emerging Adults Grow

Growing is an important theme for emerging adults, and they stick to churches where they experience personal growth. Young adults reached by bright-spot churches identity four areas in which churches contribute most to their growth: (1) serving or leading, (2) Christian community and small groups, (3) accountability and mentoring, and (4) sermons and Scripture study (see fig. 10.3). Katelyn, for instance, identified "getting

> *Growing is an important theme for emerging adults, and they stick to churches where they experience personal growth.*

more connected to like-minded people" in her small group Bible study and "being involved in leadership in the church" as ways her church fuels her growth.

There are a lot of similarities between the retention strategies just described and what young adults find attractive about their churches. They name community, service, and leading as the three key factors that help them grow.

Churches benefit as well. Sociologists of religion study why churches grow numerically and are healthy, becoming robust instead of declining.

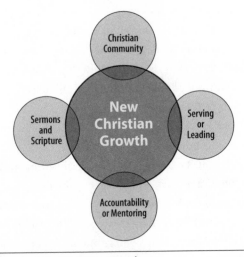

Figure 10.3. Young adults' Christian growth

There are many factors. Let's focus on why many churches that nurture young adults are stable or growing.

Why Churches Grow

The following three theories of church growth may shed some light on what I observe in churches that stand out in reaching and incorporating emerging adults.

1. Sheltered churches thrive. Popular in the last third of the twentieth century, the sheltered enclave theory assumed that orthodox religions, especially evangelicalism, when protected from culture would thrive in a "sacred cosmos" or a credible and secure moral order. An enclave is known as an enclosed or isolated community that is cut off or recedes from the broader society and culture. The sacred community affirms orthodox Christian faith and legitimizes belief in Christ by offering an alternative to the parts of society that seem to erode faith. People within the enclave find their faith, traditions, and community meaningful, so they continue to worship and adhere to the faith community that protects and shelters them. They experience belonging and faith in that protected and sheltered community.

So, secularism and religious pluralism can undermine the vitality of Christian faith and the church. When the church provides a secure and viable moral community that shelters Christians from the evil and corrupt parts of modern society and affirms their faith and belief, then people stay, and the church stays strong and grows because the community attracts people looking for these conditions within which to belong. They contribute to and raise their children in church.

Although this doesn't seem to be a good model for vibrant churches reaching young adults, effective churches do offer a moral order that makes Christian faith and practice meaningful. Young adults seem to flourish when they let go of destructive behaviors and moralities. So they're attracted to morally based subcultures. Still, the effective churches I examined aren't enclave-like in the sense of religious orders that seemingly shelter those who take religious vows. All the churches represented here are culturally engaged, as are the emerging adults that attend them. The young adults are involved with non-Christians and continue to invite them to church. And religious pluralism doesn't seem to negatively impact young adults' faith or the vitality of their churches. Emerging adults are choosing Christian identity and faith amid a profusion of religious options that don't seem to threaten their commitment to a new moral Christian community. What other model may fit the growth and vibrancy of standout churches?

2. *Strict churches thrive.* The theory that strictness creates thriving churches has been around for some time. Its proponents argue that conservative churches flourish, and lenient churches decline. The idea is that religions thrive when their adherents meet their expectations or demands in terms of time, money, energy, reputation, and so on. Some sociologists add a twist to this theory, called the rational choice theory, which adds that strict churches ban what they call "free riders"—that is, anyone who enjoys the groups' benefits without contributing to the group is not encouraged to stick around. More lenient groups will decline when the number of people who want to receive becomes more than the number who want to give. When fewer religious benefits become available, the result is apathy, disinterest, and decline.

This strictness theory may fit well with fundamentalist church cultures that require certain practices. However, bright-spot churches have few requirements. It's no surprise that they have a culture of invitation. The curveball is that they also have high expectations. They don't *require* but they *invite* everyone to participate and contribute in meaningful ways. Attenders certainly don't need to jump through hoops, such as church membership classes, to be active participants and contributors. Service and many leadership positions are not merited.

3. *High invitation and high expectancy churches thrive.* This leads me to propose a new theory: expectancy theory (an alternative theory to strictness theory), which I think much better fits the church culture of bright-spot churches and the five invitational practices. While strictness theory tends to be enclave-ish and has hard boundaries, the expectancy theory describes churches with fewer boundary markers; boundaries are porous,

encouraging the inclusion of non-Christians. Unchurched people come and go as they please. And the social script of expectancy theory is *expect to learn, grow, and serve with us.*

Churches reaching the unchurched—especially emerging adults, dones, and nones—are growing by conversions that aren't characterized by strictness but by a church culture that's inviting and has high expectations of attendees. Involvement and contribution by all those attending, regardless of profession of faith, is encouraged, appreciated, celebrated, and in other ways rewarded.

Emerging adults are challenged to grow, change, and eventually conform to the ideals of the community—without what we might call negative pressure but rather positive invitations, encouragement, and benefits—through avenues like mentoring, leadership development, ministry internships, employment, small groups, and community life. They are inspired and challenged in positive ways to learn, contribute, serve, lead, mentor, invite, share their faith, and grow in morality and belief. In turn, emerging adults receive and enjoy the benefits of being invested in by their pastors, ministry staff, and church leaders, which leads them to continue their own interest, energy, and passion.

The data suggests a reciprocity between young adults and their churches: we invest in you, and we deeply appreciate when you invest in us. The hinge swings both ways without one necessarily preceding the other. So then expectancy theory reflects the findings that bright-spot churches reaching emerging adults with high levels of social invitation, social expectation, and social engagement tend to grow and thrive.

Distinct Yet Engaged

Christian Smith and fellow scholars propose that evangelicals thrive because of their "engaged orthodoxy" in a pluralist context. "American Evangelicalism, we contend, is strong not because it is shielded against, but because it is—or at least perceives itself to be—embattled with forces that seem to oppose or threaten it. Indeed, Evangelicalism, we suggest, thrives on distinction, engagement, tension, conflict and threat."

These scholars propose the subcultural identity theory of religious persistence and strength best describes what's happening in growing evangelical churches. Basically, churches that engage with but are also in tension with the broader culture have a better chance of growing. That's because, the authors forecast, that religion thrives in pluralist societies by embedding itself in a subculture such as evangelical churches that offers a morally satisfying community where people find meaning and belonging. Basically, the idea is that thriving religious groups are sub-cultures that can engage with other groups while keeping their own distinctives. Most—if not all—bright-spot churches I examined were distinctively orthodox yet engaged with many groups, including the marginalized and the poor, at-risk youth, and unchurched emerging adults. Churches effectively reaching unchurched emerging adults are not huddled away from their surrounding communities. Many if not most of them are engaging their broader communities through caring for the homeless, providing community resources for immigrants and immigrant youth, or supplying assistance for students living in low-income communities through supporting local schools with tutoring, backpack drives, and school lunches. They offer an alternative culture to outsiders and bridge the cultural gap to make friends, be involved in bettering society, and invite those outside the church to come and check out the church.

Churches engaged with but also in tension with the broader culture have a better chance of growing.

Let's look more closely at how emerging adult Christians multiply and contribute to their thriving churches.

The wheel of multiplication. First, they are enthusiastic about their churches, and they don't keep their enthusiasm to themselves. Within a few months of their first visit, emerging adults ask their non-Christian friends and family to attend their church. Note that emerging adults don't just ask one, two, or three people to church. They invite multiple people. For instance, Michael asked eight non-Christian friends to come to church. Half of those friends visited at least once, and two now come regularly.

Michael isn't an anomaly. Katelyn decided to be baptized a month or two after first attending Life Community Church. She invited ten friends to her baptism. They all came, though half of them were unchurched. One of Katelyn's friends said, "I don't believe in God, but I'll be there for you!"

After attending Mountain View Covenant for eight months, Maddy was bringing her mom, dad, sister, aunt, and new husband to church with her.

People want to share with others what they're excited about, especially when something is helping or benefiting them. When asked why she invites and brings her family to church, Maddy replied, "Because I feel passionately about it, and I want to share my passion with them." Megan also shares online recordings of church services and her pastor's sermons with her mom. Megan described her mother's favorable reception:

> I invited my mom. And my mom's been in Arizona. So she hasn't had the opportunity to come yet. But she's totally stoked. She's really excited. I've sent her some sermons, and she said that she loved them, that she has watched them over and over and over, to, you know, get more out of them. And, as I've said, growing up, my mom was not at all any type of religion.

Why are emerging adults inviting multiple people to church? It's possible that when effective churches *initiate, invite, include, involve,* and *invest* in young adults, they become enthusiastic enough to invite others. Like Maddy and Megan, they're passionate about their loved ones experiencing what they've experienced—the benefits of the Christian community and spiritual transformation. Emerging adults who experience life-changing transformation become inviters and evangelists for their churches. So the five practices become a missional wheel of perennial evangelism and multiplication of discipleship-making.

The wheel of attraction. Let's look at the five practices as a wheel of attraction. Churches that reach and retain emerging adults perpetuate a cycle of attraction that draws in more and more young adults. The cycle begins as church members invite their emerging adult friends to church. These emerging adults start attending and begin to experience compelling community and also begin to contribute to the church as a response to a high expectancy church culture in which everyone is invited and expected to participate.

It's fair to say that church has something to offer young adults. And the church communicates clearly, "There is something here for you." As young adults begin to contribute, the church in turn begins to invest in them, helping them grow, mentoring them, and giving them even more responsibility. Emerging adults discover they are valuable to churches and worthy of investment in the eyes of churches.

In turn, young adults realize their churches have added value for them. The benefits accrued through this investment continue to attract them to the church even more, and to faith, leading young adults to reach out to invite their friends and family to receive what they have received: community and friendship; a place to meaningfully contribute, to make a difference, and to give back to the community; mentoring and leadership development and encouragement to reach their aspirations; and identity exploration and commitment. Thus the emerging adult journey comes full circle, culminating in a "wheel of attraction" (fig. 10.4).

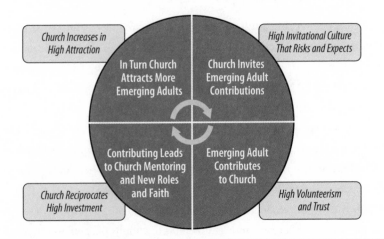

Figure 10.4. The five practices as a wheel of attraction

The wheel of discipleship. The five practices also function as a discipleship wheel. Young adults tend to find that the same things that drew them to church and faith also help them grow in discipleship. As young adults experience transforming community, they become curious about faith in Christ and begin to serve in ways they believe make a difference. In doing so, they grow toward Christ and begin to follow him in mission. As they follow Christ, they experience his love and thrive in their new identities as new creations and beloved children of God. Meanwhile, others invest in them as they continue to grow more deeply rooted in Christ, transforming into his image and making new commitments. In turn they initiate relationships and lead others to journey with them. In this way their discipleship is formed through finding a way to participate in God's mission to the world and in bearing witness to Jesus. They initiate and invest in relationships with unchurched people and invite family and friends to church.

We expect a disciple to deepen relationships with non-Christians and to invite non-Christians to church. Part of discipleship is conforming to the image of Christ through hospitality and thereby contributing to a church's invitational culture. We want disciples to be in Christian community, experiencing loving one another, praying and breaking bread together, and being devoted to Jesus' and the apostles' teaching, We expect disciples to be involved in church and to serve and to find their place in God's mission to the world. We hope that disciples are not only pouring their lives into others but also are being poured into as the church invests in them through training, teaching, mentoring, and serving. Finally, disciples are to witness to Jesus and to be inviters into God's kingdom and his church. Disciples include their pre-Christian friends in their compelling Christian community. They come full circle and begin again around the wheel. The five practices, therefore, form a discipleship wheel with mission as the context of discipleship (see fig. 10.4).

CHAPTER REWIND

A pattern in bright-spot churches where the five practices for reaching and keeping unchurched emerging adults operate is that they simultaneously retain young adults while helping them incorporate into the life of the church—before they commit to Christ—at the same time they are reaching other young adults. In fact, many seem to commit to their church before they commit to faith.

First, through relational networks, churches invite young adults to church. Second, they give them opportunity to belong to a community and to contribute through service and leadership opportunities. Third, as emerging adults both belong and contribute, they receive benefits from their churches, such as helping them; developing them; mentoring them; encouraging them to grow personally, emotionally, and spiritually; and giving them more responsibility. As a result of their church's investment and the many benefits they receive at church, emerging adults are (1) retained, (2) evangelized, (3) attracted, (4) multiplied, and (5) discipled. Emerging adults continued to be even more attracted to their churches and to faith, and they reached out to invite their friends and family to experience what they were experiencing. And so the wheel of attraction comes full circle. When these five pieces are fit together—voila! Holistic Christian identity and Christian mission fit together in a way that emerging adults get.

STARTING THE CONVERSATION

▶ Is it a paradigm shift for your church to consider praying for, encouraging, and inviting the presence of more non-Christians —especially unchurched young adults—to be a part of your church community?

▶ Use the five practices as one way to evaluate your church. Which of the five invitational practices does your church practice well? Think of several examples of excellence in one or two of the practices.

▶ Which of the five practices is a challenge for your church's ethos? If you agree that your church needs to improve, which practice will you take steps to implement? What steps does

your church need to take and in what order? How will you prepare for your first step? Who needs to be included and on
board with your plan?

▶ How may investing in unchurched young adults be perceived
negatively by church folks? How can you anticipate un-
enthusiastic reception to your plan and head that off at the
pass? How can you help people see that the benefits outweigh
the risks and drawbacks?

ACTION STEPS

Envision hospitality. Share with your church leadership the vision to
become a church that's more hospitable to non-Christians, that
invites non-Christians, that provides safe spaces for non-Christians,
and that accompanies non-Christians on their journey toward faith
in Christ.

Build for safety. Create safe community spaces where young adults
can pursue faith and discipleship without feeling pressured to be
all-in—spaces where they can explore the Christian faith.

Make small groups hospitable. Train small group leaders to recognize and practice hospitality toward those who have not made
faith commitments.

Involve the congregation. Share the vision of your church becoming
more welcoming and accepting of unchurched people, especially
young people. Let them know the church leaders are passionate
about drawing nonbelievers and creating safe spaces for them to
consider Christian faith as an option.

Ask the experts. Ask young adults at your church why they stay. Find
out if they feel they are growing as Christians and what they identify
is contributing to their growth or what is not. Use that feedback to
help you evaluate and strengthen your ministry to emerging adults.

11

Revisioning

EVANGELISM INSIDE THE CHURCH BOX

B ack in the day, before the twenty-first century, many churches were bracketed off from their broader communities. Congregational-ism, a feature of American religion, made churches similar to clubs: peo-ple joined and belonged to groups that were separated from the rest of society by boundaries such as race, class, denomination, beliefs, and party affiliation.

Evangelism Outside the Box

Over the past three-quarters of a century, American Protestant churches did much of their evangelism outside the walls of the church. Churches relied on approaches like Evangelism Explosion's door-to-door evange-lism, events outside the church, and parachurch ministries to spread the gospel. Popular among these evangelistic strategies were campaigns like the Billy Graham or Luis Palau crusades, Christian Women's Club, Bible Study Fellowship, Christian music festivals and, more recently, men's, women's, and students' religious conferences (for example, Promise Keepers, Women of Faith, Urbana missions conferences, and Catalyst). Musical concerts and tours, in which speakers and musicians give testimo-nies, evangelistic messages, and calls to faith, have also been popular.

In this traditional paradigm, evangelism was generally directed at people who were not part of a church. So most invitations to Christ were made at events and evangelistic ministries outside the walls of the church—outside the church building or context—to people who didn't participate in church life or in this particular club.

Some special occasions did provide opportunities for outsiders to be evangelized within the walls of the church, but that was only when believers were asked by pastors to invite friends, family, neighbors, and guests. Church leaders and congregants understood exactly which contexts and venues within the church were intended for evangelism efforts: Christmas Eve, Good Friday, and Easter services; vacation Bible school; and for some churches, revival meetings.

So the traditional paradigm for evangelism focused on the need to evangelize people who are not a part of a church—those "outside the box."

Incorporating and retaining *new* Christians, on the other hand, took place almost exclusively within the church's boundaries. Once people made commitments to Christ, they were received into church membership and fellowship. New Christians were retained as they participated in church-based activities such as Sunday school, Sunday worship, midweek Bible studies, evening services, and other church activities. Evangelism and retention were thus treated as separate entities, with evangelism mostly occurring outside the church box and retention occurring mostly inside the box (see fig. 11.1).

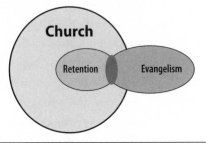

Figure 11.1. Evangelism outside and retention inside the church box

The New Paradigm: Evangelism Inside the Box

The locus of American evangelism has shifted in response to cultural changes in recent decades. My research points to the emergence of a new paradigm of evangelism and retention that appeared to be operating within every church I studied, irrespective of social or geographic location, size, or ethnicity. Its key feature is this: emerging adults are incorporated and retained either *before* or *while* they are being evangelized. The order of evangelism and retention are reversed in this evangelism paradigm. This new model is more porous than the traditional alternative, and the churches are less like clubs. Non-Christian young adults move in and out of the church with ease both through the front door (the main worship service) and on the margins (small groups, young-adult activities, mission trips, and service opportunities). Non-Christians are inside the church—and that is where they are being evangelized.

The order of evangelism and retention are reversed in this evangelism paradigm. Because non-Christians are incorporated before or while they are evangelized and are retained by becoming active within the church, they receive the benefits of church membership—previously reserved for believing church members—before they make faith commitments. In the earlier traditional evangelism paradigm, most of these benefits—like community, service, mentoring, discipleship, training, and appreciation—were awarded to church members. What these bright-spot churches demonstrate, then, is that evangelism is happening both inside and outside the church, and evangelism and retention have switched places in the chronology of emerging-adult conversion.

> *The order of evangelism and retention are reversed in this evangelism paradigm.*

Unchurched emerging adults in bright-spot churches are invited into the church and invited to receive the benefits of the church community before they make faith commitments to Christ. Churches are also using similar strategies for *evangelizing* emerging adults for *retaining* them, and both take place mainly inside the church, although sometimes on the margins of the church. For instance Pastor Lance Davis at New Zion Fellowship Church in Dolton, Illinois, now Executive Minister of Developing Leaders for the Evangelical Covenant Church said many black college students serve on Saturdays in New Zion Church's food pantry in order to receive their fraternity and sorority service credits. They begin to see New Zion as their church before they've attended on Sundays. Thus the new evangelism paradigm for churches reaching and retaining unchurched young adults is illustrated in figure 11.2.

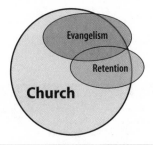

Figure 11.2. Evangelism and retention inside the church box

Similarities and dissimilarities exist between these two evangelism and retention paradigms: one reached past generations and one now reaches emerging generations. Previously, much of the retention happened within the church; now retention is happening mostly within and sometimes outside the church—often before or as emerging adults are evangelized, at the center and the margins through connecting to Christian community and service.

The shaded middle of figure 11.2, where church evangelism and retention meet, is in the space of deep, compelling community, serving, or leading, and spaces where emerging adults are invested in when mentored, trained, held accountable, and helped along in their journey. A lot of evangelism and retention is happening inside the church box, and non-Christians are retained as they are evangelized and before they make faith commitments.

In earlier chapters I mentioned two stages in the conversion process. Young adults first journey to church (fig. 11.3).

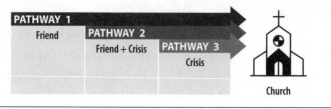

Figure 11.3. The journey to church

Once they are embedded in the life of the church in community, serving, and mentoring, they are on a journey to faith in Christ (fig. 11.4).

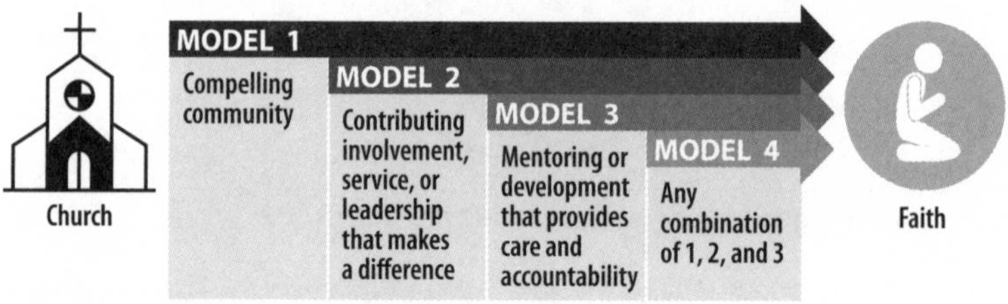

Figure 11.4. Church leads to faith in Christ

This stuff is riveting! I dug around to see if anyone else had made this discovery. Two researchers made observations that resemble my own. In 2000, Rodney Stark and Roger Finke identified a similar two-stage process for people committing to a religious identity. They referred to the process of "recruitment and conversion" in a discussion of religious choices people make. They relied partly on the work of another scholar who, in 1997, observed a similar phenomenon and described conversion as a process in which a person is able to adapt and assimilate to church culture. They argue that people don't convert for reasons of religious searching or because of doctrinal criteria. People convert because they're drawn through relationships:

People were drawn to the group through their network ties to members, thus becoming recruits, a stage of belonging prior to knowing much about what the group believed. Leatham defined conversion as the process of mastering the group's religious culture. Thus, path to full membership began with recruitment and passed through conversion.

Their conclusions are helpful to understanding the process of conversion that effective churches are experiencing among previously unchurched converts. Let's pause and acknowledge conversion as a nonbiblical term for union with God and initiation into God's rule. Only the Spirit of God can bring about regeneration: the work of the new birth, the forgiveness of sins, and the gift of the indwelling Holy Spirit. Humans are responsible for repenting and seeking forgiveness in conversion— turning from self-rule to God's reign in our lives, for Jesus calls people to repent and believe. Bright-spot churches appear to work in collaboration with the Spirit in preparing emerging adults to be receptive to new birth and guiding them and accompanying them in this process.

Somewhat similarly to what Stark and Finke observe, I'm suggesting that emerging adults are first drawn to churches through their relational networks and the invitations of good friends and close family, and not through attraction to a particular theology. However, I see more than relational networks as contributing to new faith commitments. Emerging adults jump in and engage in their new churches. They participate in Christian enactments and therefore behave or act like believers as part of trying on a Christian identity as part of the identity work young adults do in this life stage.

They jump in and contribute in meaningful ways, and they commit when given safe spaces in an anchoring, supportive moral community and friends to journey with them on their exploration. And eventually they commit to faith in Christ. As a result of contributing, they receive even

Emerging adults are first drawn to churches through their relational networks and the invitations of good friends and close family, and not through attraction to a particular theology.

more attention from the church and become the recipients of mentoring, prayer, relationships, training, and other resources before and while making faith commitments. As a result, churches increase in their attractiveness to emerging adults.

Belonging Before Believing

During the past decade or so, evangelism authors have explored the theme of *belonging before believing*—that is, inviting the unchurched into Christian communities where they experience belonging to a community of people who love and worship Jesus Christ. The big idea is that giving non-Christians the opportunity to get to know a group of caring, committed Christians exposes them to Christ. Within a loving community, the unchurched also are exposed to vibrant Christian faith that draws them to explore faith in Christ for themselves.

Many evangelism thought leaders, writers, and scholars say that the role of community has a vital influence in the conversion process. The past two decades have seen a flurry of writing on the impact of community on conversion. Rodney Stark, a Baylor University sociologist of religion, argues that conversion occurs along relational lines. Humans profoundly influence their friends, relatives, and others in their circles of connection—especially those they are close to. It follows that people influence others toward faith in Christ as they live out their Christian faith in the context of those close relationships.

In the *Celtic Way of Evangelism*, George Hunter suggests using an approach for reaching postmodern people similar to St. Patrick's approach in the ancient Celtic mission to Ireland. Patrick and his fellow monastics created communities where up to a thousand people (Bangor and Clonfert, Ireland, numbered close to three thousand!), including whole families and entire villages were living and working together. Hunter describes monastic communities that enveloped pre-Christian Celts into imaginative, hospitable, and relevant communities of Christ-followers who experienced a keen sense of belonging to the community. He suggests that postmodern people need similar experiences with hospitable Christians, who welcome unbelievers into Christian community where they have opportunity to develop friendships, connect to spiritual mentors, experience the way of life of small group community, practice prayer, and worship. Hunter proposed similarly, postmodern people need a place to belong before they believe.

Likewise, emerging-church leader and author Brian McLaren in his 2002 evangelism book, *More Ready Than You Realize* (written during his more orthodox phase) wrote, "Sometimes belonging must precede believing." He argues that at some point, non-Christians need to transition into a vibrant faith group where they can participate in the Christian community as an integral step in their process of conversion.

In my favorite book on evangelism, *Reimaging Evangelism*, Wheaton College professor of evangelism and leadership Rick Richardson affirmed, "Most people today will come to faith in the context of a community." His main point? People need to be invited to belong to a Christian community so they can come to faith in Christ. Wheaton College missiologist Ed Stetzer describes the process of evangelism similar to a journey, recognizing that people first become part of a community then convert to Christ as they journey to faith alongside other Christians. I agree that people, especially emerging adults, need to see others like them on the journey and experience being enveloped into a compelling faith community where progress in their spiritual journey is affirmed.

All of these authors illustrate that social transformation happens in the midst of community—or what sociologists call social pressure. Relationships and the Christian community are powerful, inclusive, transforming evangelism approaches. People need a Christian community to connect to before they commit to faith in Christ (see fig. 11.5).

The belonging-before-believing strategy is quite simple and aligns with the five practices. Christians *initiate* authentic and lasting relationships with non-Christian emerging adults, *invite* them to church, and *include* them in communal safe spaces connected to church (usually small groups), or *involve* them in places of service where they can experience belonging and safely explore faith in Christ before they ever

Figure 11.5. Belonging before believing

believe—so they can believe, and *invest* in providing them with guidance, care, and encouraging their development and growth. Communal space for non-Christians gives them an opportunity to get to know Christians up close, observe them, and develop meaningful and deepening relationships. Experiencing community that's compelling gives emerging adults a sandbox to play in. They can discover what this Christian thing is made of and see if it works for them. Yet in the bright-spot churches I studied, something else came even before *belonging*.

The pattern that emerged is a bit different from what many evangelism writers have noted recently. A process of belonging to Christian community before believing, which evangelism observers describe, is certainly evident in my research. Yet I observed a nuance: unchurched people are following a pattern that involves more than belonging before believing. They are in many ways belonging and *behaving before believing*. They are incorporated into a Christian community like a small group, and then they are given opportunities to contribute at church in some kind of service.

In both their community and their volunteer service, they are not just exposed to Christian behavior; they actually begin to practice Christian behavior, which I call Christian "enactments." For example, they read the Bible, pray, learn, worship, listen to Christian music, attend worship services, and serve in ministries. All of these practices—or enactments— are what disciples of Jesus do: read the Scriptures, pray, learn, worship, assemble together, and serve. Bright-spot churches *expect* unchurched emerging adults to participate as disciples of Jesus—even while their faith is not yet fully formed.

There is considerably more happening in churches reaching unchurched emerging adults than being a place to belong so people come to faith. Within the culture of many bright-spot churches, young adults are relentlessly invited to behave or act like believers before they believe. This evangelism framework is illustrated in figure 11.6.

Within the culture of many bright-spot churches, young adults are relentlessly invited to behave or act like believers before they believe.

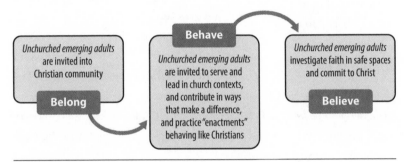

Figure 11.6. Belonging and behaving before believing

Emerging Adults Reverse the Evangelism Process

Churches reaching Generation Zers and millennials may have stumbled upon the postmodern pathway to identity commitment. For postmodern young adults who value subjective experience, conversion and spiritual growth aren't necessarily a linear process. Previously, most Protestant mainline and evangelical churches understood conversion to come first, followed by entering into Christian community and beginning to practice loving acts of service as they grow in discipleship. My research indicates that churches reaching and incorporating emerging adults are *providing a subjective experience of Christian community in which young adults are encouraged to encounter God and where acts of service often precede conversion.* Emerging adults serve and then come to faith, often through the serving process in combination with community and mentoring.

Non-Christians Inside the Box:
Almost Orthodox but Not Yet

Another thing worth noting is that churches effective in reaching emerging adults and retaining them have a lot more non-Christians attendance than churches that are not reaching them. A study by the Billy Graham Center for Mission and Ministry and LifeWay Research (2016) found that the most effective evangelistic churches have the highest percentage of

The more non-Christians in the church, the more people come to faith.

non-Christian attendees. This makes sense. The more non-Christians in the church, the more people come to faith.

What's different about these churches? Non-Christians are no longer on the fringes, the edges of church. Instead they're at the center. *These standout churches include dones and nones among emerging adults who are engaged and fully invested in by the church.* These "almost but not orthodox" are found in churches where they can engage, not just sit in the back where they can slip out unnoticed.

Rather than remaining shut off to those outside the church, where never the two shall meet, these church communities are open and porous, ready for non-Christians to cross in and out as they explore Christian faith and identity (see fig. 11.7).

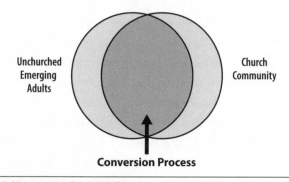

Figure 11.7. New evangelism paradigm

Taking Risks

Churches reaching emerging adults are not enclaves with armored boundaries but rather permeable and accessible to the unchurched. Their doors are wide open, and even more intriguing is the risk factor they're willing to assume.

In *More Ready Than You Realize*, Brian McLaren described the experience of evangelizing what he calls postmodern people, using a dance metaphor. Like a dance, they come together and then move apart, a push and pull, in our spiritual conversations and interaction with postmodern people, McLaren says. People need space and time to consider the

> *Churches reaching emerging adults are not enclaves with armored boundaries but rather permeable and accessible to the unchurched. Their doors are wide open, and even more intriguing is the risk factor they're willing to assume.*

information and the witness they receive from authentic friendships with Christians. Christians ought not to be pushy or alarmed by a lack of response, but they do need to keep pace with their non-Christian friends, giving them space but still engaging them regularly.

Pull factors for non-Christians are the community and the service opportunities churches provide. These are ways to keep unchurched folks engaged. My friend Stacy, a church planter in the Denver area, reminds me that people want to be generous and charitable but have no outlets for it. At meetups he helps organize, participants are encouraged to care for their community. It may mean bringing a pair of socks for the homeless shelter or stocking the shelves of a food pantry. People may push away from the message, but practical charitable giving opportunities draw them.

Both partners in this dance between emerging adults and the church are open to risk (see fig. 11.8). Allowing unchurched emerging adults to serve and even to lead in small ways before they commit to faith in Christ is risky. Churches are taking risks by assimilating non-Christians in service, supervised leadership, and community in ways they have not before. They risk (1) criticism from church members, (2) members leaving the

church, (3) those they invest in departing from the church and faith, and
(4) moral failure on the part of emerging adults.

Figure 11.8. Taking risks

Though pastors and churches encourage young adults to serve with
supervision or follow-up, failure is a real possibility. One young adult
admitted she was placed in a leadership position too soon—before she had
quit destructive and addictive behaviors. She was subsequently removed
from her position when parents reported inappropriate activity she had
posted on her Facebook page. Another emerging adult admitted to still
participating in a party lifestyle though she was serving as a church intern.
On the other hand, all the other emerging adults interviewed describe
closely following Jesus and reaching their moral and ethical aspirations.

Like children on a teeter-totter, emerging adults assume risks when
they visit and investigate churches (fig. 11.9).

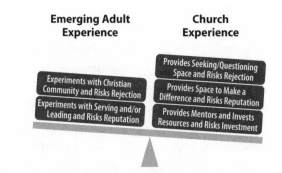

Figure 11.9. Emerging adult experiences and church experiences

Most say that before their initial visit, they were certain they wouldn't be comfortable at church. Expecting to be judged and pressured, some also feared they didn't know enough about the Bible, or they had not cleaned up their lifestyles enough to be accepted. Some, as Robert Putman reminds us, were concerned they would be influenced by the "immorality" of the church compared to their own sensibilities. Fear had to be faced and conquered in order to attend a church activity, service, or small group.

Extending Trust

Churches and young adults take a leap of faith and extend trust to each other in their process of coming together in the new paradigm of evangelism and retention. Most young adults are ignorant of the risk their churches take, but not all. Emerging adults are certainly aware of their own risk-taking as they face judgmentalism, pressure, institutionalism, and more. Many church members are unaware of this.

The scale teeters back and forth, yet the church and young adults extend trust and grace toward each other. Taking risks and extending trust characterize the ethos of churches making inroads to emerging adults.

A New Paradigm: The Five invitational Practices

The emerging adult spiritual stories shared with me were acted out against the backdrop of the new evangelism paradigm: *encouraging non-Christians to come into the church and to become included and involved and invested in before they commit.* The pathway to faith in Christ is the five invitational practices—initiate, invite, include, involve, and invest—which lead emerging adults first to church and then further along in their journey toward commitment to Jesus once they arrive at church.

So churches must not become enclaves bracketed and isolated from the rest of society, if they are to reach emerging adults. Yet they must remain faithful to traditional Christian orthodoxy—their distinctive. At the same time they must encourage congregants to engage with culture and churches to be holistic in their ministries. For emerging adults to reach their peers, they must be connected to culture and also deeply committed to Jesus, biblical authority, the church, making disciples, and missional engagement.

By "engaging friends in evangelistic conversations all along the way," I mean Christians chatting about their faith, their relationship with Christ, and their church in natural, attractive, and intentional ways that connected the dots for their friends. How did they connect the dots for loved ones? By pointing out how their faith in Christ, their church, their pastor, and their church friends met their needs. They do this in ways that their friends and family can imagine faith, church, pastors, and friends doing the same for them. Or, at least they talk in intriguing and provocative ways—so much so that non-Christians want to know more about faith or experience faith for themselves.

One-size evangelism doesn't fit every young adult, but relational evangelism is the approach most young adults pointed to when describing their own stories.

CHAPTER REWIND

The new paradigm seeks to understand and define effective evangelism within the context of North American churches among emerging generations. Generational differences are noted between evangelism methods and contexts for evangelism. In the new paradigm, evangelism and retention occur mostly *inside* the church rather than outside.

Lead pastors and ministry staff see the strong community that young adults experience through small groups and the gratification and personal satisfaction they receive from volunteering. These are the primary vehicles for retention of young adults. Emerging adults engage in volunteer opportunities when they believe they can make a difference. Such opportunities of inclusion, involvement, and being invested in encourage young adults to stay in their churches, giving them space and time to consider Christian faith as viable.

Evangelism approaches and retention strategies overlap in bright-spot churches. Church boundaries are permeable—not just at the margins but in the center of missional engagement in serving, mentoring, and even leadership. Churches use similar strategies for evangelism and retaining emerging adults, both of which take place mainly inside the church context. What draws young adults to the church and eventually to faith in Christ is often the same thing that keeps them coming to church and that helps them incorporate into the life of the church: compelling community, Scripture study, service, leadership opportunities in the context of their church, their community, and the world. But the order is reversed—or at least simultaneous: they are retained before or while they are evangelized.

STARTING THE CONVERSATION

- ▶ Again, how many non-Christians do you estimate are currently attending your church? How could you increase that number?

- ▶ What experiences have you had in helping others come to faith in Christ or helping them grow in their faith in Christ?

- ▶ Your church culture may not fit at all with what you're learning in this book about bright-spot churches. What practice *could* your church adopt so that the church community and unchurched individuals can connect and the unchurched can explore Christian faith?

ACTION STEPS

Prepare for non-Christians. Think about how to increase the number of non-Christians attending your church. Set a realistic goal and gather your leaders to pray and seek God for more non-Christians. Consider steps you and your church can take to increase the number of unchurched people invited to church.

Measure radical church hospitality. Establish a means of evaluating whether non-Christians experience your church as friendly, welcoming, inviting, accepting, and hospitable. Encourage every ministry to strengthen its ability to appeal to and to care for non-Christian guests.

Identify evangelism inside the church. Where are young adults coming to faith in Christ through your church?

Evaluate retention of emerging adults. What needs to be adjusted at your church to attract more young adults and to get them to stay long enough to connect to friends and service? What are your next five steps to make that happen?

Explore ideas that resonate with you. What plans will you make to see your exploration actually happens? Who will you invite to journey with you?

12

Balancing

ORTHODOX DISTINCTION
AND CULTURE ENGAGEMENT

Questions about how Christians should engage with culture have puzzled, eluded, and occasionally enlightened faith communities for millennia. In today's world, churches and denominations engage culture along a spectrum from no engagement to innovative engagement. Let's explore translating the gospel in the contexts of engaging culture while hanging onto Christian distinctiveness—what Christian Smith calls "engaged orthodoxy."

Churches in my study maintained connections with the broader culture and related to those within it while also cultivating deep commitment to Christ, Christian virtue, attentiveness to the Spirit, and missional passion. My findings suggest that the degree to which churches engage American society while holding onto orthodox distinctiveness is directly related to their ability to practice relational evangelism among emerging adults. Bright-spot churches reach emerging adults because they take risks to engage and stay connected with non-Christians— including individuals and groups with whom tensions are present or likely to arise. They aren't separatist, isolated, or insulated from society. Instead, they develop tools to communicate gospel truth through means such as prayer, healing, Bible studies, and recreational activities. Rather than turning their backs on controversial themes in American culture, bright-spot churches seek to be knowledgeable, empathetic, and active in addressing social ills justly. These churches engage outgroups with whom they have a history of tension.

In all these ways, churches are sending a message to emerging adults: *we are here for you, we will help you, we value you, you fit here, you can make a difference here, we care about the world and the people you care about, and we have opportunities for you to engage these concerns.* To those who respond, these churches offer an accessible and porous counterculture in which non-Christians are engaged immediately and also allowed to move in and out at the community's center and edges. Such churches grow and thrive as they build highly engaged and deeply distinctive communities.

Again . . . Why Churches Grow

Religion thrives in pluralist societies when it's embedded in subcultures that offer satisfying communities who provide meaning and belonging for adherents. Two classic interpretations can shed further light on why churches grow—especially churches that reach and keep emerging adults today. In chapter ten we explored how in the book, *American Evangelicalism: Embattled and Thriving*, Christian Smith and contributors theorize that groups grow and increase their influence when they blend distinctiveness and connectedness to build cultural bridges while also exhibiting moral strength.

Similarly Roger Finke and Rodney Stark, authors of *The Churching of America*, contend that groups grow when they are distinct yet connected to society as opposed to bracketed off and isolated from society. The bright-spot churches we've looked at closely resemble the ones these scholars' studied in that they are distinctly orthodox but not isolated. They engage with multiple marginalized populations and more generally with people they haven't previously attempted to engage.

An example from Smith confirms that churches reaching young adults are growing through engaged orthodoxy—that is, by hanging onto their Christian cultural distinctives while actively engaging society. Smith argues that twentieth-century American fundamentalists suspicious of liberal theology and the "social gospel" shifted toward "separatism, pessimistic premillennial dispensation, and concern with maintaining purity apart from the world." Fundamentalists adopted a "Christ against culture" posture, so their stance didn't supply a theological or social foundation for cultural and evangelistic engagement. Around the same time or shortly after, mainline churches and denominations began to lose hold of their distinctiveness and their differentiation from the rest of culture. Although they kept some influence, they lost the distinctions necessary to invite people into lives characterized by spiritual transformation and vibrancy.

Evangelicals, on the other hand, retained their adherence to the fundamental doctrines of orthodox Christianity, but they also built bridges to society, subsequently growing in numbers and increasing in cultural influence. As they broke with the worst features of fundamentalism—including its anti-intellectualism, defensiveness, factionalism, isolationism, paranoia, pessimism, and separatism—evangelicals were able to make inroads to influence American society by their posture of "engaged orthodoxy."

I have come to believe that churches that are both clearly distinctive *and* engaged with non-Christian outgroups are most able to translate the gospel to non-Christian young adults, so they are more likely to see new faith commitments. Churches may live in tension with some outgroups for legitimate reasons of moral or ideological disagreement, but they are able to stay engaged, not separated. These effective churches are finding cultural tools to bridge and translate the gospel truth through means like healing prayer, loving postures, Bible studies, acts of social justice and racial righteousness, and activities like sports teams. Their pastors are committed to growing in cultural fluency and speaking the language of young adults, appealing to goodness and experience and truth to build credibility for the

> *Churches that are both clearly distinctive and engaged with non-Christian outgroups are most able to translate the gospel to non-Christian young adults, so they are more likely to see new faith commitments.*

Christian faith as a viable option. Their distinctiveness includes their missional engagement in restoring social justice and evangelistic calling.

The likelihood of effective communication of the gospel is prime when both cultural engagement and orthodox distinction are high, which figure 12.1 illustrates.

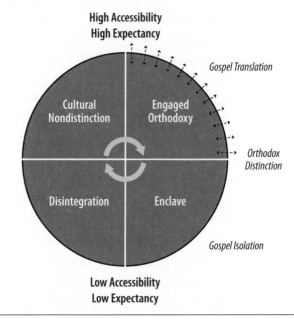

Figure 12.1. Four quadrants of cultural engagement

Two poles are significant for working with the construct of cultural engagement. The horizontal pole shows adherence to Christian orthodoxy. Using this model, positions further toward the right side of the diagram are more orthodox. The vertical pole represents culturally engaged churches relating to their local communities and American society, north being highly engaged and south being separatist and disengaged.

Unfortunately, if churches' cultural engagement is low and their orthodox distinction is also low (represented by the bottom left quadrant), they have essentially no gospel influence on culture and are likely to disintegrate eventually. There's not much to keep people coming to church, let alone attracting them. Comparably, when churches hold tightly to their orthodoxy yet have little or no cultural engagement and influence, they become enclaves set apart from society with no opportunity to communicate the gospel to those around them, much less sparking new understanding and transformation. These churches have no on-ramp for non-Christians to explore the church and Christian faith. Their posture toward culture is typically "Christ and the church against culture," and they tend toward culture-bashing without participating in solutions.

Now, if churches and denominations excel in cultural engagement to the point that they lose their Christian distinctives, as represented by the upper left quadrant of the matrix, they begin to resemble culture so much that they offer nothing distinct and actually decrease in attractiveness and numbers. In their Religious Landscape study, Pew Research Forum showed that mainline churches are no longer growing. Perhaps that's because they have so assimilated into their cultural surroundings that they have little of meaning to offer. Without Christian orthodoxy and commitment to God's missional covenants and mandates, the missionary impulse diminishes, and the result is a church that has little commitment to a distinctly Christian identity and therefore blends into the rest of the world—more *influenced by* culture than *influencing* culture. The result is no gospel translation.

The top right-hand quadrant of the matrix shows engaged orthodoxy. The church is best able to communicate the gospel when it's both fully orthodox and genuinely present in culture: interacting, engaging, justice-orienting, lamenting, healing, learning, building bridges, bearing witness to Jesus, and influencing others. Bright-spot churches are attractive to young people because of their engaged orthodoxy. Their open-hearted stance makes it easy for emerging adults to receive relational evangelism and invitations to church, community, and service.

Being Accessible and Expectant

When church culture is accessible—by that I mean non-Christians are warmly welcomed and free to come and go, and find others like them on

the journey—church culture is translated for them so they understand
the language and symbols. Due to the genuine hospitality and friendliness of the highly invitational church culture, emerging adults are able
to identify with the church community or subculture. Young adults jump
in and find their niche for serving and ministry, reach their aspirations,
and experience their burgeoning faith as salient, fulfilling, and important. They're then likely to identify with the church community and
make a faith commitment to Christian identity. On the matrix, high
accessibility equates with greater gospel translation; low accessibility
equates with gospel isolation.

In the same way, high-expectancy churches—where everyone is
included and invited and expected to pitch in, whether via community
or service—also are effective in gospel translation. Churches that have
little expectation of people pitching in—whether because service and
leadership are limited for church members or to those who have earned
that privilege—have low gospel translation and few conversions.

Bright-spot churches offer emerging adults a collective subculture
that is morally satisfying and orienting, provides belonging and meaningful identity, engages culture and is easily accessible yet runs counter
to the cultural trends offered in their emerging adult world.

Cultural Engagement in Effective Churches

One approach to drawing young adults to Christ is connecting them to
causes. Campus ministries like InterVarsity Christian Fellowship, under the
influence of thought leaders James Choung, York Moore, Doug Schaupp,
Sarah Shin, Jazzy Johnson, and many others, are combining social justice
and racial righteousness issues with evangelism, introducing non-
Christians to God's invitation to join him in healing the world's brokenness.
InterVarsity's university student conversion rate is increasing annually.

Nathan Emery White proposes that religious nones may be reached
by strongly promoting "cause," but my research did not bear out that
young adults in general are involved in social causes like social justice
and racial righteousness. In fact, I asked all the emerging adults I

interviewed, "Did you connect to any social 'causes' that resonated with your passions through your church before becoming a Christian? Do you connect your unchurched friends to causes your church supports?" Only one individual indicated these played a significant role in her spiritual journey, but she has a vocational interest as a grad student pursuing a master's degree in social work. So my findings support Christian Smith and Melinda Denton's analysis of the National Study of Youth and Religion, which revealed that only a small minority of younger (eighteen- to twenty-four-year-old) emerging adults are involved in activism to change the world.

However, the churches I studied are committed to the social welfare of their neighbors, their cities, and the world. Almost all of them have some sort of ministry focused on what Cornerstone Church in Boston calls "Compassion, Justice, and Mercy," with an emphasis on both local and global needs and injustices. The following are some examples of church expressions of commitment to social justice:

▶ Fountain of Life Church in East Los Angeles has a family center dedicated to meeting the needs of the community (such as providing tutoring and art classes for youth and English as a Second Language classes for adults). It networks with the city of Long Beach to provide resources for food distribution, shelter, medical, and other low-cost or free services with which church attendees can volunteer.

▶ High Rock North Shore is committed to "loving their immigrant neighbors by providing affordable legal services and working together toward whole community" through their ministry of Open Door Immigration Services.

▶ River City Community Church offers opportunities for church attendees to serve the greater community through reconciliation and neighborhood development.

▶ New Community Logan Square offers the homeless and economically underresourced a drop-in center and food pantry through their Open Arms Ministry for those facing food insecurity, poverty and homelessness. The drop-in center webpage states, "We gather as a family to share meals and provide access to basic needed resources. Clean clothing and toiletries, identification cards and healthcare are just a few. We also collectively work to conceive, develop, and implement further programming that will allow us to control our future!"

▶ New Zion Covenant Church in Dolton, Illinois, provides a not-for-profit organization called Building Our Own Community, Inc. (BOOC) to address the needs of the African American community of south Dolton with services that provide for growing poverty, unemployment, crime, and minimal unemployment. Their mission is to restore and strengthen the black community through targeting high-risk youth and young adults. The webpage for BOOC reads, "Today, the mission of BOOC is to provide program and activities that develop youth, enhance education, foster economic development and address health issues in underserved communities."

I could keep listing how these bright-spot congregations are involved in meeting the social needs of their surrounding communities, but I think you get the idea. Churches effectively reaching emerging adults appear to be connecting with the aspirations and values of emerging adults to be a part of making a difference for better in the world, even though many young adults do not personally participate in justice or racial righteousness ministries.

Meeting Tangible Needs

Both the pastors of bright-spot churches and emerging adults value working to meet the tangible needs of the people in their church's local context. They also focus on providing resources to meet global needs. Some pastors mentioned that connecting emerging adults to God's mission to the world is both integral to disciple-making and effective for reaching unchurched young adults.

Former pastor Alec Rahill described how compassion ministry and relationships form a persuasive combination for evangelism.

We do a thing called First Serve, where we'll do mission locally. Like we'll partner with a food pantry. We do a lot of good in the world locally. We have some regional ministry. We're part of a couple of ministries in the city that mentor students, that provide food and housing. We have international mission. We do a lot of serving opportunities, compassion-based opportunities that are one-time opportunities for people to get on board. And for millennials, relationships and compassion are the two twin kings of evangelism. They all want to be in relationship. They all want to make a difference. Giving them as opportunity for both are key reaching strategies.

The pastors I talked to strongly believe that young adults have an affinity for compassion and for meeting tangible needs of their communities and global needs. Bishop Lance Davis also commented on the significance of volunteer opportunities, observing that African American young adults find Zion Fellowship through church partnerships with local sororities and fraternities interested in service projects. Pastor Kim referred to the prison ministry that Cambridge Community Fellowship Church is involved with and the church's ministry among at-risk youth, providing job training and Bible study. Pastor Kim recognized that several young adults in the church's neighborhood have come to faith through the church's ministries.

When asked what his church was doing differently from five years ago to reach emerging adults, Pastor Daniel Hill pointed to River City's emphasis on building relationships with young people in the neighborhood.

We just did a three-week-long series called "All in Together." It was basically the heart of all three weeks, saying that we want to invest in young people—young people of any background, but particularly young people from socially challenged environments like our own. That's what it means to be a millennial in our church: to invest in young people. So, it has changed the way we engage. That was always kind of on the menu of possibilities, but now it's the main thrust. I don't know if a millennial is going to stick at River

City if they don't have an interest in participating with young people at some level.

An important consideration for reaching and keeping emerging adults is that although most emerging adults themselves didn't engage ministries of social justice, they were attracted to churches that were engaged culturally. They admired their church's attention to compassion ministries, injustice, and racial righteousness, although the young adults themselves were rarely personally engaged in these ministries. Future research on the role of compassion, justice, and reconciliation ministry in young-adult evangelism would be helpful because little information is currently available.

LGBTQ Test Case

One of the deepest fractures that divides many believers and threatens to split denominations in the first quarter of the twenty-first century involves biblical interpretation related to homosexuality and same-sex marriage. The churches in this project all affirmed a traditional position on human sexuality (that is, that sexual intimacy should take place only within a marriage between one man and one woman). Let's look at how they engage LGBTQ individuals as a test case for understanding their culturally engaged orthodoxy.

Though these churches all shared the same view on this topic, their engagement with LGBTQ individuals and communities varied. All of the pastors I spoke with reported that LGBTQ individuals attended their churches and that they were welcoming to people of all sexual orientations. They described seeking to minister to their LGBTQ congregants, leaning toward their inclusion in the life of the church. What inclusion looked like differed from church to church. The level of participation allowed varied, with positions ranging from just attending to membership (or partnership, as some churches use that term) to serving in particular roles. None of the pastors said they perform same-sex weddings.

What inclusion looks like differs from church to church.

Pastors were reticent to single out same-sex sexual activity and same-sex marriage as more egregious than other sin. One pastor noted that heterosexual marriages often fall short in terms of infidelity, while homosexual marriages fall short in terms of being same-sex. Many pastors commented that there is no reason to elevate one over the other in terms of culpability.

Pastors gave a variety of responses about preaching on the topic of homosexuality. Half said they do, and a third said they do not. The rest didn't specifically say they would or wouldn't, but they hadn't actually preached on the topic in the past three to ten years. Pastors who preach on the historic traditional view of homosexuality affirmed the importance of doing so in the context of love and humility. Pastors who were hesitant to preach on homosexuality attributed their reluctance to a desire to reach more young adults with the gospel. They said one-on-one conversations are more helpful in the context of emerging-adult discipleship. One pastor explained his position with the following analogy.

> I really wrestle with whether to teach from the stage or not. . . . What I don't want to do is lose the influence I have with this group right now. I would rather have them coming, and we have a conversation, a daily conversation of "I'm transgender. Can I lead my same group?" Can I lead, where can people serve, where can they not serve? What we find is that in the context of relationship, we can actually make a lot of progress with people.

Lead pastors who aren't publicly addressing the subject of homosexuality said they find it more helpful evangelistically to address these issues in personal conversations. This allows them to communicate theological convictions with nuance while building relationships. So among this group of pastors was strong agreement that one-to-one conversations with LGBTQ people provide opportunities to state clearly the church's traditional position on human sexuality and affirm individuals' faith journeys, allowing them to invite ongoing conversation.

Dena Davidson, a campus ministry director of Thrive School at one of the churches that takes this approach, described how her church helped a same-sex couple feel accepted at church—though the church is not yet ready to accept them into ministry. She said,

> A lesbian couple came to our church for the very first weekend, and then went straight to our 101 class. They wanted to become members and start volunteering. . . . A couple of our pastors sat down with them and said, "We are so excited that you are coming here. We are so excited about what God is doing in your life, and we want to know you. We also want to let you know our position on human sexuality. At this point, we would say it's not the right time to serve. But we want you to start getting to know us and for us to start getting to know you."

Pastors who do preach on human sexuality explain they take the opposite approach and intentionally engage publicly with homosexuality along with other issues of concern to young adults. They find that particular age group appreciates this honest approach when it's done with humility and respect. High Rock Acton is an example of churches engaging with the public on hard issues where church and culture clash, while holding firm to their orthodoxy. Senior Associate Pastor Brynn Harrington described the church's position and approach to cultural engagement.

> We want to listen to people. We want to give them a chance to tell their stories and engage with how we think, rather than just telling them what to think. Opening the door for conversations about some of these hot-buttons issues that they don't really have a lot of guided forums for—I think a lot of people in our area are just really craving that, and we are not afraid to dive into some of those harder discussions. I think that is attractive to millennials. We have a handful of gay millennials in our church who know our position on LGBTQ sexuality, on human sexuality, and they know that I would not be able to officiate at their wedding. But they feel safe; they feel welcomed. They feel like they can disagree and be respected. So I think that just crating a safe place for that type of

issue—that's an example of things we try to engage—has really helped millennials to feel like they can be part of our community.

The pastors I talked to who preach on homosexuality try to combine radical hospitality toward the LGBTQ community with theological fidelity. Pastor Peter Hong described holding these two in tension.

> At least once a year I address it for one or two Sundays. This summer I will spend six weeks on it. We spend a good chunk of time talking about it, beginning with "What is human sexuality?" "What is God's intention for marriage?" And, of course, I will talk about homosexuality, gay marriage, and so forth. I say we are a church that is biblically orthodox and yet radically loving at the same time. That means we hold to our convictions, what we believe, but we are going to do everything within our power to radically love folks who we disagree with, who have fundamentally different views on things than we do. We lay down our lives for Muslims, we lay down our lives for our LGBTQ community, we lay down our lives for Hindus, we lay down our lives for the atheist.

Pastor Larry Kim said it's best for the church to address the subject directly rather than allow people to assume the worst about the church's position. Like many other pastors, he sees differing perspectives on homosexuality as one of the most difficult barriers in reaching emerging generations.

> I think it's the stereotype they have of the church. That is where the LGBTQ issue comes up. The common narrative is they come into the church, they like the community, they like the teaching, they see something positive going on, but they're fighting against this suspicion that secretly the church is really homophobic and narrow-minded and all those stereotypes. So I feel like there is this stereotype that we as a church have to try to bust and pick apart if we're going to keep those millennials.

Overall, the pastors I met in the course of my research seek to live in the tension of being radically welcoming, accepting, and loving while remaining theologically conservative. Many preach publicly on homo-sexuality and same-sex marriage, and they often do so for evangelistic reasons. Those who choose *not* to publicly address the same issues do so for evangelistic reasons.

My data is inconclusive as to whether one approach or the other is more effective for reaching emerging adults. What we *can* observe is that pastors of churches reaching emerging adults combine high emotional intelli-gence with the strength of their orthodox convictions. They have found ways to relate to and reach emerging adults, including members of the LGBTQ young adult community. They've reflected on their approach to these complex and highly charged issues, and this thoughtfulness extends to the venues and contexts in which they choose to engage with them.

None of the pastors I talked to want to drive non-Christian LGBTQ community members away from engaging with the church that can influ-ence them over time toward faith in Christ. They are well aware of the church's reputation as homophobic, and they seek to dispel that stereo-type while hanging on to their conservative orthodoxy. They work to make room for genuine evangelism and ministry, encouraging emerging adults to continue to trust the church.

The emerging adults represented in this study expressed strong rela-tional alignment with the LGBTQ community, emphasizing acceptance, love, nonjudgmentalism, and inclusion. All said that LGBTQ people wor-ship at their churches, and most assumed that their churches shared their inclusive relational alignment with the LGBTQ community.

In terms of theological alignment with their churches, the emerging adults I interviewed fell along a spectrum of nuanced positions, rang-ing from agreement to disagreement with their churches' conservative positions on homosexuality and same-sex marriage. Theological differ-ences with their churches didn't seem to undermine their relational connections to their churches or to the LGBTQ community. Emerging adults seemed to straddle the theological interpretive divide and gave no hint of dissatisfaction or plans to disaffiliate with their churches over these questions.

Many emerging adult dones and nones leave the church or remain outside it due to their moral sensibilities and their opinion that the church is immoral due to its perceived homophobia. Yet churches that are sensitive to these emerging-adult sensibilities are drawing emerging adults from the LGBTQ community itself as well as young adults who feel passionate care and empathy for their LGBTQ friends and family members. The pastors in my study approached the issue in different ways, but all were sensitive to young adults concerns and chose to avoid divisiveness in favor of dialogue with LGBTQ church members and attendees, practicing a gracious, culturally engaged orthodoxy. Absent from their comments were any leanings toward separatism, isolationism, paranoia, factionalism, or anti-intellectualism.

CHAPTER REWIND

Pastors of standout churches engage controversial themes in emerging-adult culture. While their approaches may differ, they have thoughtful reasons behind their choices about cultural engagement. They're aware of the barriers that keep young adults away from Christians and the church, and they do their best to maintain a posture of culturally engaged orthodoxy that seeks to be welcoming, kind, and gracious while openly upholding their theological commitments.

My research suggests that barriers can often be overcome when pastors and churches welcome and accept young adults and their concerns. Emerging adults assumed the best of their churches and seek to be in harmony with them, even when their views on homosexuality and same-sex marriage diverge. Emerging adults admired their churches' postures of loving acceptance, humility, repentance, and mercy. These postures overcame social and cultural barriers and engaged moral and ethical attitudes in winsome ways.

Churches that are effective in Gen Z and millennial outreach and growth can attribute much of their success to their

Pastors of standout churches engage controversial themes in emerging-adult culture.

commitment to cultural engagement rather than withdrawal. At the same time, they recognize that maintaining their orthodox distinctiveness is key to persuasive gospel witness and translation.

STARTING THE CONVERSATION

▶ Describe your church's orientation toward political and social issues that are important to emerging adults.

▶ What groups outside your church does your church connect to, partner with, and engage?

▶ Do your church and church members communicate their stance on issues of homosexuality and same-sex marriage publicly or privately? Do they communicate in a spirit of loving and gracious conviction or with judgment?

▶ Are there attitudes and postures you or your church need to repent of, and should this be done privately or publicly?

ACTION STEPS

Locate barriers. Identify the most common barriers toward faith and church for your friends and for unchurched emerging adults that you observe.

Repent. Privately and publicly confess, reject, and lament your church's inhospitable attitudes and postures.

Plan your approach. Determine the most effective approach for engaging your LGBTQ community to minister to them. Will this approach fit with your church culture? How will you effectively implement your approach? What are your first three steps?

Plan your communication. Consider effective ways to communicate to your church community the church's stance toward cultural engagement and toward the LGBTQ community. Can this happen in a sermon series or small group curriculum? Take steps to implement your plan.

13

True North

I JUST WANTED TO KNOW YOU WERE FOR REAL

Hey, if you like this, come on out to my small group with me on Wednesday nights. We get together to eat dinner, talk about our lives, talk about God. If you like this, you'll really like it. You don't have to believe anything to come. Just come on out. You'll love it.

MEGAN AT COMMONS CHURCH

A s you, my readers, are likely armchair practical theologians, I hope that at times your radar has gone off—on the one hand due to your biblical, theological, and cultural sensibilities, and on the other hand due to recognition that your own church is falling short of practicing habits that kindly welcome young-adult strangers—those far off—to Christ and his worshiping and witnessing community—the church.

You may wonder if these churches are just a new iteration of seeker churches. I don't think so. In fact, I imagine many of the pastors in this study would shrink away from any such designation because of its resemblance to consumeristic churches seeking to make worship appealing to mainstream culture. Admittedly, each mode of church is a reaction, an attempt to autocorrect all that's gone before. By far, churches in this study pull away from anything that reminds them of excess, bureaucracy, institutionalism, consumerism, and even colonialist tendencies in the models and movements of church they regard as extrabiblical or ungospel-like.

Churches in this experiment vary in their expression of worship from ancient to contemporary; their geographic locations range from suburban to urban type. They vary in size, ethnicity, age, age of pastor(s), ethnicity and gender of pastor(s), and so forth. What they do have in common is their ability to translate church culture—Christian language, rituals, symbols, and texts—for the emerging-adult unchurched dones or nones. They are incredibly hospitable and openhearted to unchurched people arriving on their doorstep.

The biblical and theological lenses I use clearly bring into focus how bright-spot churches are following certain biblical principles and texts. They are at the same time purposefully engaging cultural outgroups. These churches' boundaries are porous to these groups and especially to people and young adults outside the church who are taking steps toward Christ, evidenced by their showing up in church contexts. Thus they are inviting unchurched people into Christian community and encouraging them to contribute to that Christian community before they have committed to faith in Christ. So the question is, is it biblically, theologically, and culturally acceptable to open the doors of the church this wide?

Is It Right?

Just because it's working—emerging adults are making new and renewed faith commitments—does that make it right? I can't answer this question for every individual church context. I therefore will appeal to Richard Osmer's model of practical theology for critiquing how the church thinks and acts.

- ▶ What is happening?
- ▶ Why is it happening?
- ▶ Should it be happening
- ▶ How do we respond?

First, I asked and observed how pastors and emerging adults describe *what is happening* within one small denomination among select churches that are reaching and keeping unchurched emerging adults. Second, I interpreted the data received by asking, *Why is it happening?* Why are these churches evangelistically fruitful among the emerging generations, and why are they attractive to the point of retaining unchurched young adults? My interpretative journey and analysis led me to the five practices of invitational church culture. So it's time for each of us to examine this phenomenon and ask, *What should be happening?* through a biblical and theological lens to find the normative church tradition and the Holy Spirit's activity.

Finally we must ask, *How do we respond to what is happening; what should we do pragmatically in response to what we have observed?* For example, if we find the five practices are biblically consistent and theologically congruent with the gospel, how ought we to support them (see fig. 13.1)? Or as Andrew Root asked in his similar practical theology framework, "Now what"?

Let's consider Osmer's third question—What should be happening?—by noting if there are any situations in the Scriptures that are similar and that may apply to inviting non-Christians into the church to participate in

Model for Critiquing How the Church Thinks and Acts

1. What is happening?
2. Why is it happening?
3. Should it be happening?
4. How do we respond?

Richard Osmer,
Practical Theology

worship, community, and contribution. Similarly we would be wise to ask if there are evangelical and orthodox biblical and theological scholars who support the presence and contribution of those far from God in community, worship, and service in the church. While no one-for-one equivalent is found, there are biblical texts and orthodox evangelical Christian scholars' careful exegeses and analytical studies of the Scriptures to guide us to further reflect on how churches are influencing life transformation among emerging adults.

Figure 13.1. The five practices: Are they biblically compatible?

As I suggested, our third question must be explored through personal study of the Scriptures and insights from Old and New Testament experts and theologians. I encourage readers to continue to study this concept prayerfully, but here I'll briefly refer to the work of New Testament professor Joshua W. Jipp. His study of multiple biblical texts reveals that God expresses his hospitality to humanity in his loving gift of Jesus Christ to a broken and lost world. This, in turn, created a people constituted for hospitality to one another, to the stranger, and to the world. The early church practiced hospitality as the primary way of fulfilling Jesus' command to love neighbor as self. *Neighbor* includes the marginalized, the stranger, and the sinner.

Particularly the Gospel of John shows how the New Testament portrays Jesus in the role of God's host who bestows God's welcome to all people, including sinners, outcasts, and foreigners, often through table fellowship and hospitality.

Jipp suggests there is a place in the public life of the church—our worship spaces—for the presence of non-Christians guests. In these spaces, the church most bears witness to the reality and presence of Christ Jesus. Through its public life of worship—the music, the confession, and the proclaimed Word—the church exhibits God's hospitality to those far from God.

So the mission of the church includes extending hospitality to unbelievers by inviting them into the church to observe and participate in the church's worship and witness to Christ the Lord, our Savior. Jipp writes, "Despite its brokenness and imperfections, then, the church should expect that Christ's hospitality is manifested in its public life of worship . . . and should therefore look for ways in which the church's public life reveals God's hospitality to non-Christians." The church not only bears witness to Jesus but also powerfully brings his presence to the world. One way it does so is by inviting non-Christians into the church to observe and participate in its public life, which manifests Christ to the world—those outside the kingdom of God.

Jipp's extensive biblical scholarship is one example of how we must examine the church's praxis from a biblical and theological lens, asking both *should this be happening* and *if so, how may we respond to it—and in this case support it?* Jipp argues that we must look for ways to further include non-Christians in the public life of the church. As such we have found biblical and theological scholarship to support the inclusion of unchurched emerging adults within the church's public life of worship and its expressions of community. I encourage further reading of Jipp's study to see that his interpretation of inclusion extends to the marginalized, the immigrant, the religious other, the incarcerated, the stranger, and the foreigner.

Similarly Chap Clark, former professor of practical theology and youth, family and culture, at Fuller Seminary, provides a theological framework for inclusion of non-Christians' presence in the church in *Adoptive Youth Ministry: Integrating Emerging Generations into the Family of Faith.* He sets forth in his "Strategy for Adoptive Youth Ministry" an intentional way of welcoming outsiders and others who are disconnected from the church community into the family of God, based on John 1:12: "to all who did receive him, to those who believed in him name, he gave the right to become children of God." Clark's strategy seeks to create and provide welcoming spaces for those left out of the Christian community as a funnel to adoption into God's family. The next level in the funnel after *welcoming* is engaging young people who begin to show signs of curiosity in personal faith by encouraging them in their faith journey in the context of the Christian community. Clark is encouraging the involvement of outsiders in the church: "This is where most ministries fail because when we promote private faith we sometimes communicate that personal faith is the end goal. This level is where leadership affirms a person's individual journey while engaging him or her toward a deeper, more intimate familial expression and corporate experience of faith."

The third level in the strategy funnel, "diverse relationships," is about connecting the disconnected with people in the family of faith, helping them understand that all believers are part of God's same family. They are encouraged and equipped through intimate, family-like relationships to live as members of God's diverse and global family.

Adoption is the final level in the funnel, in which those outside the faith are invited—not just welcomed but invited—to belong to God's family, however it gathers, "whether in small groups, missions and service, or to serve the family internally or intentionally as they seek to engage with those outside the family of faith—the rhetoric, style, and experience of the gatherings must be an intentional recognition of the reality of our station as family . . . gathering together is a comprehensive communal opportunity to collectively thank the Father who calls us his own."

Clark insists on the importance of incorporating the outsider and the disconnected into the family of God through familial-like relationships and the Christian community. He grounds his ministry philosophy in many of the Scriptures. I particularly point to Clark's emphasis on Jesus' interaction with the Samaritan woman in John 4. Clark reminds us that Jesus was always considerate, hospitable and welcoming to the vulnerable. And commenting on the Hebrews 13:2 passage Clark states, "Openness to outsiders is a core part of what it means to be a Christ-centered community. As Hebrews 13:2 puts it, 'Do not forget to show hospitality to strangers, for by doing so some have shown hospitality to angels without knowing it.'"

Churches practice the hospitality of God and adoption into God's family through their invitational culture, their welcome and reception of unbelievers, and their inclusion of them in worship, community, and contribution.

Whether in small groups, worship, or service, Clark encourages the church to embrace and gradually bring outsiders into God's family.

Isn't this exactly what we hope happens to our own children and grandchildren who have the opportunity and privilege to grow up in church—that they are lovingly embraced by God's family and nurtured along through Bible study, corporate worship, and service—and that they eventually make their own personal faith commitments in the context of the corporate family of God to become his adoptive children?

The churches described in the pages of this book practice the hospitality of God and adoption into God's family through their invitational culture, their welcome and reception of unbelievers, and their inclusion of them in worship, community, and contribution. Now let's turn to the question of the reality, the proof of emerging adults' conversions.

Are They for Real?

If you're wondering if these churches are real, let me point you to the mind shifts experienced by the emerging adults in this project in the few months to few years they had been attending church as previous dones and nones.

In a culture where attitudes toward church have moved toward indifference and "what's the point of church?" in the last several decades, it's important that we dug into the weeds a bit to understand why emerging adults do like church, stick around, and get involved—and why they are coming to faith in Christ. Or by now perhaps we should turn that sentence around: when emerging adults like church and get involved, they stick around long enough to come to faith in Christ. How is church and faith in Christ valued in a culture that is increasingly marginalizing the church, a culture that has shifted toward a postmodern outlook of denouncing metanarratives (one big overarching story of the world)? How is it valued in a culture that understands truth to be socially constructed? And, in the midst of the religious polarization in America, many emerging adults who come from a saturated Christian context have "been there, done that," and church didn't' work for them.

Barriers clutter the pathways to church and to faith in Christ. Cultural attitudes, social values, and weakening orthodox beliefs in the broader culture where emerging adults live all contribute to the hurdles churches face in reaching young adults. According to Robert Putnam, the growing number of nones has to do with the new morality of young adults (whom he believes purposefully reject the church for its lack of Christian virtues), their stance on homosexuality, right-wing politics, and exclusionary belief system. To review, Kinnaman and Lyons agree that many emerging adults denounce the church for being un-Christian, perceiving the church as hypocritical, paranoid about saving the lost, antihomosexual, sheltered, overly political, and judgmental. Previously we observed that Kinnaman and Hawkins identified six reasons why young people that are done with church have left: overprotective, shallow, antiscientific, repressive, exclusive, and doubtless.

All the young adults in this study admitted that they held unfavorable attitudes toward the church before they began attending. Most experienced acute attitude changes. Their barriers and biases toward church collapsed once they met Christians who engaged them. A former agnostic, Nathan, is representative of the group. He was disillusioned about the church, yet he went from believing Christians are uneducated and church is irrelevant to finding that Christians can be bright and intellectual and that church makes a difference in people's lives. After playing on a church sports team and getting to know people from church, his perceptions about Christianity and church were changed. From what he had seen and heard in the media, he thought the church was outdated, weird, and too political. Over a summer of hanging out with Christians, he was able to let go of the baggage he believed.

Unchurched emerging adults in this study arrived at church suspicious and cynical, but by the time I interviewed them, they had changed their minds—a shift in their attitudes toward church and Christians. They experienced six mind shifts:

- ▶ from "church is hypocritical ritual" to "church gave me a Christian identity"
- ▶ from "church is a waste of time" to "church adds value"
- ▶ from "what's the point of church?" to "church is relevant"
- ▶ from "fear based" to "scientifically credible"
- ▶ from "cultural Christianity" to "genuine Christianity"

Michael recalled his impressions of Christianity before becoming a church attender: "I thought a lot of Christians that I met growing up were hypocritical. It was very much just a ritual." He also believed church was about being a good person and living a moral life. Since he saw himself as a moral person, he didn't have any use for the church.

After visiting New Community and meeting Christians, he changed his opinion. Within a few months he began to question his own spiritual beliefs and became curious about Christianity's answers to identity and many other questions he had. Eventually Michael made a new faith commitment to Christ. No only that but he shifted from being extremely uncomfortable around Christians and church to becoming very comfortable around both. "Before, I was incredibly uncomfortable—I could not even set foot in a church. Now, any sanctuary of God, I—I just feel very much at home."

Shea, a former atheist, used to consider church a complete waste of time. A few years back a friend invited her to attend a megachurch with her. While her friend loved the experience, Shea felt it was fake—mostly because no one gave her attention or explained to her what church was about.

That experience left Shea reluctant to return. But her recent church experience has been rewarding. So rewarding that she's confident her church is shaping her into a leader. She said,

> I'm constantly being pushed outside my comfort level. I think that is a hard lesson to learn at twenty, but a very valuable one. I'm recognizing that I'm blessed. That I am being challenged at my age, and a lot of my friends outside of church are not being challenged. They're just going out and drinking a lot, and life is just all about fun.

Shea is finding meaningful purpose, opportunities to contribute, and leadership development at her church.

> Community is what stands out to me most about my church. What initially kept me going was definitely community. I love how friendly everybody is. I love how excited people are to be there. I love how excited the kids are to be there. I love that the kids know

the Scriptures, and they're participating in worship, and they're singing the worship songs and they have it in their hearts, and they teach me more than I teach them! So that all keeps me going; you know these kids are teaching me so much!

It's obvious that these young adults have reformed their thinner views of the church and negative stereotypes of Christians. The molds they believed the church and Christians fit are now broken. These churches have been able to translate an ancient institution—commonly perceived by younger people as irrelevant—so that it becomes a place where emerging adults find community and purposeful mission.

Tessa, a Taiwanese American student at Harvard, described herself as "formerly nominal" and "unchurched." Before attending Cambridge Community Fellowship Church she had little use for the church. "Prior to sophomore year of college I was like, 'What's the point of church?'" In her recent answer to the question "What do you admire or love about your church?" she said her church's mission is why she remains attached to church.

I especially love the mission of the church. There's just this earnestness to love the city, and for me it's so evident what the vertical and horizontal relationship looks like. The horizontalness of the church is very much driven by their love for Christ—there' so much heart in the fellowship. You can see how the church, they're driven by brokenness, and how Christ heals through that. I've never seen a church so active about really promoting a lot of different social causes and about loving the city. And about living a significant life and being comfortable with being uncomfortable, however that looks. I really like how the church balances those two things.

Tessa also describes how she found spiritual nurture and rest through her church:

Before it was, what is the point of church? Now? It's to get fed by the church and to really be grounded in the beginning of the week.

> And no matter if the sermon spoke to me or to something in my life
> or not, it was just like I felt CCFC was somewhere I could spiritually
> rest. Now I want to go to church. It isn't a burden for me or an obli-
> gation. I feel kind of "off" if I don't go to church. I want to go and
> hear what the pastors have to say this week, and what God wants to
> say. I love the worship at CCFC. It is very raw, and it's a time for me
> to rest too.

Tessa is typical of emerging adults who report that they had shifted in
their understanding of the church as irrelevant, outdated, meaningless,
and self-absorbed.

Jane grew up attending a Korean American evangelical Protestant
church. She dropped out of church during college. When I met up with her,
she resented her upbringing as a cultural Christian and also rejected what
she called "white, male, evangelical Christianity" for its lack of theological,
socioeconomic, and ethnic diversity. She felt that her legalistic church
background had prevented her from exploring her true spiritual self.

Recently Jane started attending a multiethnic urban church but felt
she was living in two worlds, easily "code switching" between her Christian and non-Christian worlds. Her friends in both worlds shared a commitment to social justice, but she felt lonely in her journey. She said, "I
feel like all my other Christian friends' kind of have it altogether, they
feel more stable. I feel that I'm the unstable one, like I'm the prodigal
son, like the party animal."

Jane appreciates her new pastor, who is keeping tabs on her in her
journey toward Christ and who gave her an invitation to do her graduate
internship at the church.

> I'm interning for them for a year. Which is crazy because I never
> fathomed I would stay at the church. First of all, I never thought I
> would move to a neighborhood just for a church. That was a crazy
> idea for me. My emotional state ebbs and flows. But right now, I'm
> trusting in the process because I feel like God has really orches-
> trated this in a really weird way. Like, how did it happen that a

pastor would seek me out in such an intentional way? That the university would allow such a mash placement like this. I rarely say, "It's a God thing," but I feel like it's a God thing. I think right now I am just trusting in the process, though I feel like I'm a divided Christian. I feel like my one foot is in the world, one foot is in God. I feel like "You can't do that. You can't serve both God and money. You can't serve two masters." I feel like . . . I'm serving the world, so I don't know if I'm a Christian. Should I say I'm a Christian? It's like a daily struggle for me.

Jane feels her pastor has empathy for her. Her perceptions of the church—especially the white evangelical church—are beginning to shift. Her new church has leaders diverse in ethnicity, age, and gender. Its mission is to empower minorities rather than tokenize them. Her pastor's preaching appeals to her as an emerging adult, with all her instability, and identity exploration. When I asked her how her attitudes toward church were changing, she said that her pastor has given her space to figure things out. "I feel like my perception is shifting. I'm broken and confused and all over the place, and I'm still there. I don't feel judged."

Like a lot of emerging adults in this study, Jane expected to be judged by the church. Instead, she has found hope, acceptance, mentoring, encouragement, and help to live up to her moral aspirations. Her pastor is helping her take steps to reach her vocational goals, and the church is giving her a church experience unlike the one that harmed her earlier in her life. Jane's pastor, Christian roommate, and friends are accompanying her on part of her painful journey, helping to restore her faith in Christ and the gospel of the kingdom.

Emerging adults describe something poignant about their new churches that compels them to return each week. The Spirit is doing something remarkable, restoring and healing and giving hope to young adults as they connect to churches and are enabled to linger long enough to try out Christian faith. Over time, through the love and benefits the Christian church community extends to them, they transform into kingdom people—worshiping and witnessing to the power, presence, and glory of God.

Summing Up

We've seen how non-Christian emerging adults connect to the church early in their faith journey by attending the main worship service when a trusted or new Christian friend invites them. They are incorporated into the life of the church through informal invitations to community such as, "Hey, if you like this, come on out to my small group with me. Just come on out. You'll love it." They also go through formal assimilation processes like a series of classes.

Lead pastors of bright-spot churches have a significant role as they establish an evangelistic ethos and an invitational culture. They act as cultural informants and make Christian faith plausible as they translate Christianity to unchurched people in culturally relevant ways. Pastors also act as cultural brokers, assisting young adults in navigating church culture and their new faith experiences, making familiar what may seem unfamiliar or foreign.

Emerging adults journey to faith in Christ along pathways of compelling Christian community and belonging, contributing in ways that are meaningful to them and that make a difference. They take next steps toward Christ as they receive pastoral care, accountability, and encouragement via mentoring and leadership development. The gospel is presented to them in culturally fluent ways in large and small group settings and in one-on-one meetings with pastors, ministry staff, lay leaders, and in mentoring communities like small groups.

Churches move along the preconversion process with emerging adults by

- initiating, inviting, including, involving, and investing in them
- encouraging them to engage in Christian community and to behave like Christians before they believe or commit
- incorporating and retaining them before or during the evangelization process

▶ engaging in evangelism inside the church

▶ making available retention opportunities outside the church, like service and social projects

▶ blending evangelism and retention strategies

▶ participating with young adults in mutual risk-taking

▶ giving them access to Christian friends and others like them on the journey as well as to social networks that support their growing interest and faith in Christ

▶ providing a moral community that legitimizes and sustains Christian faith

▶ orienting emerging adults in a collective Christian identity that provides them connection to something bigger than themselves, to meaning, to belonging, to expectancy, helping them navigate the tension of remaining culturally distinct and culturally engaged

Young adults look to their church for healthy relationships as well as for support in establishing healthy behaviors. Small groups provide the relational support and encouragement they need to sustain their early efforts in upholding the ethical standards they aspire to. Rick Richardson and I note the evangelistic importance of helping emerging adults succeed in achieving the moral standards they hope to attain. For example, Brooke was one of the many young people who said church provided alternatives to weekend clubbing, partying, drinking, and other destructive and addictive behaviors.

Bright-spot churches reach emerging adults by providing healthy relationships and support for moral aspirations. These churches are easily accessible and relevant, and in them young adults are engaged and not left alone to navigate church culture. They're invited to jump in and help out, and in return they are invested in and developed and mentored along the way by culturally fluent trail guides.

In this new paradigm of evangelism, unchurched emerging adults are often evangelized inside the church and incorporated before they are evangelized or simultaneous with it. Churches reaching emerging adults are willing to take risks to reach them by including them in community and giving them opportunities to contribute before they commit. Churches also provide the scaffolding that emerging adults need for conversion by allowing for the identity construction that characterizes young-adult lives and allows them to explore and experiment and try on Christian identity before committing to faith in Christ and that Christian identity.

Are You for Real?

"Are you for real?" is a question a lot of emerging adults are asking about the Christians they meet and the churches they visit. When churches give young adults the opportunity to come inside to kick the tires and critique how the church thinks and acts, they're finding emerging adults often make new or renewed faith commitments in an environment that lets them try out community, prayer, Scripture reading and discussion, meaningful service, and being invested in through mentoring, care, accountability, and resourcing. Basically, emerging adult conversions are happening in churches that provide a safe place where emerging adults are allowed to ask, *Are you for real?*

I recall an undergrad student in an evangelism course I taught at Wheaton College making an appointment with me. We met in my office, and when half the time set aside for the appointment had passed, I felt we hadn't yet gotten into any significant conversation. I wondered why he even had made the appointment; I was not his adviser. Fearing that the time would be up without us getting to his agenda, I asked him if there was anything specific he wanted to talk about. He replied, "Not really. You talk about Jesus in a way that I don't know very many people experience him. I just wanted to know you were for real."

Is this church for real? Is this Christian authentic? Or is this whole thing bogus?

Then I had one of those moments when I sensed the Holy Spirit spoke up for me. My next questions must have felt out of the blue for him: "Do you happen to struggle with cynicism?" The student nodded. "Are the friends you hang out with cynical about faith in Jesus and his church?"

Again he responded affirmatively. Together we brainstormed some ways he could begin to let go of his cynicism and journey toward deeper faith in Christ.

Emerging adults need an opportunity to spend some time inside the box—the church world—where they can kick the tires, experiment, play, try on a new identity, try out a new community to see if it fits them.

Just as that student had to check me out, emerging adults need an opportunity to spend some time inside the box—the church world—where they can kick the tires, experiment, play, try on a new identity, try out a new community to see if it fits them. But how does that happen? How do people outside the church find their way inside?

They need what every emerging adult in my research needed: the church to initiate, invite, include, involve, and invest in them. Only then do they have the opportunity to consider the claims of Christ for themselves and to deconstruct their stereotypes of church and believers. And with the help of the mentoring moral church community, they can reconstruct a fresh vision of the church and of Jesus' followers. They also learn what it means to trust and follow Christ.

Let's offer them the hospitality that God in Christ extends to us, so they too may experience spiritual transformation and be included in the kingdom of God. Or, so they too may experience spiritual transformation from the kingdom of darkness to the kingdom of light.

The Outcome: Young Adults Loving Church

It's clear that emerging adults love their churches. Somehow in a short window of time, their pastors and churches have instilled in them a strong church commitment and vision. They genuinely love their churches, highly value church, and are deeply appreciative of their pastors and ministry staff. Maddy's effervescent response represents the passionate way many respondents answered the questions, How do you feel about your church? and What do you love about your church?

I love everything. [Laughs.] The environment, the people, the message. . . . Wow, I mean there's just something about this church where I get excited to go to church. Like every morning I wake up and I'm like, yes! It's Sunday! [Laughs.] I have a lot of friends there, a lot of people that treat me like family. Every time I go there, you're always meeting new people and giving your input about God. But it's not all just about the people. They play a lot of music from Bethel, and it's really beautiful. It all echoes, like, throughout the whole church, and it's really beautiful. But then when it comes to the message, Todd just really pulls out the message. And I don't really know how to explain, but there's something—the way he relates, pulls out things [from Scripture] I've never even thought of. Like, the story about how the father kills the fatted calf for his lost son and brings him back in. He implanted in me that that story is not even about the sons. But it's about the father, and how good the father is. . . . He makes me second-think about things. Makes me take the story even deeper, and it's really amazing, because he goes beyond just the surface. He knows how to dig down deep and really make you think or see the truth beyond things.

Maddy isn't the only emerging adult who carries on about her church. What's real is that unchurched emerging adults commit to faith in Christ when they connect to welcoming, hospitable churches that reach them and love them through the five invitational practices.

It's also real that bright-spot churches stand out in reaching emerging adults, increasing the number of non-Christians attending. It's common sense: the more non-Christians attending church, the more conversions. Pastor Daniel reports,

We've crossed a threshold where now it is part of our DNA. People who are not close to God come regularly. It is funky compared to the past, where we were also trying to get non-Christians. Now we have a small number of people who are serious about their faith attending, because we have so many non-Christians come. We host people on all different stages of the journey.

What's real is that churches reaching and keeping emerging adults are hosting people on all different stages of their journey toward faith in Christ because they live out the five hospitable practices: initiate, invite, include, involve, and invest in emerging adults whose faith is "not done yet."

To God be the glory. May his kingdom reign in the hearts of emerging adults everywhere.

Acknowledgments

I am immensely grateful to the many contributors to this book and to the research behind its pages. Among them are emerging adults who enthusiastically embraced this project and gladly shared their faith stories with me out of their desire to help the church learn how to reach their peers. Thank you for your stories and your vulnerability.

I am also deeply indebted to the pastors in this study of churches that are making a difference in the lives of the emerging generations: Generation Z and millennials. Thank you for your accessibility, integrity, and transparency, and your kindness to a stranger.

Early on in this process, Evangelical Covenant Church administrators President Gary Walter, Executive Director of Ministry Development Dick Lucco, Interim Director of Make and Deepen Disciples Evelyn Johnson, and Executive Minister of Make and Deepen Disciples Michelle Sanchez graciously extended their invitation to do my research with their church. They offered continual support over the duration of the project. I deeply appreciate my denomination's tenacious pursuit of excellence as they measure how we are doing in our kingdom work.

I also thank the Billy Graham Center for Evangelism at Wheaton College for naming me a Billy Graham Research Scholar and providing financially for phase one of my research as well as the Billy Graham Center for Evangelism and LifeWay Research for their development and analysis of the Evangelical Covenant Church's online survey. In particular, Rick Richardson and Ed Stetzer were very generous in allowing my research on the Evangelical Covenant Church to be included in their project on the unchurched and the churches reaching them.

Faculty members in the Intercultural Studies and Educational Studies Departments at Trinity Evangelical Divinity School shared their wisdom and served as excellent resources, particularly anthropologist Robert Priest, missiologist Craig Ott, and sociologist Peter Cha. I also thank Deborah Colwell, associate professor of educational and leadership studies, for her significant contribution to my doctoral studies through an outstanding learning experience and an Emerging Adult Consortium. I also thank the ICS faculty for generously awarding me the Intercultural Studies Program Scholarship, which made it possible for me to pursue my studies while having three daughters in college. Of course, I couldn't have progressed very far without the encouragement and prodding of my former colleague and evangelism mentor Rick Richardson, professor of evangelism and leadership and director of BGC Research Institute. And to Hilary Duff, my first go-to in editors, who made up for what I lack in things editorial.

Many kudos to the IVP family, who guided my writing process and championed this work as important, especially Al Hsu, Ethan McCarthy, the amazing Ed Gilbreath, and Cindy Bunch.

My family, how can I articulate the countless sacrifices you have made for me or acknowledge your patience as I have been absent or not fully present during your significant milestones: college events, graduations, new jobs, moves, business startups, album releases, first homes, graduate school, study abroad, weddings, the passing of loved ones, family vacations, and more? I thank you for your enduring support during my challenging years of researching and writing this book.

Kate and Chris Matsch, Audrey and Trevor Welch, and Meredith Seversen, there are no words in English that convey my deep love and gratitude. Meredith, please find it in Farsi and teach me. My sacrificially giving and patient husband, Mark Seversen, a true champion of women whose heart beats for the *missio Dei*—without your constant encouragement, love, support, pitching in, and putting yourself second, I could not have completed this project. Guys, you are my life.

Notes

Introduction

1 *Through his younger sister's influence*: *Unchurched* refers to people who have no or little church background as well as those who have dropped out of church for six months or more.

2 *When we look at individuals'*: Christian Smith tracked the religious trajectories of emerging adults using data from the National Survey of Youth and Religion (NSYR), https://youthandreligion.nd.edu. These statistics from wave four of the NSYR were given to the author in the form of unpublished research and are used by permission of Christian Smith, October 19, 2015, showing an increasing trending drop in religious affiliation. For the definition and measurements used to determine trajectories, see Christian Smith and Patricia Snell, *Souls in Transition: The Religious and Spiritual Lives of Emerging Adults* (New York: Oxford University Press, 2009), 212-14, 242-46.

How are bright-spot churches: "America's Changing Religious Landscape," Pew Research Center, May 12, 2015, www.pewforum.org/2015/05/12/americas-changing-religious-landscape. This provides a wealth of data on America's self-identified religiously unaffiliated. The following findings are especially significant for the purposes of this book: (1) Among Americans of all ages, 22.8 percent identified themselves as religiously unaffiliated (nones); among millennials (individuals born between 1981 and 1996), the rate was 35 percent. (2) The number of older millennials (born between 1981 and 1989) who identify as nones increased by 9 percent between 2007 and 2014. (3) Between 2007 and 2014, the percentage of college graduates affiliated with Christianity decreased by 9 percent, from 73 to 64. A similar decline (8 percent, from 81 to 73) was seen among individuals with less than a college degree. (4) Millennial nones were among those least likely to change their religious affiliation between 2007 and 2014. (5) Data from both the Pew report and the Survey of Youth and Religion show that young adults are at a heightened risk of experiencing a decline in religious commitment and affiliation between the ages of twenty-two and twenty-nine. Seemiller and Grace draw attention to findings that show over time each entering college generation is less religiously affiliated than the generation before it. For instance in 2001 only 15.8 percent of entering college millennials were religiously unaffiliated

compared to 2015 when the rate climbed to 30 percent of entering college
Generation Z were religiously unaffiliated. The data points to rising rates
of religiously unaffiliated among emerging adults. "So, if a larger share of
those in Generation Z are religiously unaffiliated compared to members
of older generations when they were young adults, we could expect relatively high rates of unaffiliation as this generation ages." "Thus, between
one-quarter and one-third of Generation Z first-year students do not identify with a religious affiliation." Corey Seemiller and Meghan Grace, *Generation Z: A Century in the Making* (New York: Routledge, 2019), 174.

younger eighteen to twenty-three year olds: James Emery White, *Meet Generation Z: Understanding and Reaching the New Post-Christian World* (Grand
Rapids: Baker, 2017), 24, 49.

the least-supported cohort: Robert Wuthnow, *After the Baby Boomers: How
Twenty- and Thirty-Somethings Are Shaping the Future of American Religion*
(Princeton, NJ: Princeton University Press, 2007), 70, 232.

And we need to hear the stories: Nones are now the largest religious group
in the United States, according to the latest data available from the
General Social Survey (2015) and fastest growing (Pew). White, *Meet
Generation Z*, 22.

3   *I call them* bright-spot *churches: Bright-spot* is a term used by Chip Heath
and Dan Heath to refer to places where things are working right, and
in *Growing Young*, the largest body of research currently available on
churches retaining young adults, to refer to effective churches. In keeping with this pattern, I use the term *bright-spot churches* to refer to
churches that have shown exceptional effectiveness in reaching and
incorporating unchurched emerging adults. See Chip Heath and Dan
Heath, *Switch: How to Change Things When Change Is Hard* (New York:
Broadway Books, 2010); and Kara Powell, Jake Mulder, and Brad
Griffin, *Growing Young: Six Essential Strategies to Help People Discover and
Love Your Church* (Grand Rapids: Baker, 2016).

4   *third space venues:* The term *third space* was attributed to sociologist Ray
Oldenburg, who coined the word in his book *The Great Good Place*,
2nd ed. (New York: Paragon, 1999), xiii-xxx, to define a social space for
the purpose of informal public gatherings for community, inclusion,
and democratic public discourse outside of home or work spaces (e.g.,
coffee shops, cafes, bars, bookstores, libraries, and hair salons). Star-
bucks is an example of capitalizing on the concept of providing a third
space where people can enjoy the significant informal public life that
Oldenburg argued for.

5   *The information in this book: Not Done Yet* is based on and includes parts
of my unpublished qualitative research: Beth Seversen, "Millennials
Connecting to Contemporary Congregations: Effectively Reaching
and Incorporating Emerging Adults in North American Evangelical

Covenant Churches" (PhD diss., Trinity International Evangelical School, 2017). Material in *Not Done Yet* may also appear in "Churches Reaching Emerging Adult 'Nones' and 'Dones,'" in *Against the Tide: Mission Amidst the Global Currents of Secularization*, ed. W. Jay Moon and Craig Ott (Littleton, CO: William Carey, 2019), 83-105.

identified by George Barna and David Kinnaman: George Barna and David Kinnaman, eds., *Churchless: Understanding Today's Unchurched and How to Connect with Them* (Austin, TX: Barna Group, 2014), 6.

data is from a small qualitative study: Demographics of the nineteen churches I identified and researched that were reaching and keeping young adults follow: *Ethnicity:* nine white, eight multiethnic, one black, one Asian. *Type:* eleven urban, eight suburban; *Size:* two megachurches over ten thousand, three churches of attendance over one thousand, three churches between 500 and 999, and nine churches between 175 and 499 participated. Church geographic locations ranged from the Pacific Northwest, Pacific Southwest, Midwest, Mid-South, New England, and one Canadian church. No Hispanic churches or churches from Alaska, Hawaii, or the Southeast United States were included. Pastors ranged from age twenty-nine to seventy, and two pastors were female. Emerging adults were age twenty to thirty-two, male and female, African American, Asian American, Chinese Taiwanese American, Korean American, Filipino American, and white. Their length of connection to their church and rebirth fell along a spectrum from four months to five years. Eight had attended church for less than one year. All were religiously unaffiliated. Eight had dropped out of church in middle or high school and the other young adults had never attended church.

1. Journeying

9   *During emerging adulthood:* Originally, Jeffrey Arnett and Susan Taber defined the time frame for emerging adulthood to be ages eighteen to twenty-five and then later extended it to age twenty-nine. Jeffrey Jensen Arnett and Susan Taber, "Adolescents Terminable and Interminable: When Does Adolescence End?" *Journal of Youth and Adolescence* 23, no. 5 (October 1994): 517-37; and Jeffrey Jensen Arnett, "Emerging Adulthood: A Theory of Development from the Late Teens Through the Twenties," *American Psychologist* 55, no. 5 (2000): 469-80. And for the metaphor of the "long winding road" to identity development, see Jeffrey Jensen Arnett, *Emerging Adulthood: The Winding Road from the Late Teens Through the Early Twenties*, 2nd ed. (New York: Oxford University Press, 2015).

Emerging adulthood is sometimes divided: Christian Smith, Notre Dame sociologist of religion, worked with the National Study of Youth and

Religion, the largest longitudinal study in the United States on young
adults, to provide much-needed research on the religious and spiritual
lives of young adults age 18-23, to what he calls the first half of emerging adulthood. That research is presented in his book *Souls in Transition*. Christian Smith with Patricia Snell, *Souls in Transition: The Religious
and Spiritual Lives of Emerging Adulthood* (New York: Oxford University
Press, 2009), 7.

Although not everyone agrees: James Côté and some other scholars strongly
disagree with Arnett that there is new data suggesting emerging adulthood can be distinguished from Erik Erikson's early adulthood stage,
ages twenty to thirty-five, as a definitive life development stage. See
James E. Côté, "The Dangerous Myth of Emerging Adulthood: An
Evidence-Based Critique of a Flawed Developmental Theory," *Applied
Developmental Science* 18, no. 4 (2014): 177-88.

10   *While "emerging adulthood" refers to:* Becka A. Alper, "Millennials Are Less
Religious Than Older Americans, but Just as Spiritual," *Fact Tank*
(blog), Pew Research Center, November 23, 2015, www.pewresearch
.org/fact-tank/2015/11/23/millennials-are-less-religious-than-older
-americans-but-just-as-spiritual. William Strauss is credited with naming the cohort and originally set their births between 1982 and 2004.
However, Pew Research dates are now the more commonly accepted
birth guidelines. See Bruce Horowitz, "After Gen X, Millennials, What
Should Next Generation Be?" *USA Today*, May 4, 2012, www.usatoday30
.usatoday.com/money/advertising/story/2012-05-03/naming-the
-next-generation/54737518/1?loc=interstitialskip.

Generation Z first born in 1995: Corey Seemiller and Meghan Grace, *Generation Z: A Century in the Making* (New York: Routledge, 2019), xix.

Generation Z first born in 1997: Pew sets the start year for Generation Z at
1997. "Defining Generations: Where Millennials End and Generation
Z Begins," Pew Research Center, accessed August 20, 2019, www
.pewresearch.org/fact-tank/2019/01/17/where-millennials-end-and
-generation-z-begins.

Scholar James Emery White marks the birth years: James Emery White, *Meet
Generation Z: Understanding and Reaching the New Post-Christian World*
(Grand Rapids: Baker Academic, 2017).

Combined, the two youngest generational: White, *Meet Generation Z*, 37.

the 78 million millennials: Thom S. Rainer and Jess W. Rainer, *The Millennials: Connecting to America's Largest Generation* (Nashville: B&H, 2011),
2. Seemiller and Grace conclude, "Millennials are expected to surpass
their Boomer parents in population size by 2019 and have eclipsed their
Generation X predecessors." Seemiller and Grace, *Generation Z*, 9.

Generation Z surpassed millennials: Anthony Cilluffo, "6 Demographic Trends Shaping the U. S. and the World in 2019," Pew Research Center, April 11, 2019, www.pewresearch.org/fact-tank/2019/04/11/6-demographic-trends-shaping-the-u-s-and-the-world-in-2019.

11   *So who are Generation Z?* White, *Meet Generation Z*, 39.

Only two-fifths (41 percent): White, *Meet Generation Z*, 49. In the *Generation Z Goes to College* study, 47 percent of college students reported they participate in organized religion, and in 2015 first-year college students identified as participating frequently or occasionally in a religious service. Seemiller and Grace, *Generation Z Goes to College*, 176.

while only 27 percent of Millennials: Becka A. Alper, "Millennials Are Less Religious Than Older Americans but Just as Spiritual," Pew Research Center, November 23, 2016, www.pewresearch.org/fact-tank/2015/11/23/millennials-are-less-religious-than-older-americans-but-just-as-spiritual.

Christian churches that care about: I recommend the following resources for the most up-to-date research for understanding Generation Z: Seemiller and Grace, *Generation Z: A Century in the Making*; Seemiller and Grace, *Generation Z Goes to College*.

How are churches reaching the least-reached: "America's Changing Religious Landscape," Pew Research Center, May 12, 2015, www.pewforum.org/2015/05/12/americas-changing-religious-landscape, provides a wealth of data on American's self-identified religious affiliation. The following findings are especially significant for the purposes of this book: (1) Among Americans of all ages, 22.8 percent identified themselves as religiously unaffiliated (nones). Among millennials (individuals born between 1981 and 1996), this rate was 35 percent. (2) The number of older millennials (born between 1981 and 1989) who identify as nones increased by 9 percent between 2007 and 2014. (3) Between 2007 and 2014, the percentage of college graduates affiliated with Christianity decreased by 9 percent, from 73 to 64. A similar decline (8 percent, from 81 to 73) was seen among individuals with less than a college degree. (4) Millennial nones were among those least likely to change their religious affiliation between 2007 and 2014. (5) Data from both the Pew report and the Survey of Youth and Religion show that young adults are at a heightened risk of experiencing a decline in religious commitment and affiliation between the ages of twenty-two and twenty-nine.

Much of the literature proposing: Smith and Snell, *Souls in Transition*, 6.

12   *possibilities and optimism*: Jeffrey Arnett, *Emerging Adulthood: The Winding Road from the Late Teens Through the Early Twenties*, 2nd ed. (New York: Oxford University Press, 2015).

The trail through emerging adulthood: Smith and Snell, *Souls in Transition;* and Christian Smith et al., *Lost in Transition: The Dark Side of Emerging Adulthood* (New York: Oxford University Press, 2011), 5, 11, 15.

13 *Emerging adults are disposed toward:* Smith and Snell, *Souls in Transition;* and Smith et al., *Lost in Transition,* 2011.

For many emerging adults: Smith et al., *Lost in Transition,* 5, 9, 11-13, 34, 60-62, 108-9, 141-42, 146-47, 193, 229, 232.

14 *But let's be real:* Smith with Snell, *Souls in Transition,* 5.

Smith reports parents spend: Smith and Snell, *Souls in Transition,* 5.

Fifty-nine percent of millennials: John Fleming, "Gallup Analysis: Millennials, Marriage and Family," *Gallup.com,* accessed February 6, 2020, https://news.gallup.com/poll/191462/gallup-analysis-millennials -marriage-family.aspx.

Eighty-three percent do not: Pew Research 2015. Gallup reported that statistic at 60 percent in 2016. Fleming, "Gallup Analysis."

These two factors contribute: Rodney Stark, *What Americans Really Believe: New Findings from the Baylor Surveys of Religion* (Waco, TX: Baylor University Press, 2008), 183.

Think about it. Between 1950: Robert Wuthnow, *After the Baby Boomers: How Twenty- and Thirty-Somethings Are Shaping the Future of American Religion* (Princeton, NJ: Princeton University Press, 2007), 21-23, Wendy Wang and Kim Parker, "Record Share of Americans Have Never Married as Values, Economics and Gender Patterns Change," Pew Research Center, September 24, 2014, www.pewsocialtrends.org/2014/09/24/record -share-of-americans-have-never-married/#will-todays-never-married -adults-eventually-marry.

Many who study the religious: Stark, *What Americans Really Believe.*

15 *Developmental psychologists believe:* Shahram Heshmat, "Basics of Identity: What Do We Mean by Identity and Why the Identity Matters?" *Psychology Today,* December 8, 2014, www.psychologytoday.com/us/blog/science -choice/201412/basics-identity.

In the United States, personal identity: Vivian L. Vignoles, Seth J. Schwartz, and Koen Luyckx, "Introduction: Toward an Integrative Theory of Identity," in *Handbook of Identity Theory and Research,* ed. Seth. J. Schwartz, Koen Luyckx, and Vivian L. Vignoles (New York: Springer, 2011), 1-28.

The guru of identity work: Mark Christian, *Multiracial Identity: An International Perspective* (New York: St. Martin's Press, 2000), 1.

Identity is a sociological concept: Paul Gilroy, "Roots and Routes: Black Identity as an Outernational Project," in *Racial and Ethnic Identity:*

Psychological Development and Creative Expressions, ed. Herbert W. Harris, Howard C. Blue, and Ezra E. H. Griffith (New York: Routledge, 1995), 19.

It is also believed to vary: Identity is changeable according to social context while at the same time identity maintains a sense of continuity and is both historically rooted and socially constructed. Mark Christian, *Multiracial Identity: An Internal Perspective* (New York: St. Martin's Press, 2000), 4; Peter Weinreich, "The Operationalisation of Identity Theory in Racial and Ethnic Relations," in *Theories of Race and Ethnic Relations*, ed. John Rex and David Mason (Cambridge: Cambridge University Press, 1986), 299-320; Peter Weinreich and Wendy Saunderson, eds., *Analyzing Identity: Cross-Cultural, Societal and Clinical Contexts* (New York: Routledge, 2003).

Erikson believed that the work: C. H. Hoare, *Erikson on Development in Adulthood: New Insights from the Unpublished Papers* (New York: Oxford University Press, 2002), 10, 13, 17, 31. Sharon Daloz Parks describes Erikson's work this way: "Erikson described the formation of self-identity as an adolescent task that included achievement of both self-awareness and an effective social role." Sharon Daloz Parks, *Big Questions Worthy Dreams: Mentoring Emerging Adults in Their Search for Meaning, Purpose, and Faith* (San Francisco: Jossey-Bass, 2011), 85.

16   *Over time, the two major questions:* Dan P. McAdams, Ruthellen Josselson, and Amia Lieblich, eds., "Introduction," in *Identity and Story: Creating Self in Narrative* (Washington, DC: American Psychological Association, 2006).

During this season of life: Erickson viewed "ego-identity" as a lifelong formation spanning all eight of his psychosocial stages and not, as many believe, only during the identity stage (James E. Côté and Charles Levine, "A Formulation of Erikson's Theory of Ego Identity Formation," *Developmental Review* 7, no. 4 (1987): 276. He considered identity formation from both a stage specific sense and as a continual part of the life cycle. Erickson's concept of psychosocial moratorium was an inclusive term representing that period of time during adolescence and early adulthood in which there is a delay in adult commitments within the bandwidth of time a society gives youth to resolve their identity stage before sanctions are invoked (Côté and Levine, "Formulation of Erikson's Theory," 295). This period of selective permissiveness in society gives young adults an opportunity to "play" and also to experiment with future roles culminating in a "transitory commitment" from youth and a "ceremonial confirmation of commitment" by society (Erickson 1968a, 157; Côté 2006; Côté and Levine, "Formulation of Erikson's Theory," 277).

Marcia built on Erickson's work: James E. Marcia, "Development and Validation of Ego Identity Status," *Journal of Personality and Social*

Psychology 3, no. 5 (1966): 551-58, in David P. Setran and Chris A. Kiesling, *Spiritual Formation in Emerging Adulthood: A Practical Theology for College and Young Adult Ministry* (Grand Rapids: Baker Academic, 2013), 62.

Setran and Kiesling describe moratorium: Setran and Kiesling, *Spiritual Formation in Emerging Adulthood*, 62.

Often this period of "social moratorium": Seth J. Schwartz, James E. Côté, and Jeffrey J. Arnett, "Identity and Agency in Emerging Adulthood: Two Developmental Routes in the Individualization Process," *Youth & Society* 37, no. 2 (December 2005): 278, 303.

17 *These include supportive parents:* Côté and Levine, "Formulation of Erikson's Theory," 280; Brian Simmons, *Wandering in the Wilderness: Changes and Challenges to Emerging Adults' Christian Faith* (Abilene, TX: Abilene Christian University Press 2011), 121; and William S. Aquilino, "Family Relationships and Support Systems in Emerging Adulthood," in *Emerging Adults in America: Coming of Age in the 21st Century,* ed. Jeffrey Jensen Arnett and Jennifer Lynn Tanner (New York: American Psychological Association, 2006), 195.

Making their own decisions: Schwartz, Côté, and Arnett, "Identity and Agency," 224.

When they don't have those opportunities: James E. Côté, *Arrested Adulthood: The Changing Nature of Maturity and Identity in the Late Modern World* (New York: New York University Press, 2000), 42.

Choices of a college, career, location: Orrin Edgar Klapp, *Collective Search for Identity* (Austin, TX: Holt, Rhinehart & Winston, 1969); James E. Côté and Charles Levine, *Identity Formation, Agency and Culture: A Social Psychological Synthesis* (Mahwah, NJ: Erlbaum, 2002); and Setran and Kiesling, *Spiritual Formation in Emerging Adulthood*, 57.

Cultural observers argue: Setran and Kiesling, *Spiritual Formation in Emerging Adulthood*, 58.

When identity work excludes a supportive: Setran and Kiesling, *Spiritual Formation in Emerging Adulthood*, 59; and Côté, *Arresting Adulthood*, 3.

18 *Life choices that young adults:* Schwartz, Côté, and Arnett, "Identity and Agency in Emerging Adulthood, 201-29; and Smith and Snell, *Souls in Transition*, 73.

For example, they take on enormous: Wuthnow, *After the Baby Boomers*, 70.

Identity commitments are nurtured: James E. Côté and Seth J. Schwartz, "Comparing Psychological and Sociological Approaches to Identity: Identity Status, Identity Capital, and the Individualization Process," *Journal of Adolescence* 25 (2002): 571-86.

Community and religious involvement: Constance A. Flanagan, "Volunteerism, Leadership, Political Socialization, and Civic Engagement," in *Handbook of Adolescent Psychology*, ed. Richard M. Lerner and Laurence Steinberg, 2nd ed., (Hoboken, NJ: Wiley, 2004), 721-45; and Pamela Ebstyn King, "Religion and Identity: The Role of Ideological, Social, and Spiritual Contexts," *Applied Developmental Science* 7, no. 3 (July 2003): 197-204; and Marie Good and Teena Willoughby, "The Identity Formation Experience of Church-Attending Rural Adolescents," *Journal of Adolescent Research* 22 (2007): 387-412.

Community involvement often provides: Jodi B. Dworkin, Reed Larson, and David Hansen, "Adolescents' Accounts of Growth Experiences in Youth Activities," *Journal of Youth and Adolescence* 32 (2003): 17-26.

Community participation especially seems: Sam A. Hardy et al., "Community and Religious Involvement as Contexts of Identity Change Across Late Adolescence and Emerging Adulthood," *International Journal of Behavioral Development* 35, no. 2 (2010): 127.

Through religious involvement, emerging adults: Good and Willoughby, "The Identity Formation Experiences of Church-Attending Rural Adolescents," 387-412; King, "Religion and Identity," 197-204; James Youniss et al., "The Role of Community Service in Duty Development: Normative, Unconventional, and Deviant Orientations," *Journal of Adolescent Research* 14 (1999): 248-61; and Hardy et al., "Community and Religious Involvement," 126-27.

19   *Basically, social research confirms:* Laura B. Koenig, Matt McGue, and William G. Iacono, "Stability and Change in Religiousness During Emerging Adulthood," *Developmental Psychology* 44, no. 2 (2008): 532-43.

Religious contexts encourage emerging adults: Hardy et al., "Community and Religious Involvement," 127.

They offer accountability and support: Setran and Kiesling, *Spiritual Formation in Emerging Adulthood*, 79.

Richard Dunn and Jana Sundene write: Richard R. Dunn and Jana L. Sundene, *Shaping the Journey of Emerging Adults: Life-Giving Rhythms for Spiritual Transformation* (Downers Grove, IL: InterVarsity Press, 2012), 20.

Without mentors and mentoring: Sharon Daloz Parks, *Big Questions Worthy Dreams*, 229, 233-34, 236.

Faith communities provide a social: Tory Baucum, *Evangelical Hospitality: Catechetical Evangelism in the Early Church and Its Recovery for Today* (Lanham, MD: Scarecrow, 2008).

20   *mentoring communities are very significant:* Parks, *Big Questions Worthy Dreams*, 174.

21   *During their identity construction:* Smith and Snell, *Souls in Transition*.

One result of religious disassociation: Smith and Snell, *Souls in Transition.*

If young adults spend a long time: Jonathan Hill, "Religious Involvement During the Transition to Adulthood" (PhD diss., University of Notre Dame, 2008), 138.

When I traveled to the Burning Man: Burning Man, a self-expression and arts festival held annually over Labor Day weekend in Black Rock City, Nevada, with seventy thousand-plus participants, is another contemporary "moratorium" where Lee Gilmore finds people come to experiment and play with alternative identities and spiritualties. They embrace fluid spiritual self-descriptions and not fixed identities with *spiritual, not religious* being one set of markers and self-descriptions among many. They piece together their hybrid spiritual identities, drawn from a limitless pool of global resources to engage their spiritual beliefs and aspirations. Three of the ten core principles of Burning Man pertain to immediacy, participation, and gifting. Emerging adults are a large part of the attenders of the Burning Man festival, and they desire to fully engage and participate, to bring their gifts, and to have encounters. Lee Gilmore, *Theatre in a Crowded Fire: Ritual and Spirituality at Burning Man* (Los Angeles: University California Press, 2010), 66-67.

22   *Bricoleur has its roots:* Nasrullah Mambrol, "Claude Levi Strauss' Concept of Bricolage," *Literary Theory and Criticism,* March 21, 2016, www.literariness.org/2016/03/21/claude-levi-strauss-concept-of -bricolage; and Wuthnow, *After the Baby Boomers.*

2. Initiating

28   *These outsiders or nones:* The number of American nones doubled between 2000 and 2010. Robert D. Putnam and David Campbell, *American Grace: How Religion Divides and Unites Us* (New York: Simon & Schuster, 2010), 121, 123.

reject the church for what they perceive as immorality: Putnam and Campbell, *American Grace,* 3.

hypocrisy, enclaving, and imposing: David Kinnaman and Gabe Lyons, *Unchristian: What a New Generation Really Thinks About Christianity—and Why It Matters* (Grand Rapids: Baker, 2007), 41, 67, 91, 121, 153, 181.

30   *Unchurched young adults:* Other researchers also reveal the significance of friends and family inviting friends and family to church. Ed Stetzer, Richie Stanley, and Jason Hayes also found invitations to be an important part of reaching young adults. See their *Lost and Found: The Younger Unchurched and the Churches That Reach Them* (Nashville: B&H, 2009). George Barna and David Kinnaman also found that an invitation from a friend was the most likely way to connect unchurched people to

church. George Barna and David Kinnaman, *Churchless* (Wheaton, IL: Tyndale House, 2014), 27-28.

The most effective outreach pattern: George Barna and David Kinnaman, eds., *Churchless: Understanding Today's Unchurched and How to Connect with Them* (Austin, TX: Barna Group, 2014). 156-57.

There was declining interest: Barna and Kinnaman, *Churchless*, 150.

31 *Actually, there's a bit more to it:* Thom Rainer, "Relationships That Click," in *Surprising Insights from the Unchurched and Proven Ways to Reach Them* (Grand Rapids: Zondervan, 2001), 69-84.

Apart from the contest: Rick Richardson, *You Found Me: New Research on How Unchurched Nones, Millennials, and Irreligious Are Surprisingly Open to Christian Faith* (Downers Grove, IL: InterVarsity Press, 2019), 61-65.

second, enthusiastically invite friends: church-bridging opportunities are activities and events that connect unchurched people with church apart from attending the main worship services. For instance, in my study, young adults were invited to bridging activities like feeding the homeless, camping trips, playing on church sports teams, and to board game nights in friend's homes.

32 *In interviews with two hundred:* Don Everts and Doug Schaupp, *I Once Was Lost: What Postmodern Skeptics Taught Us About Their Path to Jesus* (Downers Grove, IL: InterVarsity Press, 2008), 47.

33 *At the time when most social services:* Robert Wuthnow argues, "After providing significant institutional support for the developmental tasks that occurred before then, we provide almost nothing for the developmental tasks that are accomplished when people are in their twenties and thirties. And since most of those tasks are happening later, this is a huge problem. It means that younger adults are having to invent their own ways of making decisions and seeking support for those decisions. Whereas dating and mate selection used to happen within the social milieu of the high school, congregation, or campus, it now occurs increasingly in bars, at parties, and through the internet. Other major decisions, such as when to have children and how to raise them, or where to live and what kind of career to pursue, are also being made on an improvisational basis, largely without firm institutional grounding. It is little wonder that social critics write about the problems of *individualism*. In the absence of any institutional sources of support and stability, young adults are forced to be individualistic. They have no other resources but themselves." Robert Wuthnow. *After the Baby Boomers: How Twenty- and Thirty-Somethings Are Shaping the Future of American Religion* (Princeton, NJ: Princeton University Press, 2007), 12-13.

3. Inviting

44 *Christian Smith, the author:* Christian Smith et al., *Lost in Transition: The Dark Side of Emerging Adulthood* (New York: Oxford University Press, 2011).

45 *She was captivated by:* These were Brooke's words. Interestingly, the church website does not actually mention anything about being a light but simply says, "Go serve others." The website is not cited to protect the identity of the young adult.

emerging adulthood is: Jeffrey Arnett, *Emerging Adulthood: The Winding Road from the Late Teens Through the Early Twenties,* 2nd ed. (New York: Oxford University Press, 2015).

46 *No wonder Commons: The Covenant Yearbook: Statistical Data & Resources for Churches,* 2015–2016 ed. (Chicago: Evangelical Covenant Church, 2015), 373; and *The Covenant Yearbook: Statistical Data & Resources for Churches,* 2016–2017 ed. (Chicago: Evangelical Covenant Church, 2016), 361.

4. Welcoming

55 *Millennials actually like:* One study found that emerging adults report interest in relationships with "mentors and friends of all ages who have gone through experiences that they are about to encounter." Ed Stetzer, Richie Stanley, and Jason Hayes, *Lost and Found: The Younger Unchurched and the Churches That Reach Them* (Nashville: B&H, 2009), 129.

Unchurched emerging adults often: David Kinnaman reports that young Christians who leave the church regard the church as morally repressive, especially in the area of sexual expression. One group of young people who have left the church described the church as "controlling, joyless, and stern when it comes to sex, sexuality, and sexual expectations." David Kinnaman and Aly Hawkins, *You Lost Me: Why Young Christians Are Leaving Church and Rethinking Faith* (Grand Rapids: Baker, 2011), 149-50.

others view churches themselves: David Kinnaman and Gabe Lyons found that people outside the church accuse churches of being un-Christian due to hypocrisy, judgmentalism, homophobia, narrow-mindedness, and exclusivity in calls for absolute allegiance to Christ. David Kinnaman and Gabe Lyons, *Unchristian: What a New Generation Really Thinks About Christianity—and Why It Matters* (Grand Rapids: Baker, 2007).

57 *"Life.Church has a special way":* "Life.Church—which relies on video sermons—is the largest multisite church in the United States, reporting over 85,000 attendees in 2018 according to Michael Gryboski, Life. Church Has Grown to 30 Campuses and 85,000 Attendees," *Christian Post,* September 12, 2018, www.christianpost.com/news/life-church

-has-grown-to-30-campuses-and-85000-attendees.html. And it is still growing rapidly.

This may seem surprising: George Ritzer, *The McDonaldization of Society: An Investigation into the Changing Character of Contemporary Social Life* (Newbury Park, CA: Pine Forge Press, 1993).

58 *Maddy, Megan, and Michael:* Maddy is quoted to say, "The sense of family and home and welcome-ness, that's what I love." Taking the notion of home more literally, Mountain View and CCFC ran community houses designed for young adult discipleship and supervised by staff or situated in staff homes. Several emerging adults—Chelsea, Shea, Brooke, and Garrett—lived with their college pastor or another church staff member.

59 *Church provides a community:* Jonathan Hill proposed that religious faith and practice are legitimized where religious behavior is integrated into social environments. Jonathan P. Hill, "Higher Education as Moral Community: Institutional Influence on Religious Participation During College," *Journal for the Scientific Study of Religion* 48, no 3 (2009): 515-34; Small and Bowman's research suggest that university students' social networks can legitimate religious faith and decrease skepticism. Jenny L. Small and Nicholas A. Bowman, "Religious Commitment, Skepticism, and Struggle Among US College Students: The Impact of Majority/Minority Religious Affiliation and Institutional Type," *Journal for the Scientific Study of Religion* 50, no. 1 (2011): 167.

60 *She learned about Community Church:* A pseudonym is used for Zoe's church to protect her identity.

5. Changing

63 *We don't need to design:* Willow Creek Church is known for creating the seeker-service model. The Willow Creek strategy is to design every element of their weekend church service with one primary goal in mind: "to convert unchurched Harrys and Marys [described as unmotivated unchurched individuals] to Christ." Willow offers a midweek evening service designed to nurture believers. The seeker service has been critiqued by G. A. Pritchard and others questioning whether the Willow strategy is consumeristic, manipulative, unethical, anti-intellectual, and lacking theological moorings, among many other assessments. G. A. Pritchard, *Willow Creek Seeker Services: Evaluating A New Way of Doing Church.* (Grand Rapids: Baker, 1996), 23, 26-27, 216, 240-49, 272-87.

64 *They constantly recalibrate:* Chapter nine will be devoted to what pastors of churches reaching young adults are doing and how they are communicating. Here I solely mention that pastors are communicating

with the unchurched in mind and giving regular and frequent calls to faith.

This process, called co-communicating: Andy Stanley refers to co-communicating as "double-barrel preaching" and devotes a chapter of his book to engaging a dual audience of Christians and non-Christians. Andy Stanley, *Deep and Wide: Creating Churches Unchurched People Love to Attend* (Grand Rapids: Zondervan, 2012), 227-59.

two-degree vectoring: Kevin G. Harney, *Organic Outreach for Churches: Infusing Evangelistic Passion in Your Local Congregation* (Grand Rapids: Zondervan, 2011), 141.

66   *And it saw a 69 percent growth*: Comparison of the 2016–2017 and 2018–2019 editions of *Covenant Yearbook: Statistical Data and Resources for Churches* (Chicago: Evangelical Covenant Church, 2016, 2018).

68   *their book on leading change*: Chip Heath and Dan Heath, *Switch: How to Change When Change Is Hard* (New York: Broadway Books, 2010). See especially chapter six, "Shrink the Change."

75   *InterVarsity Christian Fellowship has*: The following are examples of Inter-Varsity Christian Fellowship's evangelism training: "Give a Call to Faith" (evangelism.intervarsity.org/share-gospel/give-call-faith); "A Theology of Calls to Faith" (evangelism.intervarsity.org/resource/theology-calls -faith); "How To: Invite to Faith in Large Groups (evangelism.intervarsity .org/resource/large-group-guide); and "Small Groups Call to Faith" (2100.intervarsity.org/resources/small-group-calls-faith).

6. Including

76   *The full invitation on the church website*: See the homepage of LifeChurch Canton at www.lifechurchcanton.org.

77   *Let me introduce myself*: Email correspondence provided by Brooke to author and used with permission.

Brooke was also asked: Starting Point resources include a video series by Andy Stanley at Northpoint Church and a conversation guide available from Zondervan. Andy Stanley and The Starting Point Team, *Starting Point: A Conversation About Faith* (Grand Rapids: Zondervan, 2014). The focus of Starting Point is to create a community experience and conversational environment for people beginning or considering beginning a life with God. It's designed for seekers, starters, and returners. The table of contents includes Start, Problem, Trust, Rules, Jesus, Grace, Faith, and Invitation. Adjacent to the main worship service time is a strategic location for Starting Point—where guests can easily access their next step toward "including" in Christian community.

78   *First, as we've already seen*: Not surprising, Thom Rainer found five key factors that made significant impressions on formerly churched visitors

that encouraged them to return: friendliness of the people; nice or excellent facilities; the high quality of the nursery, preschool, or childcare facilities and care; a sense of being well-organized; and, friendly helpful greeters and a welcoming center. Also interesting is Rainer found formerly unchurched people were more impacted on their second visit than their first. Thom Rainer, *Surprising Insights from the Unchurched and Proven Ways to Reach Them* (Grand Rapids: Zondervan, 2008), 92-103.

79   *George Barna and David Kinnaman reported:* George Barna and David Kinnaman, eds., *Churchless: Understanding Today's Unchurched and How to Connect with Them* (Austin: Barna Group, 2014), 46.

     In the conclusion of his book: James Emery White, *The Rise of the Nones: Understanding and Reaching the Religiously Unaffiliated* (Grand Rapids: Baker, 2014), 47.

80   *Further research suggests that:* David Kinnaman and Gabe Lyons, *Unchristian: What a Generation Really Thinks About Christianity—And Why It Matters* (Grand Rapids: Baker, 2007), 5, 41, 67, 91, 121, 153, 181.

     overprotective, shallow, antiscience: David Kinnaman and Aly Hawkins, *You Lost Me: Why Young Christians Are Leaving Church—And Rethinking Faith* (Grand Rapids: Baker, 2011), 90–93. *Doubtless* refers to people who leave the church because of the people in the church that never doubt anything the church teaches.

     It's not surprising: Christian Smith and Patricia Snell, *Souls in Transition: The Religious and Spiritual Lives of Emerging Adults* (New York: Oxford University Press, 2009), 152.

     Sociologists have observed: Christian Smith writes, "Rarely do people's thinking and feeling and behaving change dramatically (or stay the same) without significant social relationships exerting pressures to do so and facilitating these outcomes." Smith with Snell, *Souls in Transition* (New York: Oxford University Press, 2009), 209.

81   *like-minded Christian community*: Jenny Hill found more students experience a strengthening of religious convictions than those whose faith is weakened as a result of attending college. Jenny Hill, "Religion and College Attendance: Change Among Students." *Review of Higher Education* 25, no. 4 (2002): 382. Roberts, Koch, and Johnson found that religious and secular students with religious friends became more religiously active in college than students with nonreligious friends. A. E. Roberts, J. R. Koch, and D. P. Johnson, "Religious Reference Groups and the Persistence of Normative Behavior: An Empirical Test," *Sociological Spectrum* 21 (2001): 81-98. Jonathan Hill found students belonging to religious subcultures often flourish in religious identification through association of like-minded students in religiously diverse

student populations. Jonathan Hill, "Higher Education as Moral Community: Institutional Influences on Religious Participation During College," *Journal for the Scientific Study of Religion* 48, no 3 (2009): 515-34. Jenny Small and Nicholas Bowman suggests students' social networks legitimate religious commitment and socializing with students who have similar religious beliefs is related to greater religious commitment and decreased skepticism. Religious engagement in college is strongly associated with an increase in religious commitment and a decrease in religious skepticism. Jenny L. Small Small and Nicholas A. Bowman, "Religious Commitment, Skepticism, and Struggle Among US College Students: The Impact of Majority/Minority Religious Affiliation and Institutional Type," *Journal for the Scientific Study of Religion* 50, no. 1 (2011): 157, 167, 168; and Hill, "Religion and College Attendance," 379. Faculty support for religious development and engagement is positively related to student's religious engagement and increase in spiritual identification (Small and Bowman, "Religious Commitment"; Hill, "Religion and College Attendance," 379). It is not that the university has no secularizing influence on Christian students, but rather the literature shows in some university contexts some Christian students maintain religious commitments, some decline, and some students commit to Christian faith, grow and maintain religious identity, especially when their faith is legitimated. Three conditions seem especially legitimizing for sustaining Christian faith, new Christian faith and incorporation into Christian communities: (1) The role of certain types of communities (Hill, "Higher Education as Moral Community," 515), (2) socializing peer networks that validate faith (Roberts, Koch, and Johnson, "Religious Reference Groups"), and (3) exposure to relationships with legitimating supportive adults—faculty and mentors—that include leadership training and opportunities (Small and Bowman 2009; and Hill, "Religion and College Attendance," 3). Factors from the literature that support religious stability and discourage decline include attending college where religious behavior is integrated into the university ethos (Hill, "Higher Education as Moral Community"), having and socializing with religious friends (Roberts, Koch, and Johnson, "Religious Reference Groups"), being connected to social networks that legitimate faith (Small and Bowman, "Religious Commitment"), professors that encourage, model and verbally interact about their religious faith (Small and Bowman, "Religious Commitment," Hill, "Religion and College Attendance"), and leadership training (Hill, "Religion and College Attendance"). Is it possible effective evangelizing churches are replicating these conditions in their engagement of emerging adults?

When we belong: Pierre Bourdieu and Loïc J. D. Wacquant, *An Invitation to Reflexive Sociology* (Chicago: University of Chicago Press, 1992), 119.

Bonding social capital: Tristan Claridge, "What Is Bonding Social Capital?" *Social Capital Research & Training*, January 6, 2018, www
.socialcapitalresearch.com/what-is-bonding-social-capital.

Robert Putnam calls bonding: Robert D. Putnam, *Bowling Alone: The Collapse and Revival of American Community* (New York: Simon & Schuster, 2000), 22-23.

83   *They are attracted to churches:* Kara Powell, Jake Mulder, and Brad Griffin, *Growing Young: Six Essential Strategies to Help Young People Discover and Love Your Church* (Grand Rapids: Baker, 2016), 170-71.

86   *As political scientist Robert Putnam:* Robert D. Putnam, *Our Kids: The American Dream in Crisis* (New York: Simon & Schuster, 2015), 213-14. Putnam provides multiple examples of formal and informal mentoring relationships involving teachers, pastors, coaches, and family friends. He argues that mentoring matters for the development of healthy relationships with adults, citing academic and psychosocial benefits.

mentoring community offers: Sharon Daloz Parks, Big Questions, *Worthy Dreams: Mentoring Emerging Adults in Their Search for Meaning, Purpose, and Faith* (San Francisco: Jossey-Bass, 2011), 132.

87   *Parks wrote that:* Parks, *Big Questions, Worthy Dreams,* 123.

89   *Community, whether experienced:* Beth Seversen, "Millennials Connecting to Contemporary Congregations: Effectively Reaching and Incorporating Emerging Adults in North American Evangelical Covenant Churches" (PhD diss., Trinity International University, 2017).

7. Involving

95   *In his book* The Rise of the Nones: White does not point to any research studies that support his thesis, but he does base his hypothesis in the Pew Forum's finding that nones believe religious institutions are overly consumed with money, power, and politics. However, 77 percent hold that religious organizations do benefit society when they care for the poor, and 78 percent of nones appreciate that religious institutions foster community. James Emery White, *The Rise of the Nones: Understanding and Reaching the Religiously Unaffiliated* (Grand Rapids: Baker Academic, 2004), 100.

96   *Involving them is a necessary:* Interestingly, Jenny Lee found religious behavior leads to stronger religious convictions and personal faith. Jenny J. Lee, "Religion and College Attendance: Change Among Students," *Review of Higher Education* 25, no. 4 (Summer 2002): 382.

103 *Pastor Craig Groeschel:* See Johnnie Moore, "Newsmax's Top 50 Churches in America," *Newsmax,* November 11, 2015, www.newsmax.com/TheWire /megachurches-top-united-states-newsmax/2015/11/11/id/701661.

Their hope is that young adults: Missiologist Paul Heibert, former professor of mission and anthropology at the School of World Mission, Fuller Theological Seminary, Pasadena, California, was the first to apply set theory to evangelism. See Paul G. Hiebert, "The Category 'Christian' in the Mission Task," *International Review of Mission* 72, no. 287 (1983): 421-27.

8. Investing

107   *Rightly or wrongly*: Pew Research reported 46 percent of millennials age 25 to 37 were married in 2019. Kristen Bialik and Richard Fry, "Millennial Life: How Young Adulthood Today Compares with Prior Generations," February 14, 2019, www.pewsocialtrends.org/essay/millennial -life-how-young-adulthood-today-compares-with-prior-generations/. Gen Zs were aged fifteen to twenty-three in the year 2020; and Kim Parker, Nikki Graf, and Ruth Igielnik, "Generation Z Look A Lot Like Millennials on Key Social and Political Issues, Pew Social Trends.org, January 17, 2019, www.pewsocialtrends.org/2019/01/17/generation -z-looks-a-lot-like-millennials-on-key-social-and-political-issues.

        During a recent young adult ministry: Young Adult Ministry Consultation hosted by the author on behalf of the Evangelical Covenant Church, Chicago, February 2018.

109   *If they miss the close-knit*: Harvard Graduate School reports loneliness at epidemic proportions in need of intervention in the United States. See Hannah Schulze, "Loneliness: An Epidemic?" *Science in the News*, accessed October 11, 2019, sitn.hms.harvard.edu/flash/2018 /loneliness-an-epidemic.

110   *When five thousand Gen Zs*: "What 5000 Gen Z'ers Tell Us About the Nature of Work," *Door of Clubs*, November 30, 2017, https://medium.com /@doorofclubs/what-5-000-gen-zers-tell-us-about-the-future-of -work-6dd00f796e8f.

        According to a national: David L. DuBois and Naida Silverthorn, "Natural Mentoring Relationships and Adolescent Health: Evidence from a National Study," *American Journal of Public Health* 95, no. 3 (March 1, 2005): 518-24, www.ncbi.nlm.nih.gov/pmc/articles/PMC1449212.

        These findings suggest: DuBois and Silverthorn, "Natural Mentoring Relationships," 518.

        The report noted: Kara E. Powell and Chap Clark, *Sticky Faith: Everyday Ideas to Build Lasting Faith in Your Kids* (Grand Rapids: Zondervan, 2011), 100. Powell and Clark discuss mentoring on pages 105-7, and provide a link to a website with mentoring ideas.

111   *After Powell's second study:* Kara Powell, Jake Mulder, and Brad Griffin, *Growing Young: Six Essential Strategies to Help Young People Discover Your Church* (Grand Rapids: Baker, 2016), 181-82.

Looking across disciplines: David L. DuBois and Michael J. Karcher, eds., "Youth Mentoring: Theory, Research, and Practice," in *Handbook of Youth Mentoring* (Thousand Oaks, CA: Sage, 2005), 3.

The mentor is ordinarily: University of South Florida, 2003, adapted from D. J. Levinson et al., *The Seasons of a Man's Life* (New York: Knopf, 1978), in DuBois and Karcher, "Youth Mentoring: Theory, Research, and Practice," 3.

114 *In fact, it can be*: In Sharon Daloz Parks, *Big Questions, Worthy Dreams: Mentoring Emerging Adults in Their Search for Meaning, Purpose, and Faith* (San Francisco: Jossey-Bass, 2011), Parks warns against the dangers of exposure only to individual mentors, which is without the checks and balances of the mentoring community.

Intentional mentoring communities: Parks, *Big Questions*, 176, 185; DuBois and Silverthorn, "Natural Mentoring Relationships," 518; Jim Wilhoit, *Spiritual Formation As If the Church Mattered: Growing in Christ Through Community* (Grand Rapids: Baker Academic, 2008), 124; Constance A. Flanagan, "Volunteerism, Leadership, Political Socialization, and Civic Engagement," in *Handbook of Adolescent Psychology*, ed. Richard M. Lerner and Laurence Steinberg, 2nd ed. (Hoboken, NJ: Wiley, 2004), 721-45; James Youniss et al., "The Role of Community Service in Duty Development: Normative, Unconventional, and Deviant Orientations," *Journal of Adolescent Research* 14 (1999): 248-61; Erik H. Erikson, *Identity: Youth and Crisis* (New York: Norton, 1968); Marie Good and Teena Willoughby, "The Identity Formation Experiences of Church-Attending Rural Adolescents," *Journal of Adolescent Research* 22 (2007): 387-412; Pamela Ebstyn King, "Religion and Identity: The Role of Ideological, Social, and Spiritual Contexts," *Applied Developmental Science* 7, no. 3 (July 2003): 197-204; and Sam A. Hardy et al., "Community and Religious Involvement as Contexts of Identity Change Across Late Adolescence and Emerging Adulthood," *International Journal of Behavioral Development* 35, no. 2 (2010): 125-35.

115 *As a result, young adults*: David P. Setran and Chris A. Kiesling, *Spiritual Formation in Emerging Adulthood: A Practical Theology for College and Young Adult Ministry* (Grand Rapids: Baker Academic, 2013), 57; and Robert Wuthnow, *After the Baby Boomers: How Twenty- and Thirty-Somethings Are Shaping the Future of American Religion* (Princeton, NJ: Princeton University Press, 2007), 70.

Christian communities help young: Parks, *Big Questions, Worthy Dreams*, 190-97; and Thomas Landefeld, *Mentoring and Diversity: Tips for Students and Professionals for Developing and Maintaining a Diverse Scientific Community* (New York: Springer, 2009), 11.

Participation in mentoring communities: Hardy et al., "Community and Religious Involvement," 127.

9. Leading

124 *Training resources I highly recommend*: Please visit the websites of Organic Outreach International (organicoutreach.org), the Amplify Conference (amplifyconference.tv), and the Church Evangelism Institute (ceicohorts.com).

142 *Young adults value authentic*: Edrin Williams, Young Adult Ministry Consultation, Evangelical Covenant Church, Chicago, February 2018.

144 *Pastor John Teter said*: Robert K. Johnston, professor of theology and culture at Fuller Theological Seminary, attributes this analogy to Karl Barth, not John Stott. See Johnston's *Reel Spirituality: Engaging Theology and Film in Dialogue* (Grand Rapids: Baker Academic. 2006), 111. Stott likely quoted Barth. The point: Bright-spot lead pastors don't have their head in the sand. They are aware of what's happening in the broader culture and how it is impacting emerging adults across ethnicities and social locations.

145 *Church hasn't been a place*: Dominique Gilliard, Young Adult Consultation.

Gilliard says that young adults: Dominique Gilliard, personal interview with author, Evangelical Covenant Church offices, Parkridge, IL, winter 2018.

146 *a bifurcation where they hold*: Edrin Williams, Young Adult Ministry Consultation.

10. Attracting

161 *Popular in the last third:* James Davison Hunter, *American Evangelicalism: Conservative Religion and the Quandary of Modernity* (New Brunswick, NJ: Rutgers University Press, 1983); and Christian Smith et al., *American Evangelicalism: Embattled and Thriving* (Chicago: University of Chicago Press, 1998).

People within the enclave: For discussion of secularism and religious reactions, as well as several case studies, see Peter Berger, ed., *The Desecularization of the World: Resurgent Religion and World Politics* (Washington, DC: Ethics and Policy Center, 1999). For the concept of the "sacred canopy" see Peter Berger, *The Sacred Canopy* (Garden City, NY: Anchor, 1967).

162 *Its proponents argue:* Dean Kelley, *Why Conservative Churches Are Growing* (New York: Harper & Row, 1972), 36-46.

More lenient groups will decline: Laurence R. Iannaccone, "Sacrifice and Stigma: Reducing Free-Riding in Cults, Communes, and Other Collectives," *Journal of Political Economy* 100, no. 2 (April 1992): 271-91; Laurence R. Iannaccone, "Why Strict Churches Are Strong," *American Journal of Sociology* 99, no. 5 (March 1994): 1180-1212; Roger Finke and

Rodney Stark, *The Churching of America, 1776–1990: Winners and Losers in Our Religious Economy* (New Brunswick, NJ: Rutgers University Press, 1992), 252-55; and Rodney Stark and Roger Finke, *Acts of Faith: Explaining the Human Side of Religion* (Berkeley: University California Press, 2000).

When fewer religious benefits: Christian Smith, *American Evangelicalism: Embattled and Thriving* (Chicago: University of Chicago Press, 1998), 72-73.

163 *American Evangelicalism, we contend:* Christian Smith et al., American Evangelicalism: Embattled and Thriving (Chicago: University of Chicago Press, 1998), 89.

That's because they forecast: Smith et al., *American Evangelicalism*, 118-19.

11. Revisioning

175 *People were drawn to:* Rodney Stark and Roger Finke, *Acts of Faith: Explaining the Human Side of Religion* (Berkeley: University of California Press, 2000), 123, 137.

Let's pause and acknowledge conversion as: Rick Richardson, *Reimagining Evangelism: Inviting Friends on a Spiritual Journey* (Downers Grove, IL: InterVarsity Press, 2006), 137. See also William Abraham's argument for conversion as initiation into Christ and his kingdom in William Abraham, *The Logic of Evangelism* (Grand Rapids, MI: Eerdmans, 1989), 84, 120-39.

Gordon Smith identifies seven critical elements of conversion: (1) belief in Jesus Christ, (2) repentance, (3) trust in Christ Jesus, (4) transfer of allegiance, (5) baptism, (6) reception of the gift of the Spirit, (7) incorporation into congregational life. See Gordon T. Smith, *Beginning Well: Christian Conversion and Authentic Transformation* (Downers Grove, IL: InterVarsity Press, 2001), 125, 138-41.

Bright spot churches appear: Smith, *Beginning Well*, 19-20, 26, 31. Smith argues conversion is a complex experience that is not to be understood as punctiliar and definitive but is "drawn out over many years" and is the beginning of spiritual transformation, for the "goal of our conversion is transformed humanity." In response to revivalism that defined conversion as a one-moment-in-time event, and in response to the reactionary view of revivalism that conversion is a continual, ongoing lifelong turning, Smith proposes conversion is both an extended process and a beginning to the Christian life: "The weight of the evidence suggests that most if not all people come to faith in Christ through a protracted series of events. These events in concert constitute a Christian conversion and thus a good beginning. . . . For most if not all, conversion is a protracted experience, a series of events over many months or even years" (31). Scot McKnight defines conversion at its core as a process of identity formation in which the person comes to see himself or herself in accordance with the gospel of Jesus Christ and is a "transformation of identity, involving both affirmations and behavior." McKnight too defines conversion as a process and argues that what we may observe as a partial or "less -than-a-full conversion" may merely be the beginning dimension of that process. It is how the church serves that process of conversion that concerns this researcher. Scot McKnight, *Turning to Jesus: The Sociology of Conversion in the Gospels* (Louisville, KY: Westminster John Knox, 2002) 3, 10.

176 *conversion occurs along relational lines*: Rodney Stark, "Why Religious Movements Succeed or Fail: A Revised General Model," *Journal of Contemporary Religion* 11, no. 2 (1996): 133-46. Stark's thesis is reminiscent of Donald McGavran's major contribution to the church-growth movement. McGavran proposed "relational bridges of God" as a key strategy to church growth and evangelism. In other words, evangelism runs along relational networks. Donald A. McGavran, *Understanding Church Growth* (Grand Rapids: Eerdmans, 1970).

177 *Sometimes belonging must precede:* Brian McClaren, *More Ready Than You Realize: Evangelism as Dance in the Postmodern Matrix* (Grand Rapids: Zondervan, 2002), 84.

Most people today will: Rick Richardson, *Reimagining Evangelism: Inviting Friends on a Spiritual Journey* (Downers Grove, IL: InterVarsity Press, 2006), 50.

Ed Stetzer describes the process: Ed Stetzer, *Planting Missional Churches: Planting a Church That's Biblically Sound and Reaching People in Culture* (Nashville: Broadman and Holman, 2006), 188.

180 *A study by the Billy Graham Center:* In churches where non-Christians are attending, the Billy Graham Center study found that the most new faith commitments are happening where "at least one in five attendees are not Christian in 30 percent of top churches and 15 percent of others," and that "for 44 percent of top evangelistic churches in the national survey, more than 50 percent of all new attendees were unchurched." Rick Richardson, "Reaching the Unchurched," presentation at Amplify Conference, Wheaton, Illinois, June 27, 2016; Rick Richardson and Beth Seversen, "The Unchurched and the Churches Reaching Them," *YouTube*, August 24, 2016, www.youtube.com/watch?v=NPkR68hT7Dw &list=PLxZddGvRSn2EPb-TGe9xmFcNLTWr4Y2T8&index =11&t=0s.

181 *In* More Ready Than You Realize: Brian D. McClaren, *More Ready Than You Realize,* 11-12.

183   *Some, as Robert Putnam reminds us:* Robert D. Putnam and David Campbell, *American Grace: How Religion Divides and Unites Us* (New York: Simon & Schuster, 2010), 3.

12. Balancing

188   *Christian Smith and contributors theorize:* Christian Smith, *American Evangelicalism: Embattled and Thriving* (Chicago: University of Chicago Press, 1998), 118-19. The subcultural identity theory of religious persistence is this: "Religion survives and can thrive in pluralistic, modern society by embedding itself in subcultures that offer satisfying morally orienting collective identities which provide adherents meaning and belonging" (97). And the subcultural identity theory of religious strength is this: "In a pluralistic society, those religious groups will be relatively stronger which better possess and employ the cultural tools needed to create both clear distinction from and significant engagement and tension with other relevant outgroups, short of becoming genuinely countercultural" (118-19).

Similarly Roger Finke: Roger Finke and Rodney Stark, *The Churching of America 1776–1990: Winners and Losers in Our Religious Economy* (New Brunswick, NJ: Rutgers University Press, 1992).

Smith argues that twentieth-century American: H. Richard Niebuhr, *Christ and Culture* (New York: Harper & Row, 1951), proposed a spectrum of five positions churches and denominations take toward culture. In his typology, the "Christ Against Culture" pattern reflects the sectarian impulse of churches that withdraw from society to protect themselves from being contaminated by the world's polluted morals and anti-gospel ideologies and philosophies. This position stresses the idea that the world is corrupted by sin and the church is set apart from the world. Christians of this persuasion, such as fundamentalists, typically do not participate in "worldly" affairs such as politics.

189   posture of "engaged orthodoxy": Smith, *American Evangelicalism*, 10.

193   *Almost all of them:* "Ministries," Cornerstone Church, accessed April 18, 2019, cornerstoneboston.org/serve.

It networks with the city: "The Family Center," Fountain of Life Covenant Church, accessed April 18, 2019, www.folcov.org/family-center.

High Rock North Shore is: "Open Door Immigration Services," Highrock North Shore, accessed April 18, 2019, www.highrocknorthshore.org/open-door-immigration.

River City Community Church offers: See the homepage of River City Community Church (rivercitychicago.com).

New Community Logan Square offers the homeless: See the homepage of Open Arms Ministry (openarmsministry.org).

194   *Today the mission of BOOC is to*: See the "About" page of BOOC (booc
      .org/about.html).

      Churches effectively reaching emerging adults: Mark Chaves, professor of
      sociology at University of Arizona, found that most congregations do
      not engage in social services. If they do, it is only marginally. He also
      observed that in the congregations that do engage, only a handful of
      individuals are actually involved. Mark Chaves, *Congregations in America*
      (Cambridge, MA: Harvard University Press, 2004), 54-55.

201   *Many emerging adult dones:* David Kinnaman with Aly Hawkins, *You Lost
      Me: Why Young Christians Are Leaving Church and Rethinking Faith* (Grand
      Rapids: Baker, 2011), 171, 175; David Kinnaman and Gabe Lyons,
      *Unchristian: What a New Generation Really Thinks About Christianity—and
      Why It Matters* (Grand Rapids: Baker, 2007), 91-119. Robert Putman and
      David Campbell argue that nones purposefully reject the church due
      to the church's lack of Christian virtues, and particularly for its stance
      on homosexuality, its conservative politics, and its exclusionary belief
      system. Young adults have a new moral sensibility and reject the church
      for being immoral. Robert D. Putnam and David Campbell, *American
      Grace: How Religion Divides and Unites Us* (New York: Simon & Schuster,
      2010), 3.

13. True North

204   *I therefore will appeal*: See Richard Osmer, *Practical Theology: An Introduc-
      tion* (Grand Rapids: Eerdmans, 2008), 8. In a conversation, a col-
      league of mine—Joel Willitts, professor of biblical and theological
      studies and practical theology at North Park University—gave me a
      useful definition of practical theology: "a critique of how the church
      acts and thinks."

205   *Or as Andrew Root asked:* Andrew Root, *Christopraxis: A Practical Theology
      of the Cross* (Minneapolis: Fortress Press, 2014), 23-26.

206   *Particularly the Gospel of John:* Joshua W. Jipp, *Saved by Faith and Hospital-
      ity* (Grand Rapids: Eerdmans 2017), 12, 22, 37, 94-95. Jipp further
      argues, "The witness of Luke-Acts calls for a recovery of the practice
      of sharing meals with one another as opportunities to 'remember' and
      to celebrate the presence of Jesus who, as the risen Lord, continues to
      extend divine welcome indiscriminately to those who come to him.
      Jesus' meals, and the meals in the early church as well, were the means
      whereby the sinner, the outcast, and even the enemy encountered
      God's hospitality and were transformed into friends who were fully
      included in God's people. As such, we have seen that these meals were
      marked by joy, inclusivity, the satisfaction of hunger, and the presence
      of the risen Jesus. This calls for the church to recommit itself to inten-
      tional times of eating together with the expectation that, in

obedience to both the example and the command of Jesus, the risen Jesus is powerfully present in our communities, and that these meals will continue to provide the hospitable context whereby all people may encounter God's hospitality. The church's hospitality meals testify that the defining marker of the church is that they are recipients of God's hospitality and nothing else. If the sacrament of the Last Supper ritualized and brought to memory all of Jesus' eating and drinking with sinners and outcasts, then the church needs to recover a greater role for meals of fellowship in remembrance of Jesus. Craig Blomberg states this well when he notes that the right response of seeing Jesus' hospitality meals with sinners 'is to elevate the significance and "sacramentalize" the role of other fellowship meals, *when Christians celebrate them intentionally for the sake of creating greater intimacy with fellow human beings before reconciling them to each other and to God.'"* Jipp, *Saved by Faith and Hospitality*, 37. The Blomberg quoted comes come Craig L. Blomberg, *Contagious Holiness: Jesus' Meal with Sinners*, New Studies in Biblical Theology 19 (Downers Grove, IL: InterVarsity Press, 2005), 179.

Despite its brokenness and imperfections: Jipp, *Saved by Faith and Hospitality*, 94-95.

207   *Strategy of Adoptive Youth Ministry:* Chap Clark, "The Strategy of Adoptive Youth Ministry," in *Adoptive Youth Ministry: Integrating Emerging Generations into the Family of Faith*, ed. Chap Clark (Grand Rapids: Baker Academic, 2016), 19.

  expression and corporate experience of faith: Clark, "Strategy of Adoptive Youth Ministry," 20.

  They are encouraged and equipped through: At this point the funnel is very much like the five practices, but I didn't come across *Adoptive Youth Ministry* until a year after my research, analysis, and defense of my study. You can imagine how excited I was to find a model that corroborates my research.

208   *Adoption is the final level in the funnel:* Chap Clark, *Adoptive Church: Creating an Environment Where Emerging Generations Belong* (Grand Rapids: Baker Academic: 2018), 20.

  He grounds his ministry philosophy: Clark, *Adoptive Church*, 16.

209   *According to Robert Putnam:* Robert D. Putnam and David Campbell, *American Grace: How Religion Divides and Unites Us* (New York: Simon & Schuster, 2010), 3.

210   *To review, Kinnaman:* David Kinnaman and Gabe Lyons, *Unchristian: What a New Generation Really Thinks About Christianity—and Why It Matters* (Grand Rapids: Baker, 2007), 5.

Previously we observed: David Kinnaman and Aly Hawkins, *You Lost Me: Why Young Christians Are Leaving Church—And Rethinking Faith* (Grand Rapids: Baker, 2011), 90-93.

216   *Rick Richardson and I:* Beth Seversen and Rick Richardson, "Emerging Adults and the Future of Evangelism," *Witness* 28 (2014): 31-51.